Charles Wentworth Dilke

Twayne's English Authors Series

Herbert Sussman, Editor
Northeastern University

TEAS 300

CHARLES WENTWORTH DILKE
(1789–1864)

Photography by Christopher Oxford
Reproduced by permission of
London Borough of Camden
from the collections at Keats House, Hampstead

Charles Wentworth Dilke

By William Garrett
University of South Florida

Twayne Publishers • *Boston*

Charles Wentworth Dilke

William Garrett

Copyright © 1982 by G. K. Hall & Company
All Rights Reserved
Published by Twayne Publishers
A Division of G. K. Hall & Company
70 Lincoln Street
Boston, Massachusetts 02111

Book Production by John Amburg
Book Design by Barbara Anderson

Printed on permanent/durable acid-free
paper and bound in The United States
of America.

Library of Congress Cataloging in Publication Data

Garrett, William, 1928–
    Charles Wentworth Dilke.

    (Twayne's English authors series ; TEAS 300)
    Bibliography: p. 233
    Includes index.
    1. Dilke, Charles Wentworth, 1789–1864.
2. Critics—England—Biography. 3. Editors—
England—Biography. 4. Keats, John, 1795–1821—
Friends and associates. I. Title. II. Series.
PR29.D5G37   1982   820'.9 [B]   82–9342
ISBN 0–8057–6792–4

Contents

About the Author

William Garrett, born January 21, 1928, was educated in public schools in southern Illinois, graduating from high school in 1946. After a two-year stint with the occupation forces in Japan, he entered the University of Colorado as a freshman in 1948. Shortly thereafter he transferred to Eastern Illinois University and graduated there in 1952. After teaching for one year in Sheldon, Illinois, he began graduate work at the University of Florida, receiving the M.A. in English in 1955 and the Ph.D. in English in 1958. Upon completion of a two-year teaching assignment at the University of Guam, he returned to America to become a charter member of the faculty at the University of South Florida in Tampa. He is currently Professor of English and Director of Academic Affairs at the University of South Florida, St. Petersburg Campus.

Professor Garrett has published several articles generally on the Romantic Period, particularly on Keats and his circle. Other special interests include William Blake and Lady Sydney Morgan, feminist, and close friend of and talented writer for the subject of this present study. Professor Garrett has also written a book on Modern Grammar.

Preface

"Charles Wentworth Dilke and the March of Intellect" is an alternate though inappropriate title for this book, which purports to be a biography of a man, not of an idea. The man, Charles Wentworth Dilke (1789–1864), friend of Keats and his Circle, editor of the *Athenaeum*, and respected scholar and critic of several eighteenth-century figures, took the idea of the March of Intellect and made it his own. It was his passion, which for the greater part of his life amounted almost to an obsession. The passion assumed the form of several questions: how to improve the world; how to leave it to succeeding generations in better shape than his generation found it; and finally, how to insure that succeeding generations would venerate and embrace the same high purpose. That idea has since been called by several names, but the one which Keats gave it—the "grand march of intellect"—contains a number of related associations included in most such names.

Such related ideas as are contained in such terms as "the march of civilization," "the doctrine of progress," "the doctrine of perfectability" were by no means original with the Romantic age. For the general concept in its then-present form, the poets of that age rightly credited and venerated Rousseau and Godwin; and though they inherited it from writers of the Enlightenment, who in turn had inherited it from antiquity, Rousseau and Godwin had examined it, had turned it over to discover its various implications, and had set about fashioning it into a dynamic, new world-view, congruous to what Hazlitt with admirable insight would term "the Spirit of the Age." Central to all such concepts relating to progress is a sense of historical continuity; ironically that sense had recently been provided by the politically conservative Burke. Though from time to time Dilke altered his Godwinian faith, he retained from Godwin that which Godwin preserved from Burke: the sense of historical continuity, which was, Burke said, the "continuous life of mankind."

That sense of historical continuity would in time undergo subtle shifts of emphasis. For Burke it meant that history and history's institutions were to be venerated, preserved, and hence interpreted as a bulwark of conservatism which would militate against change. Godwin too (unlike Paine) venerated history but modified the faith by blending it with the revolutionary idealism of Rousseau, so that the product was a new dynamic theory of historical evolution, a new sense of cultural continuity which proved eminently palatable to certain later young Romantics, particularly to Keats and Shelley and to a few of their friends. This consciousness of cultural development and thrust would undergo yet another modification before it could serve as the basis for Dilke's theory of art. Owing probably to Dilke's influence, that modification had been foreshadowed in Keats's *Endymion* and the two *Hyperion*s. Whereas Godwin had believed that a high sense of duty and morality would save the world, Keats and Shelley were among those for whom the old "poetry of concern" had begun to manifest itself in a new social consciousness directly concerned with the role of the poet himself. The awesome task of saving the world from itself, so went the rationale, had been abdicated by religion; traditional Christianity had failed miserably in affording mankind much more than a mere continuation of the deprivation of spirit and meaningless struggle which, in Glaucus's terms, it had known for a tragic millennium. Thus, the office of leading civilization out of the wilderness was now no longer that of the priest. Perhaps among a few others, Keats, Shelley, and Dilke believed that the high calling had fallen to art and literature in general and to the artist and poet in particular.

Keats, Shelley, Dilke, and others felt that Burke and Rousseau, great as their gift to posterity was, had slighted one essential element necessary to the march of intellect. It needed the idealistic impetus given it by Rousseau; it needed likewise the historical impetus which Godwin had blended with that idealism; it needed, in addition, Godwin's "moral force." But "moral force," as it seemed to the Romantics, was too general, and therefore smacked of time-worn precepts and authoritarianism which a tragic history of civilization had proved woefully inadequate. A moral force, emphatically yes; but not such a moral force as religion had foisted off onto an "embruitified race" fit only as a description of Hobbes's Leviathan. What was needed was something more to make that moral force more meaningful and viable. What was needed was art and literature.

Thus said in particular the later Romantics: Shelley in the "Defense of Poetry" and Keats in the two *Hyperions*. And thus said Dilke in the fifty years of his active publishing life. But—and this was peculiarly Dilke's insistence—mere art and literature were in themselves not enough: there must be *good* art and *good* literature, as well as the right kind of morality. The greatest surety for this striving toward excellence in art and literature is constant vigilance on the part of critics. The *Athenaeum* and others like it were in an especially favored position to guarantee such vigilance. In the periodical press this "poetry of concern" found new and vigorous expression in a new prose of concern.

But Dilke said another thing that Shelley and Keats did not say, that only two or three others said, and even so, said less effectively than did he: the enunciation of his *system*; and the system existed for the purpose of merging art and literature with societal good. That system can best be termed an "ethnos of art and literature." This book is about his efforts to refine that system as it develops into a matured ethnos having far-reaching effects on art and society.

Chapter 1 shows Dilke in his relationships with the surviving members of the Keats Circle, focusing especially on the central role he played in the "Keats Brothers' finances" controversy and the effect it had on the subsequent scholarship about Keats. Chapter 2 shows his "apprenticeship" in two senses: apprenticeship to periodical editorship, and to a matured ethnos of art and literature. Accordingly, it traces the growth and development of his system from 1815 to 1830, largely via periodical literature. Chapter 3 gives an account of his "art" and "causes" groups of personages who served him in his editorship of the *Athenaeum* (1830–1846). The bulk of this chapter—the longest in the book—is concerned with tracing Dilke's direct influence on the many liberal causes espoused in his journal: all designed to advance the march of intellect. The concluding pages of this chapter are given over to discussion of how such causes affect and in turn are affected by Dilke's ethnos of art. This subsection is called "The March of Intellect." Chapter 4 touches on his brief period of newspaper editorship and then focuses on his numerous contributions—some 450 items—to his two favorite periodicals: *Athenaeum* and *Notes and Queries.* It is in this period that he establishes himself as a respected scholar and critic. At the conclusion of this final chapter is an estimate of his influence.

My obligations are many. I believe that the most pressing is to two of Dilke's descendants, Captain Stephen W. Roskill, C.B.E., D.S.C., Litt D., F.B.A., R.N., and Sir John Dilke, Bart, (owner of Roskill-Dilke Collection and owner of copyright, respectively), both of whom graciously made it possible for Churchill College, Cambridge Library to lend me the use of unpublished Dilke documents and letters from the Roskill-Dilke Archive, created by a bequest from Captain Roskill in 1974. To Miss Marion Stewart, Archivist at Churchill College, I am likewise deeply grateful for assistance on numerous occasions. I wish also to express my thanks to the good and kind people in the offices of the *New Statesman* in Great Turnstile Street, who for three weeks provided desks and office space for me, my wife, Helen, and my daughter, Pamela, to work in. In particular, I wish to thank Mr. Neville Rhodes, General Manager, and Bob Sharp and Eve Suckling, who have often looked up specific information for me in the Marked File. I wish also to thank Professor Leslie A. Marchand, who some years ago permitted me to copy his notes on the Marked File from 1830–1846. I am grateful to the administration of the University of South Florida, particularly to Dean Carl Riggs and Dean William Scheuerle for providing grants to enable me to visit libraries in England to search for Dilke materials. Also, to those individuals and libraries that sent valuable information: Professor Barbara

Preface

McCrimmon of Florida State University; to Mr. Geoffrey Langley
of Avon County Library; to Sir J. L. W. Cheyne, Curator of Keats-
Shelley Memorial House in Rome; to Dr. M. A. E. Nickson, Department of Manuscripts in the British Museum; to Elizabeth
Stege Teleky, MSS Specialist for the Joseph Regenstein Library at
the University of Chicago; to Mr. Frank D. Cole Curator of Keats
House, Hempstead, and especially to Mrs. Gee and her assistants,
whose hospitality and kind assistance I shall remember with pleas-
ure; also to W. N. Yates, City Records Office of the City of Ports-
mouth; to Miss Rosemary Graham, Manuscript Cataloguer of
Trinity College, Cambridge; to E. Hargreaves of the Reference
Library of the City of Birmingham; to the Hon. David Lytton
Cobbold, owner of the unpublished letters of Sir Edward Bulwer-
Lytton, and County Archivist Peter Walne at Hertfordshire Record
Office, which houses these letters; to Marjorie Robertson of Edinburgh University Library; to Frank Paluka, Special Collections in
the University of Iowa Library; and finally to some 200 librarians
in England who searched through their archives—most of the time
fruitlessly—for Dilke memorabilia, I wish to acknowledge my
gratitude. To other individuals I am likewise grateful: to V. Reilley
of the Naval Historical Library for information on the Dilke
family's long connections with the Navy Pay Office; to Leslie
Blanchard for assistance with the bibliography; to Carol Moore for
assistance in the preparation of the index; to Edward "Bill" De
Young for frequent researches in English libraries and other less
accessible places; and to Doris Martin, whose patient assistance
in collating and preparing the manuscript I shall always remember
with gratitude; to these and to many others unnamed who helped
make this book possible, I wish to express my thanks.

William Garrett

University of South Florida

Chronology

1789   Born, December 8, to Charles Wentworth and Sarah Blewford Dilke, in Bedhampton near Parish of Portsea, Hampshire.

1794–1805   Education, largely tutorial; move to London; resumes education; perhaps meets Charles Brown in a school, though more likely Dilke and Brown families were long acquainted; employed at Navy Pay Office as "Extra Clerk" at £75+ per annum on same day as John Dickens.

1806   Marries Maria Dover Walker, daughter of Edward Walker, official in East India Company.

1810   Birth of son, Charles Wentworth.

1814–1816   Editor *Old English Plays*, with "Introduction" (6 Vols.); begins building Wentworth Place (completed 1816); meets Keats (through Reynolds).

1817–1818   Cements his "most affectionate friendship" with Keats; writes for the *Champion*; Keats moves to Wentworth Place.

1819   Dilke and family move to Great Smith Street.

1820   Keats departs England for Italy (dies February 23, 1821); Dilke a reporter on Proceedings at Parliament.

1821   "Letter to Lord John Russell: The Course and Remedy of the National Difficulties...."; writes for *London Magazine*; also occasionally (1822–30) for *Westminster Review, Retrospective Review, New Monthly Magazine, London Review.*

1822   Becomes guardian to Carlino Brown.

1824   Editor of *London Magazine*; has probably become trustee to Fanny and Margaret Brawne; as trustee to Fanny Keats, Dilke succeeds in wresting Fanny's inheritance from "that consummate villain, Abbey"; establishes correspondence with George Keats.

1825(?)   Moves to #9 Lower Grosvenor Street.

1826   Tours Continent with Wentworth; visits Brown in Florence and Keats's tomb in Rome; leaves Wentworth in Brown's charge ostensibly for two years (Wentworth actually stayed eight months); serves as "Arbitrator" for Leigh Hunt.

1829–1830   Writes in Hood's *The Gem*; quarrels with Brown over Keats Brothers' finances; begins writing for *Athenaeum*; buys the *Athenaeum* along with Thomas Hood, John Reynolds, James Rice, Allan Cunningham and others; immediately assumes editorship; establishes *Athenaeum* in the first rank of literary journals; dedicates journal to the advancement of literature, art and liberal societal causes to create an "ethnos of art and literature."

1833   Brown visits England and establishes a temporary truce with Dilke.

1836–1837   Retires on a pension from Admiralty on abolishment of Navy Pay Office; visits Hood and family in Coblenz and Ostend.

1838   Break with Brown; becomes personally active in societies, causes, institutions in behalf of "ethnology of art."

1843   Birth of Charles Wentworth (Numero Three); possible (temporary) break with Hood.

1846   Retires from active editorship of *Athenaeum*; becomes "Managing Editor" of *Daily News*; embroilment with "Committee" of the Literary Fund.

1849–1854   Retires from managing editorship of *Daily News* and from public life; writes extensively on Junius and frequently on Burke, Wilkes, and others.

1850–1852   Establishes *Notes and Queries* with W. Thoms; assists Wentworth in planning the "Great Exhibition" of 1851; Maria dies; travels in Wales, Ireland, Scotland, and on the Continent, often with his grandson; moves to 76 Sloane Street, home of Wentworth.

1853   Resumes active interest in *Athenaeum*.

1854–1863   Acquires Caryll Papers; extensive writings on Pope and occasionally on Swift.

1856–1862   Dilke-Elwin-Murray correspondence.

1858   Dickens, Forster, Dilke in final effort to "reform" Literary Fund.

1862   Moves to Alice Holt, Hampshire.

1863   Makes final contribution to *Notes and Queries*; begins gradual demise, owing to a "granular disease"; makes final contribution to *Athenaeum*.

1864   Dies at Alice Holt on August 10.

Chapter One

Dilke and the Keats Circle

The Early Years

Dilke's Ancestry. "Old Mr. Dilke, of Chichester," as he would come to be known to Keats scholars in later times, did not consider himself a very important person. He could have nothing to say to anyone, he apologized once, because "no one says anything to me."[1] But then Old Mr. Dilke was a modest, humble, unassuming man, more so, perhaps, than his stature in the friendly agrarian community of Bedhampton warranted. For a clerk in the Navy Pay Office—Chief Clerk, to be sure—he owned a very respectable amount of property, both in lands and rents and also in investments, chiefly in terms of speculations on goods transported by ships which docked where he worked. His salary as Chief Clerk of £230 per year (up to 1799) appears to have been about one-third of his annual income. His interests were catholic: he read often in sixteenth- and seventeenth- and widely in eighteenth-century literature; he was engrossed in English politics both local and national, though strictly as an observer; he talked knowledgeably of painting and painters; but his first love seems to have been architecture, on the subject of which he wrote a carefully illustrated, bound manuscript dedicated to Henry Flitcroft.[2] In addition, he was fond of and expert in heraldry and was particularly proud of his family history, which he is said to have traced back to the eighth century. This Dilke never became famous for anything he did; but by Keats scholars he will always be remembered gratefully for his kind hospitality and fatherly concern for the great poet, who would in times of wretchedness repair to his home for solace. He was also the father of the subject of this study, who was one of Keats's closest friends.

The family of the "London Dilkes"[3] dated back to the late sixteenth century to Fisher Dilke of Shustoke, a "bitter puritan" born
in 1595. Fisher Dilke had married into a Wentworth family distinguished for their connections with Cromwell's Council of State;
he inherited property through his wife on the condition that the
heirs should assume the name of Wentworth. His descendants, in
keeping with this pledge, were known through succeeding generations as the Wentworth Dilkes or Dilke Wentworths until the
end of the seventeenth century. In 1698 Wentworth Dilke Wentworth, Old Mr. Dilke's father, was born "in poverty," like his
father before him; but he entered the navy in early life, retired as
a lieutenant, and became Secretary of the Earl of Litchfield and
afterwards clerk to the Board of Green Cloth at Kew Palace.
According to Sir Charles Dilke, his great-great grandson, he
amassed a modest amount of property in his lifetime. In the early
1740s he married Winifred Street, and they apparently lived in
London until the death of Winifred in 1762.[4] Wentworth and
Winifred had one surviving son, "Old Mr. Dilke," born in 1743;
this son would know Keats and would father a son who would
profoundly affect the course of English literature and history. In
1762 this then young Mr. Dilke (only nineteen) was employed
in the Admiralty.[5]

By 1774, he was in Portsmouth, clerk in the Room of Edward
Clark, and on June 11, 1781, was promoted to the Victualing
Branch; and again on January 29, 1784, he moved to the Paymaster branch.[6] In the meantime, being a man of compassionate
parts, as he later explains, he secured for himself on February 17,
1783, a beautiful bride named Sarah Blewford, who was twenty-
three years his junior, and took her to live in neighboring Bedhampton.

Six years after that, the year his first son was born, Mr. Dilke,
Sr., became Chief Clerk. The first son, friend of the Keats Circle,
antiquary, and prolific contributor to periodicals, was born on December 8, 1789; he was also named Charles Wentworth Dilke, the
second of five in succession who would bear that name.[7] Elder
sisters Letitia and Jane had been born in 1784 and 1785, though

the latter died in infancy. A brother William was born in 1796. Joanna Richardson observes that Dilke's birth date was an appropriate one for the "future radical," though the term may be a bit too strong as a description of his political inclinations for the greater part of his life.[8]

Education and Charles Brown. Since there was no school in the Parish of Bedhampton, Charles Wentworth Dilke probably attended the one in the neighboring Portsea Parish, where his father worked in the dockyards. In the year 1800 Old Mr. Dilke's fortunes were increased materially when he transferred from Portsmouth dockyards to the Navy Pay Office in London, where as "1st clerk" he "superintended the making up of accounts" related to Her Majesty's naval expenditures.[9] There, tradition goes, in a school in London Dilke first met Charles Brown,[10] who was for forty years to have a direct influence on Dilke's life, if not on his opinions. In his unfinished autobiographical novel *Walter Hazlebourn*, Brown describes his and Dilke's headmaster:

Our clerical master, no doubt unconsciously, neglected the manly feeling and inward morality of his pupils in the persuasion that pious precepts, constantly enforced, must indubitably be followed by the purest moral conduct. His solemn and austere demeanour rendered, together with himself, his sermons and his tasks repulsive to youth; though the lads never thought of appearing otherwise than pleased and attentive.[11]

Later, both Brown and Dilke were removed from that school and were favored with private tutoring.[12] Old Mr. Dilke had intended his son for a career in law, says Brown, but seeing it useless, procured for him a position in the Navy Pay Office. Accordingly, on April 5, 1805, Dilke entered into a profession as "extra clerk," a position which Brown says he "heartily despised," but which he tolerated for more than thirty years.[13]

Maria and Wentworth. If we may trust Brown's "full length caricature" in *Walter Hazlebourn* in youth Dilke was insolent, quick-tempered, and vain, though when occasion demanded he was clever enough to conceal these shortcomings.[14] Scrupulously honest, however, Brown acknowledged his congeniality, his quickness, his wit, and his "wide reading" in English literature and history.

At sixteen, Dilke is pictured as physically large, fiercely independent, and ambitious of making some mark in the world of literature. He had for nearly a year been employed at the Navy Pay Office in London. He was given, unfortunately, to keeping late hours which, according to Brown's account, caused arguments with his father. After one such particularly painful altercation, Dilke left home. Entreaties to him to return were unavailing. Finally in desperation, Old Mr. Dilke sent his "nephew" Gerald to persuade Dilke to rejoin the family; Dilke pleaded not only the late-hour conflicts, but cited his low standing among other members of the family as well. He would therefore not return, and Brown closes that chapter with the mournful notation that some weeks later Mr. Rydel (Old Mr. Dilke) "... was allowed to learn, as he could, that his son had married a milliner."[15] This was in the year 1806, when Dilke was just over sixteen years old, and the "milliner" was supposedly Maria Dover Walker, daughter of Edward Walker, an official in the East India Company. The Walkers were Yorkshire people "related to Blades, Milnes, Dovers, and Culverlys," people of sturdy stock, as Sir Charles liked to think of them, and as his grandfather taught him to think.

Brown does not so indicate, but if it ever occurred, the rift between father and son was soon healed. Almost immediately the bride and groom returned to live in the "dwelling house," which Old Mr. Dilke procured for them.[16] From the many chatty and warm letters passing back and forth between the lively, engaging Maria and the obviously pleased father-in-law, there is no reason to believe that the relationship between father and son thereafter was anything but one of the most cordial intimacy and mutual respect.

On February 18, 1810, Maria Dilke gave birth to their only child, another Charles Wentworth, upon whom Dilke doted and whom he undoubtedly spoiled. At about this time, too, Dilke began his researches into sixteenth and seventeenth century letters, particularly Shakespeare and Milton, into Old English Ballads, into the poetry of his somewhat older contemporaries, and into the prose writings of Godwin and Rousseau. Brown, too, was a "particular student" of Rousseau and Shakespeare, his favorites at that time, and undoubtedly read with Dilke when he was not tutoring young William.[17] He rather berated Dilke's efforts to learn other languages, but acknowledged that he "read much on every subject" in his own.[18] Their mutual interest in all phases of English letters and philosophy was both competitive and supportive and paradoxically would later prove to be both the cementing and undoing of their lifelong friendship.

Nevertheless, out of this competitive but supportive relationship between the two friends there developed in Dilke a certain attitude toward art and literature, toward history, and toward civilization itself, an attitude that may be described as essentially culturally oriented.[19] It was to permeate his thinking and writing for the remainder of his life.

In 1814 Dilke began work on his first major literary venture. When finished in 1815, published anonymously, it was a six-volume edition of old Elizabethan, Jacobean, and early Caroline plays. He called it *Old English Plays, Being a Selection from the Early Dramatic Writers*, and explained in the preface that he was issuing the old plays not necessarily because they were the best samples that could be obtained, but because they were rare and hence not generally available.[20]

The Keatsian Years

Shortly after the publication of Volume 6, Dilke, together with his friend Brown, embarked on what was to prove, if not more important, then certainly a more renowned venture: together they built a house that would become a literary shrine as the home of the poet Keats. It was a modest dwelling, compared to Belmont Castle, where his sister Letitia lived, or even to the spacious home on Newman Street, which his father had kept for the past fourteen years, passing rich at £700+ per year; but the surroundings were quiet and peaceful, the grounds were rolling, the air was pure, and must have reminded Dilke of lovely, agrarian Bedhampton, which forty years later he would still visit and remember from childhood. The structure later to be known as Wentworth Place was "a pair of semi-detached houses . . . standing in a common garden." Brown occupied the lesser half, which indeed was quite ample; Dilke, Maria and Wentworth lived in the larger portion "in the most complete happiness."[21] Years later in 1878 William Dilke would write to his grand-nephew:

There are few in [for if] any one living who could speak with such authority [on Wentworth Place] as myself who, with Mrs. Dilke, named it and had it painted up during my Brother's absence from home, on a visit to Chichester, I think.—There were three houses at the time, but the name was only thought of in connection with the 2 in one block in which my Brother and Brown resided. The 1st built house stood on its own ground & did not adopt the name so long as I lived there, though of late years the name has been lost to the 2 and adopted by the 1st which is now called Wentworth *House.*[22]

Very soon the house began to show promise of its later fame for its hospitality. Chatty, unpunctual Maria was a lovely hostess, and Brown and Dilke loved to talk about literature, politics, the sciences, the rise and fall of civilizations, the causes thereunto appertaining; and both genuinely liked people and fun. Dilke mentions in his letters some literary people at that time. Perhaps the best known of these was the critic William Gifford, editor of the influential Tory magazine, the *Quarterly Review*, who knew Dilke or his work well enough to give him encouragement in the editing of the *Old Plays.*[23]

About this time Dilke and Brown began to be drawn into the group that was later to be known as the Keats Circle. It is not known exactly how or when Dilke became acquainted with Keats, with whom, according to his grandson he formed his "most affectionate friendship." In a letter to Keats's biographer, R. M. Milnes (later Lord Houghton), John Hamilton Reynolds states that Dilke "knew Keats through me."[24]

Brown states in his memoir that he first met Keats on Hampstead Road in late summer of 1817,[25] but Dilke had met him much earlier, perhaps by as much as seven or eight months.[26] The first mention of the Dilkes by Keats is in a letter to Reynolds, dated March 17, 1817. By September of that year, Keats had spent some days at the Wentworth home; and in a letter to the Reynolds sisters, the tone of a passage (wherein Keats jokes at the Dilkes' expense) offers reasonably strong proof of their quickly ripening friendship:

...tell Dilk[e] that it would be perhaps as well if he left a Pheasant or Partri[d]ge alive here and there to keep up a supply of Game for next season—tell him to rein in if possible all the Nimrod of his disposition, he being a mighty hunter befor[e] the Lord—of the Manor. Tell him to shoot fa[i]r and not have at the poor devils in the furrow—when they are flying he may fire and nobody will be the wiser. Give my sincerest Respects to Mrs. Dilk[e] saying that I have not forgiven myself for not having got her the little Box of Medicine I promised her for her after dinner flushings—and that had I remained at Hampstead I would have made precious havoc with her house and furniture—drawn a great harrow over her garden—poisoned Boxer—eaten her Cloathes pegs,—fried her cabbages fricacced (how is it spelt?) her radishes—ragouted her Onions....[27]

By December he is having "not a dispute but a disquisition" with Dilke about negative capability. He is "daily with the Dilkes," with whom he is "getting to be capital friends,"[28] and at whose hospitable house he is "in the habit of taking my papers and copying [Endymion] there," so that he can "chat and proceed at the same time."[29] In the same letter to George and Tom (then in Teignmouth), he writes "I dined with Brown lately. Dilke having taken the Champion theatricals was obliged to be in town."[30] By February he had become intimate with Brown, with whom, along with Dilke, he was "very thick; they are very kind to me." In the following summer, after *Endymion* was published and *Hyperion* was being contemplated, Brown and Keats took a walking tour of Scotland, from which Keats had to return prematurely because of a sore throat.[31] In the meantime Dilke had written to him urging his quick return to care for the youngest brother Tom, who had become afflicted with tuberculosis—"the family complaint," as George called it. Keats returned on August 17 or 18, "as brown and shabby as you can imagine,"[32] only to find Dilke himself ailing and under a doctor's care. Shortly thereafter, Dilke went to the seashore at Brighton to recover (according to Maria's "Wentworth Place Bulletin"), perhaps accompanied by Brown,[33] but had left by September to complete his recuperation at the "mansion" of his sister Letitia, Mrs. John Snook of Belmont Castle in Bedhampton.[34] Within a month Dilke was back home and "poor little Mrs. D" was herself in Brighton recuperating, Keats says, "from another gall-stone attack."[35]

It was during this period that Keats met Fanny Brawn. Following his customary practice of renting his side of Wentworth Place for the summer, Brown had let his house to a Mrs. Brawne and her three children, the eldest of whom was Fanny. Dilke reports that in October or November Keats "met Miss Brawne for the first time at my house."

Brown let his house when he and Keats went to Scotland to Mrs. Brawne, a stranger to all of us. As the house adjoined mine in a large garden, we almost necessarily became acquainted. When Brown returned, the Brawnes took another house at the top of Downshire Hill; but we kept up our acquaintance and no doubt Keats, who was daily with me, met her soon after his return from Teignmouth.[36]

During this time Keats was caring for his dying brother Tom at Well Walk, Hampstead, across the heath from Wentworth Place. He had begun *Hyperion*, had regained his own health, and had apparently weathered the attacks on *Endymion* in *Blackwood's Magazine* and the *Quarterly Review*.[37] Through October and November Tom's condition made it imperative that he be attended almost constantly, especially in the last stages of his consumptive illness. As perhaps his only respite from the long, lonely hours at Tom's bedside, Keats "was daily" with Dilke, for it was only a few minutes' walk from Well Walk to Wentworth Place. There with Brown they talked of "different and indifferent Matters—of Euclid, of Metaphysics of the Bible, of Shakspeare, of the horrid System and conseque[nce]s of the fagging at great Schools...."[38] But Tom grew steadily worse. Finally, on the morning of December 1, Tom died, and by mid-December Keats had moved in with Brown and Dilke. Toward the end of the month, though still bothered by "a plaguey sore throat," Keats's strength, his good humor, and much of his good spirits gradually returned, so that, accompanied by Mrs. Dilke, he could visit his sister Fanny and solicit from her guardian a visit in return; he could go "with Dilke a shooting on the heath"; he could be cheered by Dilke's "great confidence" in the eventual outcome of George's migration to America; and in turn he could give encouragement to Dilke, who was "up to his ears in Walpole's Letters." He tells George and Georgiana about a battle with Mrs. Dilke with celery stalks, and though "nothing particular passed," he and the Dilkes welcomed the new year at a dinner at Mrs. Brawne's.[39]

On January 21, Keats joined Brown at Chichester, who since before Christmas had been a house guest of Old Mr. Dilke. Maria writes to her father-in-law, "You will find him a very odd young man, but good-tempered, and good hearted, and very clever indeed."[40] Two days later Brown and Keats walked seven miles to the home of Letitia Snook, Dilke's sister in Bedhampton, with whom Keats some twenty months later spent his last night in England. From Bedhampton Brown and Keats composed a letter to Maria:

Bedhampton, 24th Jany 1819.

Dear Dilke,

This letter is for your Wife, and if you are a Gentleman, you will deliver it to her, without reading one word further. *"read thou Squire,"*[41] There is a wager depending on this.

My charming dear Mrs Dilke,

It was delightful to receive a letter from you,—but such a letter! what presumption in me to attempt to answer it! Where shall I find, in my poor brain, such gibes, such jeers, such flashes of merriment? Alas! you will say, as you read me, Alas! poor Brown! quite chop fallen! But that's not true; my chops have been beautifully plumped out since I came here; my dinners have been good & nourishing, & my inside never washed by a red herring broth. Then my mind has been so happy! ...I am sorry—*that Brown and you are getting so very witty—my modest feathered Pen fizzles like baby roast beef at its entrance among such tantrum sentences—or rather ten senses... Mrs. Snook I catch smoaking it every now and then and I believe Brown does—but I cannot now look sideways—Brown wants to scribble more so I will finish with a marginal note—Viz. Remember me to Wentworth Place and Elm Cottage—not forgetting Millamant —your's if possible J. Keats....*

This is abominable! I did but go up stairs to put on a clean & starched hand-kerchief, & that overweening rogue read my letter, & scrawled over one of my sheets, *and given him a counterpain,—I* wish I could blank-it all over *and beat him with a* {^kertain rod... *he shan't ticlke me pillow the feathers,*—I would not give a tester for such puns, *let us ope brown* (erratum—a large B—*a Bumble B*) *will go no further in the Bedroom* & not call Mat Snook a relation to Mattrass—*This is grown to a conclusion—I had excellent puns in my head but one bad one from Brown has quite upset me* but I am quite set-up for more, but I'm content to be conqueror. Your's in love,
                                                         Cha Brown.

   N.B. I beg leaf to withdraw all my puns—they are all wash, an bas uns—[42]

Probably Keats was not trying to be modest when he wrote to George and Georgianna in mid-February that during his visit to the Snooks' and Old Mr. Dilke's: "Nothing worth speaking of happened," although he did take some thin paper and wrote on it "a little poem called 'St. Agnes Eve.'"[43]

Beginning at this time Keats has a great deal to say about Dilke and "his boy," on whom, no doubt too much attention was centered. He explains that Dilke had long been uneasy about the manner of educating Wentworth:

...—he [Dilke] at length decided for a public school—and then he did not know what school—he at last has decided for Westminster; and as Charley is to be a day boy, Dilke will remove to Westminster...—Dilke is at present in greek histories and antiquit[i]es—and talks of nothing but the electors of Westminster and the retreat of the ten-thousand—...[44]

Brown, too, was critical of Dilke's "parental mania." In a letter inviting Dilke's nephews to visit him at Hampstead Brown speaks of his regret that Dilke will be no longer his neighbor:

Hampstead, 3 April 1819.

My dear Boys,

On Thursday next I expect to see you. I shall be in Great Smith Street at about 11 o'Clock to meet the Tooting Coach; unless I hear from you to the contrary. I shall rely on your coming at that hour. My Lord Sands and the Marquis of Carrots, my illustrious nephews, will be met at the same time, by their father, at the other end of the Town. On Saturday Miss Jin and Miss Fanny, with half a dozen other Misses (my sweetheart Emma among them) are to try how much cake it will be possible to consume at one sitting. And on Easter Day we are all invited to dine at Mrs. Davenport's.

Your Uncle has this morning begun to move off from Wentworth Place I don't like it at all. He has taken a house in Westminster to be near Master Charley at school. You will be sorry not to find them my next door neighbours. Mrs. Brawne has taken the house.

Present my Comp[s] to Mr Lord, and request to know when the first full school day will take place after the holidays.

Dear Boys, I am ever

Your affectionate friend

Chas. Brown[45]

Shortly afterwards, Keats confirmed that Dilke, Wentworth, and Maria had in fact moved to new lodgings in 3 Great Smith Street

(April 3, 1819). Agreeing with Brown, Keats breaks his reserve and tells of Dilke's "obsession":

The Di[l]kes like their lodging in Westminster tolerably well. I cannot help thinking what a shame it is that poor Dilke should give up his comfortable house & garden for his Son, whom he will certainly ruin with too much care—The boy has nothing in his ears all day but himself and the importance of his education. Dilke has continually in his mouth "My Boy" This is what spoils princes: it may have the same effect with Commoners. Mrs. Dilke has been very well lately— But what a shameful thing it is for that obstinate Boy Dilke should stifle himself in Town Lodgings and wear out his Life by his continual apprehension of his Boys fate in Westminsterschool with the rest of the Boys and the Masters. Eve[r]y one has some wear and tear—One would think Dilke ought to be quiet and happy—but no— this one Boy makes his face pale, his society silent and his vigilance jealous—He would I have no doubt quarrel with anyone who snubbed his Boy—With all this he has no notion how to manage him.[46]

Dilke's obsession, Keats feared, was like any obsession: what normally passed for a relatively harmless and quaint failing may in this case have serious consequences for both father and son:

Dilk is entirely swallowed up in his boy: 'tis really lamentable to what a pitch he carries a sort of parental mania. I had a letter from him at Shanklin. He went on a word or two about the isle of Wight which is a bit of [a] hobby horse of his; but he soon deviated to his boy. "I am sitting" says he "at the window expecting my Boy from School." I suppose I told you somewhere that he lives in Westminster, and his boy goes to the School there, where he gets beaten, and every bruise he has and I dare say deserves is very bitter to Dilke.[47]

He tried in various ways to restore some balance to Dilke's "parental mania"; on one occasion he undoubtedly put their friendship to a severe test when he jokingly referred to Wentworth as "the Westmonisteranian."[48] On another occasion he tried to sooth Dilke into a philosophical acceptance of the "wear and tear":

I am sorry to hear that Charles is so much oppress'd at Westminster: though I am sure it will be the finest touchstone for his Metal in the world—His troubles will grow day by day less, as his age and strength increase. The very first Battle he wins will lift him from the Tribe of Manassah. I do not know how I should feel were I a Father—but I hope I should strive with all my Power not to let the present trouble me—When your Boy shall be twenty, ask him about his childish troubles and he will have no more memory of them than you have of yours.[49]

Owing to a variety of reasons, September 1819 probably marks the peak of friendship between Keats and Dilke. To be sure, they remained on generally friendly terms right up to Keats's death, and letters and visits were exchanged nearly up to the time Keats left England more than a year later. Indeed, Dilke may never have been aware of any real lessening of affections.[50]

But a lessening of sorts there assuredly was, and while it may have been partly owing to a "morbidity of temperament," itself exacerbated by his approaching consumptive illness, it is nonetheless true that for the first time Keats began to discover serious flaws in the character and motives of his closest friends: Hunt, Reynolds, Bailey, Hayden, not excepting even Dilke and Brown; and later not even his brother George.

Writing in September 1818, Keats had reminded George of Dilke's liking for the sociopolitical theories of Godwin. He had called him, rather accurately for the time, a "Godwin-perfectabil[it]y man,"[51] and meant it, if not as a compliment, at least approvingly. Keats himself was of two minds on the matter, but ultimately opted in favor of the "Grand march of intellect,"[52] owing partly, no doubt, to Dilke's unflinching certainty on the issue. But by October 1819, Dilke's unflinching certainty on almost all other issues as well began to annoy Keats, so that the designation "Godwin perfectability man" of October 1818, became the less imaginative, prosaic "Godwin-Methodist" nearly a year later.[53]

Even so, during the ensuing period from September 1819 through July 1820, Keats probably saw more of the Dilkes than of any other of his old acquaintances except Brown. In early October he wrote from Shanklin to ask Dilke to procure rooms near Westminster, where Dilke lived. From rooms thus procured on 25 College Street he sent word that on any fine day Mrs. Dilke would be glad to accompany him to Hampstead to visit Fanny Brawne. He in turn called upon Dilke in the Navy Pay Office to talk about George. He had Christmas Dinner with Mrs. Dilke, where he agreed to serve as one of the judges of a fairy tale contest between Brown and Dilke.[54]

In the meantime, sometime before the ninth of January, George Keats had arrived from America and left again on the thirtieth, on which departure he was believed by Brown and others to take money which he then knew belonged to his brother.[55] Four days later on February 3, Keats had the attack of blood-spitting which signalled the commencement of his final illness.

In March, however, he writes a cheerful enough letter wherein he very justifiably chides Dilke for his illegible handwriting.

You must improve your penmanship; your writing is like the speaking of a child of three years old, very understandable to its father but to no one else. The worse is it looks well—no that is not the worst—the worst is, it is worse than Bailey's. Bailey's looks illegible and may perchance be read; your's looks very legible and may perchance not be read.[56]

In April he assured his sister that he would ask Mrs. Dilke to pay her a visit, that her dog "was being attended to like a Prince" (probably its name), and shortly afterwards that "Mrs. Dilke's Brother was caring for it."[57] There are no more extant letters from Keats to the Dilkes.

In June 1820 Keats's illness had reached an advanced stage; he had parted with Brown at Gravesend (Brown having let his house for the summer), and he was miserable in Kentish Town in his voluntary exile from Fanny. In this state of mind, in some of his letters—often painful letters revealing a soul in torment—Keats makes surprising and curious statements regarding Dilke and Brown:

Brown is a good sort of Man—he did not know he was doing me to death by inches. I feel the effect of every one of those hours in my side now; and for that cause, though he has done me many services, though I know his love and friendship for me, though at this moment, I should be without pence were it not for his assistance, I will never see or speak to him until we are both old men, if we are to be.[58]

And again, probably in August:

Mr. Dilke came to see me yesterday, and gave me a very great deal more pain than pleasure. I shall never be able any more to endure to [for *the*] society of any of those who used to meet at Elm Cottage and Wentworth Place. The last two years taste like brass upon my Palate[59] ... I will indulge myself by never seeing any more Dilke or Brown or any of their friends.[60]

These are feverish statements, of course, for the wearying, slow, consumptive illness had long been having its morbid effects on the heightened sensitivity and imagination of Keats. But though he realized to some extent some unfairness on his own part, Keats felt he had reasons for such statements. Certain distractions undoubtedly contributed to Keats's coolness toward Brown and the Dilkes. We saw how Keats disapproved of Dilke's handling of Wentworth; likewise, Dilke appeared at times to be too forceful in his dissemination of the gospel of Godwin: "At Dilkes I fall foul of politics,"[61] but all of these are minor sins and could and would easily have been forgiven; for by remaining aloof from people, he said, he could "like their good parts without being eternally troubled with the dull processes of their every day lives."[62] But there was one overriding paramount cause for such strange utterances: his frustrations and anger over their well-meant advice concerning Fanny Brawne.

Dilke and The Keats Circle

Fanny Brawne. Fanny was just over eighteen when she met Keats at Dilke's house. In that very first week, he says later, he wrote himself her vassal, though, if his multiplicity of interests at that time (as compared to a year or so later) is evidence, he was probably exaggerating somewhat. Whatever may have been her "true nature" or whatever her feelings may have been toward him in the early months of their courtship, she conveyed the impression to virtually all his friends that she was vain, flippant, and insincere in her attentions toward Keats. Reynolds called her "that poor idle thing of womankind"[63] and his sisters (probably very biased judges) were even more vehement in their censure. Jane Reynolds wrote to Maria that Keats's proposed journey to Rome "must please all his friends on every account...I sincerely hope it will benefit his health, poor fellow! His mind and spirits must be bettered by it; and absence may probably weaken, if not break off a connexion that has been a most unhappy one for him."[64] George, who saw her only during the three weeks he was in London in January 1820, opined that while he could not speak conclusively of her love for John, she had in his presence behaved badly toward her sister and mother and that he had heard from others whose opinions he respected (probably the Reynolds family) that she was an "artful bad-hearted girl."[65] Brown's granddaughter, Maria Osborne (who must have had it from Carlino after Brown's death), said, "My grandfather did not like Fanny Brawne; he thought her superficial and vain, and he considered her flirtatious manner, in the company of every man she met, accounted for Keats's jealousy."[66] In 1883, William Dilke, who was Keats's age and who remembered him at Chichester in 1819, wrote to his grand-nephew:

My recollection of Miss Brawn as a girl agrees with your grand-mothers description. She was of a very sallow complexion not a lady with whom a Poet so sensitive as John Keats would be likely to fall in love. Your grandfather would probably say she made the advances to him without really caring much for him.—[67] She did not accompany him to Italy which she might have done with her brother when Keats went there as a last resource for his health—[68]

And as late at July 3, 1819, Old Mr. Dilke and possibly even Maria believed that the affection was "all on one side;" "I do not think" he wrote to Maria, "that Brawne will ever change to

Keats."[69] Rollins puts it quite succinctly: "She was young and gay; Keats, a jealous, possessive, suspicious lover as well as a desperately sick man. The two were star-crossed...."[70]

Fanny's flirtations with Brown, among others, partly explain Keats's outbursts against him; but what of those against Dilke, who was not a man to flirt?[71] Indeed, Dilke and Maria always liked Fanny, always defended her; and Dilke was her trustee in later years, and remained friends with her for the remainder of his life. Undoubtedly, they would have liked to see Keats and Fanny happily married, but the circumstances of Keats's finances, not to mention his illness, obviously dictated at least a prolonged postponement. In the summer of 1819 Keats had evidently discussed with Dilke his love for Fanny and the advisability of proposing marriage to her, whereupon Dilke no doubt unhesitatingly delivered himself of his sentiments on the matter.[72] Later Keats himself acknowledged that "our friends think and speak for the best."[73] He knew theirs was good, logical advice; but as he grew worse from February onward he came increasingly to resent the advisors.

The comment from William Dilke probably was an accurate statement of Dilke's opinion of Keats and Fanny's early relationship, the period of courtship before their engagement. However, as Keats's letters after February 1820 indicate, and later as her letters to Fanny Keats prove, Fanny did in fact "change to[ward] Keats." Dilke and Maria recognized that change, but still they saw, as did Fanny's mother, the impossibility of any early matrimonial expectations; even so, the star-crossed lovers may have become engaged as early as December 1818.[74] Had their friends known of that engagement, undoubtedly they would have tempered their advice, or at least would have tried to ameliorate the harsh and seemingly heartless tone of it; but in view of the hopeless situation, nothing could have changed their sentiments as to the prospects of an early marriage. Maria accordingly wrote to her father-in-law:

It is quite a settled thing between John Keats and Miss ―――――. God help them. It's a bad thing for them. The mother says she cannot prevent it, and that her only hope is that it will go off. He don't like anyone to look at her or to speak to her.[75]

By summer of 1820 something had happened to cause Keats to distrust even Maria: whether it was something sudden and overt or merely the cumulative effect of good but by then unsolicited advice, it is difficult to say; he wrote to Fanny:

When your mother comes I shall be very sudden and expert in asking her whether you have been to Mrs Dilke's, for she might say no to make me easy.[76]

However, it is quite likely that before he left London to sail for Italy the Dilkes knew of Keats's engagement, and if so, it is almost a certainty that they learned it from Keats himself, not from Fanny, who like Keats, was extremely averse to anyone's knowing her private thoughts or intimacies concerning her betrothal. Before he departed from her, Keats elicited from Fanny Brawne a promise to establish correspondence with his sister in Walthamstow. This she did with an admirable consistency, introducing herself in her first letter to Fanny as "a great friend of Mrs. Dilke's."[77]

When Keats departed London for Italy on September 19, 1820, he had first put in at Gravesend, but after being blown about ten terrible days in the channel, the *Maria Crother* put in again at Portsmouth. From there he and Severn walked the three miles to Bedhampton to visit Dilke's sister. There Keats spent his last night on English soil: he closed a letter to Brown:

The Capt the Crew and the Pasengers are all illtemper'd and weary. I shall write to dilke. I feel as if I was closing my last letter to you.[78]

We cannot know whether he ever wrote Dilke that letter, though he did send word by Letitia Snook that "he was much better than when he left London." But he was not better, and after he reached Italy, he grew steadily worse. He was not deceived about his "complaint," as Fanny noted later, and the letters Severn sent back to England grew more and more ominous. He could read no letters "for fear of agitating himself," but he did express a wish that Mrs. Brawne and Mrs. Dilke call on Fanny Keats.[79] Though the worst "was kept from her," Fanny Brawne had no misconception as to the seriousness of Keats's illness. Brown reports to Severn that when the tragic news of Keats's death did reach England she

—was to have it told her; and the worst had been concealed from her knowledge, ever since your December letter. It is now five days since she heard it. I shall not speak of the first shock, nor of the following days,—it is enough she is now pretty well,—and thro'out she has shown a firmness of mind which I little expected from one so young, and under such a load of grief.[80]

After an extended period of mourning, Fanny Brawne set about carrying out her betrothed's wish that she and his sister become friends. Also pursuant to Keats's wish, Maria accompanied Mrs. Brawne to see Fanny Keats in Pancras Lane. Their object was to persuade Fanny Keats's guardian to allow her to visit Wentworth Place. In the heat of the ensuing discussion Maria apprised Mrs. Abbey of Keats's and Fanny Brawne's engagement, though Mrs. Abbey "appeared to know it already."[81] For the next few years Fanny and Maria were intimate, exchanging daily and sometimes weekly visits and corresponding often. Especially in the months that followed Keats's death Maria Dilke tried to see to it that both sister's and lover's minds were occupied.

Fanny was understandably bitter toward the Reynolds family, whom she resented not only for their animosity toward her, but whom she included among those who she felt contributed to Keats's despondency over his courtship: for the "want of feeling in those who ought above all to have felt for him." When for some reason in late November 1821, Maria quarreled with the Reynolds family, Fanny remarks

—I have been a few days at Mrs Dilkes there I heard only one thing to please me, she has quarrelled, I hope for ever with the Reynolds. My dear Fanny if you live to the age of the Methuselem and I die tomorrow never be intimate with the Reynolds, for I dare say they

will come your way—Mrs Dilke cannot keep up a feud and perhaps will be friends again. Every day I live I find out more of their
malice against me—[82]

Fanny was right: Mrs. Dilke could not keep up the feud, though
by October 1822 it had drawn on for nearly a year. The occasion
for their reconciliation was the marriage of John Reynolds to
Elizabeth Drewe. When they called on the bride and groom, the
Dilkes were informed that the Reynolds sisters were "very anxious
to make up the quarrel."[83] They promptly did so, undoubtedly
a relief to Dilke who with Reynolds could not but have felt the
strain on the otherwise close friendship which had lasted at least
seven years (that it was to continue for at least two dozen more
proved a boon to literature).

By January 1836, after Fanny Brawne had married Louis Lindo
(or Lindon, 1812–72) and the couple had begun their rather extensive travels on the Continent, she became close friends with
the former Jane Reynolds, now Mrs. Hood,[84] living in Coblenz,
Germany. At one point she was "commissioned" to hand-carry to
the Dilkes some letters and parcels, some of which she forgot;[85]
later she wrote to Jane from Düsseldorf, mentioning her efforts in
the culinary arts.[86] In April 1838 Maria wrote to Jane Hood in
Ostend an intriguing note which may throw some light on the
reasons for the Lindo family's frequent movements on the continent:

I have not heard from Mrs. Lindo—but we saw in the paper the
other day that Capt. Lindo and another paymaster had now settled
all their business—that of course he is at liberty again—however he
has been fortunate in being kept on so long—they of course will
reside there.[87]

Finally, in December 1838 Jane wrote that she and Hood had
temporarily lost touch with the Lindo family and supposed they
must have left Bayonne. Fanny continued to be mentioned and
"remembered" by both Hood and Jane at least through 1839.[88]
Fanny continued also to correspond with the Dilkes. In Novem-

ber 1848 she wrote to Maria, probably in reference to Milne's *Life of Keats*:

> ...you must not be surprised at Mr. Lindons mentioning the *"memoirs."* He has a very imperfect idea of the real case. *Perhaps thinks his wife had an admirer, no more.* He never would have heard of it, had it not happened about seven or eight years ago, he noticed the portrait in your room; and asked who it was. As you hesitated in answering, he felt puzzled & I, to prevent awkward mistakes in future, when we got home explained as much as was necessary.[89]

By 1851 both Jane Hood and Maria had died, and with them passed the last of Fanny Lindon's close associates who had known Keats. This excepts, of course, Dilke (with whom, however, they kept only sporadic communication), and Fanny Keats, who had ungenerously broken off all correspondence with Fanny Brawne because she "never understood nor excused" her marriage to Louis Lindo.[90] By this time Dilke was occupying himself in eighteenth-century studies after having retired from public life. He and the Lindons may have renewed acquaintances in the early 1860s when the Lindon family returned to London after nearly thirty years of living in various countries on the Continent. Louis Lindon is said to have secured a position as one of the Secretaries of the 1862 [Great] Exhibition, but more accurately was a secretary to one of the Exhibition Commissioners; tradition has it that Wentworth, by then himself a respected and influential public figure and one of the four commissioners to the second Great Exhibition, secured this appointment for him.[91]

One further transaction, often misunderstood, between Fanny and the Dilkes should be mentioned. At about this time Fanny, beset with financial difficulties, was forced to part with one of her treasured Keatsian relics: Severn's miniature of Keats. In so parting she doubtless gave aid and comfort to her later critics, though posterity could as well honor her who would render up something precious in an effort to help support her family. Sir Charles preserved this much of her letter:

... It is towards enabling me to do this that I am induced to ask whether it would suit you to purchase that miniature of Mr. Keats which has been for so long a time in my possession. It would not be a light motive which would make me part with it, but I have this satisfaction, that next to my own family, there is no one whose possession I should....[92]

Though the letter breaks off here, it is evident that Sir Charles looked with disdain upon the transaction. But his grandfather bought the miniature and was grateful.

In 1862 Dilke retired to a secluded estate in his beloved native Hampshire, to Alice Holt, near Farnham. There, pursuant perhaps to the guidance of his son, considered by now an authority in horticulture, Dilke became a gardener; there, Richardson opines, occasionally Fanny Brawne and her husband would visit him, "hands in pockets making observations."[93] And there to him, and only to him, Richardson further surmises, Fanny would talk of Keats.[94]

Fanny Keats Llanos.   Until at least 1846 Dilke and Maria continued also to keep in touch with Fanny Keats, whose communications with Fanny Brawne were severed. After coming of age in 1824, she visited often with the Brawnes in Hampstead and with the Dilkes in Lower Grosvenor Street. In 1826 Fanny married a dashing, cosmopolitan Spaniard who had met her brother during his last days in Italy. Fanny Brawne heartily approved of him, had written to Fanny Keats about him, and after they met in late 1821 had encouraged their friendship. She must have been very pleased with Fanny's choice. Dilke liked the author of *Sandoval* and *Don Estaban* personally—as who did not—but later had cause to regret his business acumen.[95]

Shortly before Miss Keats came of age in 1824, she began to experience much difficulty in extracting her inheritance from her guardian, that "consummate villain," Abbey. Unknown even to George at the time, it was Dilke who came to her aid and succeeded in forcing Abbey to relinquish all the property that was rightfully hers.[96] Already trustee to Fanny Brawne and to her sister Margaret, he became cotrustee (with Rice) to Fanny Keats, in which relationship he continued probably until well into the 1850s. Sometimes given (it must be admitted) to a degree of self-centeredness and narrowness of sympathies, Fanny Keats herself was nevertheless sensible of Dilke's great exertions on her and her brother's behalf. On his wresting her funds from Abbey, she wrote to George, "When you write to Mr. Dilke I must beg you to thank him most warmly for his great kindness to me...."[97] Later in 1828, when George Keats was himself in great consternation about his own financial affairs in England (the settlement of which had dragged on since Fanny's coming of age in 1824), Dilke came to his aid and after a great deal of attention and labor, managed to conclude them favorably. George wrote to Dilke:

Fanny says that I have been unjust to you in imputing to you carelessness of my interests: in what words and to whom I made the imputation I don't know; I certainly never willed it—She *has* painted your exertions to shame me.[98]

Sometime after their marriage in 1826, the Llanos couple apparently went to Paris to live, where Fanny gave birth to their first child in September 1827. They probably remained there until early 1828 before returning to England to the same famous semi-detached house that the Dilkes, Brown, and her brother had lived in eight years earlier, and where her dearest friend Fanny Brawne was then living in the "larger half."[99] Sam Brawne, Fanny's ailing consumptive brother, would die in April. When in November of the following year Mrs. Brawne died tragically, Fanny Brawne apparently moved into the other half of Wentworth Place to live with Fanny Llanos.[100]

Shortly before this, against Dilke's advice, Valentine Llanos and Fanny had entered into a foolish financial scheme that was to result in a temporary coolness toward Dilke for his alleged indifference to her interests. To get rich quickly, Llanos had turned from author to inventor of what he termed "a clever and useful patent" of bridle bits, though it appears that he and Fanny were alone in thinking so. Out of Fanny's remaining funds which Dilke had "wrested" from Abbey, Llanos spent upwards of "£1000 in the establishment" of his patent and had some £780 left over. The trustees, Rice and Dilke, handed over to Reynolds, his solicitor, the £780, about half of which the latter forwarded to Llanos. When Llanos approached Reynolds for the other half, he was rebuffed, Reynolds perhaps claiming it as his fee for his efforts in behalf of previous Llanos affairs. Llanos explained to George Keats:

Mr. R. though well acquainted with our circumstances and aware of the deep injury he is doing me, by the delay, not only [does not pay me] continues withholding the money but has adopted the plan of never being at home to us, or even vouchsafing an answer to our repeated letters. On the other hand Mr. Dilke, to whom I have communicated the facts, declines interfering on the ground that it would involve him in a quarrel with his friend Rey.[101]

Dilke, however, gave a slightly different slant on the affair; when it was for practical purposes over and the Llanos family was preparing to depart England forever, Dilke wrote to George:

From the first I declined all interference. I do not see how it is possible that Llanos can be wrong, but unfortunately being right does not alter his position, or at all tend to a settlement—I knew too much of Reynolds affairs to intermeddle—they have long been desperate. I should not choose to say so if you were this side the Atlantic— When delay arises from total incapacity to pay money, there is no interference can serve, & as *I had no chance* myself, it would have been ridiculous to intermeddle for others.—You must not return this information to England—The Llanos must be aware of it—but my name would be authority & place me in a position of great difficulty.— As to advising Llanos about Spain, he is unfortunately not the man to take advice or to think he wants it—I believe him to be a very honorable man, but as weak as a child. There never was any speculation so silly as his patent bits— I was *compelled to tell him so*, because application was made to Rice & myself to lend the trust money —we had three sides of an argumentative letter to prove that as the money was put in trust by your grandmother &c for the benefit of his wife and children & as this speculation was for the benefit of his wife & children we were bound &c &c he & *your Sister* were agreed on this, although when the scheme *failed* the latter said it would have been very wrong & had totally forgotten that *she* had ever thought otherwise.[102]

Adami confirms that Dilke, irritated by Llanos's efforts to bring him into the quarrel, "retaliated by placing [what was left] of her marriage settlement funds in the Court of Chancery, and by withdrawing in some degree, from his position as confidential advisor."[103] Indeed, though Fanny declared that "This matter might have been greatly simplified had either of the trustees stepped forward in the business,"[104] it is not clear as to just what kind of pressure Dilke could have applied on Reynolds even had he willed to do so.

After Fanny moved to Spain, however, Dilke and Maria maintained infrequent correspondence with friends either in Spain or America. Dilke still served, if not as "confidential advisor," then at least as "financial executor," for he saw to it that proceeds from her property in England were periodically mailed to her in Spain. On one occasion in April 1838, when the Dilkes heard from Fanny through friends, Maria writes to Jane Hood:

Young Montessino—a friend of the Drs[105] has come over to dine with us on Sunday. He says Mr. Llanos has an excellent situation— only he *don't* get *any salary*.[106]

This "excellent situation" had come about when in 1835 liberalism triumphed under the leadership of Mendizabel, whom Llanos had known in London. Adami states that Llanos "was supplied with money from the family purse."[107]

In 1840 Espartero seized power, and, fortunately for Llanos, managed to retain it for a few years. In the meantime, Llanos made according to Adami "the one fortunate speculation of his life"[108] in an investment in church property. By 1846 he was apparently in easy circumstances, for Dilke wrote to Milnes, who was collecting materials for a *Life of Keats*:

While in office he managed to *buy* some church property, & in this way or someway, has become a reasonably prosperous gentleman. I infer so for, curiously enough, I have this day received a letter from him, wherein he request[s] me to receive & pay the dividends due to Mrs. Llanos from June 1842! Now a man must be reasonably well off who leaves dividends unclaimed for four years & a half.[109]

When Milnes had completed his *Life of Keats* in August 1848, he sent a copy (two volumes) to Dilke to forward to Mrs. Llanos. Dilke replied that he supposed she was residing in Valladolid, but that in any event, he had no way at present of getting the volumes to her.

Her last letter, the *third* of enquiry after *George* and his family, I received only *six weeks* since! ...I was so ignorant of the authority on which George's death was reported, that heretofore I evaded the subject.[110]

Milnes himself could have enlightened Dilke on this subject, and it is curious why he did not do so then and there. Milnes knew for a certainty that George had died in December 1841.[111]

After 1861, Fanny struck up a long and fruitful correspondence with Severn, whom she had never met. But in the intervening years, between 1833 and 1861, Dilke and Maria were apparently her only link with her past acquaintances in England and until 1841 with her only surviving brother in America.

George Keats and the Dilke-Brown Controversy. Similarly, through the Dilkes the brother in America maintained to some extent his ties with former friends and interests (largely financial) in England. Presumably Georgiana corresponded often with members of her family, but few records remain of that interchange.

The Dilke and George Keats correspondence extended over a fourteen year period (1824–38) and consists of at least two dozen letters, of which sixteen are preserved (including one unpublished from George to Maria, and not including one unpublished from Georgiana to Maria).[112] Their long interchange of letters concerned two paramount interests: Dilke's attending to and settlement of numerous financial problems which George, a continent away, could not attend to himself; and, more important to Keats students, the Dilke-Brown controversy over the extent of George's culpability, if any, regarding the Keats family's inheritance.

Throughout the George Keats-Dilke correspondence George shows himself extremely grateful for Dilke's efforts in his behalf. In letter after letter he affirms his gratitude in expressions like "I ... look upon y[ou] as the best Friend I have in the world;[113] ... "My good and kind friend Dilke,"[114] "you are the man of all others to whom I am most closely allied in feeling."[115] To Maria he writes somewhat later:

I have not any correspondent in England who understands me, or the things that interest me, Assured by his repeated kindnesses, I took to Mr. Dilke as my anchor in my native sod, and so long as my cable of love of Country, and kindly feeling lasts, I shall cherish a hope that I shall one day haul my vessel to his hearth.[116]

And to Dilke himself:

I found so much evidence of your great kindness to me, that you performed so much disagreeable labour on my acc, that you waded thro so many calculations and figures for my benefit, of a nature so disagreeable to your particular frame of mind, that I could not for an instant cherish any of those sp[l]enetic feelings your supposing me capable of abstracting an item from the acc of a supposed bankrupt and placing it to yours, was calculated to raise.—I now most earnestly beg that you will assure yourself of my endless gratitude for the services you have rend^d me, and more [o]ver my most particular partiality for you independently of any gratitude for benefits confered, which would alone have protected you from any wrong on my part, did not my good principles protect every man.[117]

However, George remained largely unaware of the details concerning Dilke's defense of him against charges that he knowingly took money belonging to his brother. These charges were made primarily by Brown and Haslam but echoed by Taylor and Hessey and apparently at first Abbey. With his bride Georgiana Wylie,

George had sailed to America in June 1818, intending to proceed to the Birkbeck settlement, about five miles west of what is now Albion, Illinois. Before reaching that settlement, however, he turned back eastward at Princeton, Indiana, and proceeded to Louisville, Kentucky, where he promptly lost £500 in a scheme not fully understood but involving apparently a sunken boat, some of the merchandise on which he had bought from Audubon, the naturalist.[118] He then returned briefly to England in January 1820 to procure his share of Tom's inheritance and to settle other aspects of the money dealings between him and John. When George returned to America at the end of January 1820, his brother John indicated to Brown and possibly to others his displeasure with George for taking money which actually belonged to John.

This controversy has received numerous extended treatments. Nearly all Keats biographers since Colvin have recognized that, important as they were, the questions regarding the extent of George's culpability or of Dilke's or Brown's lack of complete disinterestedness, or of both, were among the lesser considerations surrounding the issue. The main issue was the result that an adequate Keats *Life* had been delayed (perhaps fortunately so) for more than twenty-six years—longer than the life of the poet himself.

In 1825 Dilke contemplated writing a *Life of Keats* and was encouraged by George, who agreed to furnish him, or Reynolds, all the materials in his possession. Brown, who had made copies of many of Keats's poems and who still possessed many of the letters, likewise dreamed of publishing a *Life* and did in fact write a *Memoir*, which figured prominently in Milne's *Life* in 1848. But neither side could write an adequate life without access to the materials in the possession of the other.

To their credit most biographers have charitably ascribed the long-standing argument between Dilke and Brown to each one's honest conviction that he was in the right. Thus far no biographer has conclusively shown either to be in the wrong.[119] Nearly all biographers have revealed a bias, however, and have elected to take sides depending on whether Brown's charges or Dilke's rebuttal appears more convincing. If one finds George guilty, Dilke becomes a positive, obstinate, inflexible dogmatist who would not see, or who affected not to see, the mathematical proofs before his eyes. Even his motives may be suspect. If George is deemed innocent, Dilke becomes a hero who defends to the end his helpless friend. One must then question Brown's assertions of George's guilt. No one would accuse Brown of ulterior motives; but in their more charitable constructions, defenders of George will point to a combination of circumstances to support their side, among which are (1) Brown relied too much not only on Keats's imperfect knowledge of his financial affairs, but could find "no fault" or error in some of Keats's utterances even when disease racked him; (2) "though a good man," Brown was vindictive: recalling Keats's injunction "If I die, you must ruin Lockhart,"[120] Brown was for the remainder of his life obsessed with that enjoinment. Since he believed then and continued to believe that Keats's disease was "in his mind," he was vindictive likewise for the pain that John suffered in his grievence toward George—legitimate or not; (3) it is easier to level charges than to prove them unfounded.

The crux of the Dilke-Brown controversy is this: When George left England the second time in January 1820, he reminded his brother John of his offer to lend him all the money at his disposal. George later explained that the money was his own in the first place, but that he, who had always arranged money matters between them, led his brother to believe otherwise. His reason for so misleading John, he said, was to shield him, if possible, from the knowledge of how truly serious his financial state actually was, for that desperate news would have plunged him even deeper in despair. Besides, George argued, since it was ever his intent ultimately to support and maintain John so that he might fulfill his poetic destiny without being encumbered by mundane pecuniary worries, he would have been justified in taking John's money as an investment in their partnership. But, he adds, even in that circumstance he did not and could not have taken John's money, for the simple reason that John had none to take! George's contention was essentially that, unknown to John, he (George) had "given" him some £375, which, for purposes stated above, he let John believe was the amount remaining of his own share of their grandmother's estate. Actually, contended George, there was nothing remaining, and the £375 was George's own. When, therefore, in January 1820 he "borrowed" £170 from John, he was thus borrowing his own money and was in fact a creditor to John by some £200.[121]

But these facts, if true, were unknown to the poet. He was hurt by the indifference to his welfare and happiness apparent in the behavior of George who left him with only £60 though he, John, already owed £80. John confided to Brown that George "did not act rightly" in leaving him so. When Brown inquired why Keats kept secret his promise of assisting George, Keats replied "Because I knew you would oppose it, and because your opposition must have been in vain against my promise."[122] Thinking that Keats's consumption was severely aggravated by George's duplicity, Brown vowed revenge. "What is to be done with George? Will he ever dare to come among his brother's friends?"[123] A month later, he wrote again "You have heard, or may hear, of my letter to George,— I read a copy of it to Taylor; —should you hear news of that *money brother* pray let me know,—as for remittances from him,— we must dream about them.—Wait a month, and if George remains still silent, give him such a sting as he has had from me.—"[124] Later while Keats was still alive, Brown called George a "canting, selfish, heartless swindler, and shall have to answer for the death of his brother,—if it must be so."[125] He wrote to Severn that

...you and I well know poor Keats' disease is in the mind,—he is dying broken hearted. You know much of his grief, but do you know how George has treated him? I sit planning schemes of vengeance upon his head. Should his brother die, exposure and infamy shall consign him to perpetual exile. I will have no mercy,—the world will cry aloud for the cause of their Keats' untimely death, and I will give it, O Severn, nothing on my part could stop that cruel brother's hand,—indeed I knew not, till after he quitted us the second time for America, how cruel he had been.[126]

So matters stood until Brown decided a year later to live in Italy. Earlier he had determined to "follow Keats," as he said, though Dilke pointed out that some eighteen months passed before he did so. A part of the reason for Brown's delay undoubtedly was the added responsibility of his baby son Carlino (born July 16, 1820).[127] In March of 1822 Brown wrote to his friend Thomas Richards listing objections to Richard's offer to care for young Carlino for a few years during Brown's absence in Italy; the final objection concerned "the extreme trouble in rearing a child, whom you are to lose at a certain period, unless I myself die & then you & Dilke may settle him as you please."[128] In an intriguing afterthought he adds, "You must know from what I said to you a fortnight ago, it never was my intention to leave the child with Mrs. Dilke, and she knew it." For some unspecified time he did, however, leave the child with Mrs. Richards, as shown by the following letter assigning Dilke and Richards his executors and guardians to Carlino:

My Dear Dilke,
    Yesterday I deposited in the hands of Mr. Robert Skynner, of No. 62 Great Portland Street, my last Will and Testament, wherein I have appointed you my Executor, together with Mr. Thomas Richards of the Storekeeper's Office in the Ordnance Department in the Tower; and likewise I have appointed him and you Guardians to my natural Son, Charles Brown, during his minority. In order to prevent any mistake, I hereby declare that my said natural Son, Charles Brown, is the child who lately resided with me in Wentworth Place, Hampstead, and who at present resides with Mr. Thomas Richards in his house at No. 9 Providence (or Sidney) Place, near Vauxhall Gardens, and whom I have hitherto always acknowledged as my Son. I intend to take him with me to Italy. He was baptized in the Spanish Chapel in London, and will have completed the second year of his age on the 16th of this month.
    Wishing you health and happiness, and no trouble as my Executor, I remain,

My dear Dilke,
Your sincere friend,
Chas. Brown[129]

After Brown and Carlino left for Italy in September 1822, excepting Maria's exculpation of George to Fanny Keats,[130] for the next two years the issue of his guilt or innocence seemed to die down. George himself revived it when on April 10, 1824, he wrote to Dilke, whom he thought the least likely among his brother's friends "to be influenced by those reports so injurious to [his] honor."[131] In this letter George outlined his defence, claiming effect that he had in 1818 given Keats money (though he acknowledged that Keats may not have realized that it was George's money and not his own);[132] so that when he "borrowed" on his return to America the second time (January 1820) he was actually borrowing from himself.[133] Finally he voices his desire, though he does not specifically ask, that Dilke give appropriate publicity to his defense.

Dilke did so on July 31, 1824, sending the "heads," as Brown called them, of George's letter prefaced by a few sociable remarks of his own:

Upon my conscience, Brown, I believe I am one of the most kind, considerate, affectionate, pleasant, sociable, unsociable fellows that "lard the lean earth,"—I have not had your letter six hours, but, though perplexed with more than my usual no-occupation, here I am having a chat with you.—I believe there is something in good spirits & warmheartedness, more infectious than plague, pestilence, methodism, or hunting, & your letters have the spot upon them, so that one half of my amiability is to be set off to your account.—I know not that you are a "good letter writer," or any other thing that is *good*; but somehow you contrive to put one in a good humour, & the first feeling after the second reading is to do one's best to thank you.—[134]

After giving a judgment (or perhaps a "no-opinion") on whether Severn's time and effort would be well spent were he to exhibit a copy of a Raphael fresco, Dilke introduces George's defense:

—Having thus made a clearance of the old account, I think I should, to be in character, say, struck the Balance, I am about to open a new one; & as I reduced your odd hundred thousand specious truths, to *one*, on a former occasion, I now have to score up another, that may stand as a cypher at the *right* end of the Balance.—What will you say, or how open your eyes & fix your attention, when I tell you that I have had a letter from Geo Keats.—Aye and just *such* a letter, mind I have nibbed my pen, as in "my strange obstinacy" I always maintained he would write, when he wrote at all.[135]

It is not clear to what the "thousand specious truths" part of this passage refers; the later part is significant, however, for its suggestion that George's fate had been previously argued and that both Brown and Dilke had already made up their minds on the matter. If so, George's explanation left the principals exactly as it had found them. Dilke asked Brown to "have the goodness to convey the spirit of what follows to Mr Hunt & any other likely to have heard of the charge, which, as he understands it assumes its most tangible shape in form 'that he on his second return to America took with him £700 of his Brother's money.' "[136]

Brown replied doubtfully to Dilke and quite negatively to Severn:

Geo. Keats has written a very long letter to Dilke, to exculpate himself from the charge against him, and expressing himself very angry that ever it was made. Dilke thinks his letter conclusive in his favor, and sends me the heads of it. I am sorry I cannot agree with him, as his George's assertions are directly in opposition not only to what John Keats said (who might on money affairs be easily in error) but to what Mr Abbey told me.[137]

By coincidence Dilke's letter came at a time when Brown was immersed in another financial embroilment, this one between Leigh Hunt and his brother John. It, too, would consume much of Dilke's time and attention. Briefly, the cause of their contention was as follows: perhaps partly for reasons of health, perhaps also partly for reasons of economy, but primarily for the purpose of establishing a profitable Journal, Leigh Hunt betook himself, his wife, and their seven children to Italy in July 1822. There, together with Shelley and Byron, he began preparation as coeditor of a promising periodical to be called the *Liberal*. All parties looked upon the venture as "the means of great enrichment,"[138] and indeed, considering the talent in abundant attendance, one must allow that the view was not overly optimistic. In coming to Italy, however, Hunt had of necessity to relinquish a portion of his close relationship with the *Examiner*, produced conjointly by him and his brother John since 1808.[139] Even so, the brothers agreed that Hunt would continue to write for the *Examiner* and that they were to divide equally his share of the profits of the *Liberal*. He had barely arrived in Italy, however, when Shelley drowned in the Gulf of Spezzia. Hunt made a valiant effort to launch the *Liberal*, devoted his entire attention to it, even to the extent of writing his brother John that he could contribute no more articles to the *Examiner*. John apparently acquiesced in this contingency in that he registered no objections. But with Shelley dead, Byron became increasingly uninterested in the once-promising venture. Though Byron had paid a good part of Hunt's expenses in coming to Italy, he soon grew impatient with what he felt was a great bother. After the *Liberal* collapsed, John Hunt sent word from England that because Leigh was no longer affiliated with the *Examiner*, he (John) would no longer forward half its profits. By the following year the brothers had worked out a compromise whereby Leigh would contribute and be paid two guineas for every article printed in the paper; in addition, John would settle on him an annuity of £100 charged to the paper and subject to increase, provided the fortunes of the *Examiner* may allow. In the following year when some of Hunt's articles failed to appear in the *Examiner*, his already precarious financial state became desperate. Byron had by now departed for Greece. In failing health, left with one or two friends nearly as penniless as he, and in a foreign land with a family of nine to support, Hunt was in despair. He wrote to Brown asking for assistance in straightening out his affairs and, if possible, to persuade John to resume payment for uninserted articles or to consider him still a partner in the enterprise.

To his great credit Brown not only responded to Hunt's request to analyze and order Hunt's finances, but in letter after detailed letter he painstakingly reviewed every pertinent transaction between the two brothers. From the first, however (August 1824), Brown believed that Leigh Hunt had the better side of the argument. Since he was close friends with both brothers, he understood and feared the possibility of alienating one or both of them.

Having at length found in favor of Leigh Hunt, Brown duly sent his conclusions to John Hunt, who remained inflexible in his conviction that Leigh deserved no increase of monies from the *Examiner*. There seemed no solution to the impasse short of legal recourse, which Leigh Hunt was unwilling to inflict on John, not merely because of the added expense, but primarily because such an action would signify a complete break between the two brothers who together had endured for many years privations, hardships, and even imprisonment.

Brown then suggested that the argument be submitted to "arbitration," that is, that each brother appoint an "arbitrator" and that each should agree to abide by the decision of the two arbitrators—not advocates, Brown insisted, but arbitrators. If such arbitrators could not come to an agreement they would themselves appoint a third, whose judgment would be binding. It was some months before John Hunt reluctantly agreed to this arrangement. In due course, however, the dispute was ultimately referred to "arbitration" according to the format recommended by Brown.

By this time the year was 1827. Dilke had visited Brown in Italy the preceding year and had left Wentworth in Brown's care for eight months. As Wentworth, in July 1827, returned home to England to enter Cambridge, Brown sent by him to Dilke all the pertinent material he had collected on the Hunt Brothers. Why to Dilke? Because as early as May 7, 1825, Leigh Hunt had selected Dilke and Dilke had consented to serve as his "arbitrator."[140]

After Dilke had forwarded the "heads" of George's defense and Brown had answered (September 6, 1824), still with grave reservations about George's probity, apparently some further discussion on the matter took place. Dilke had relayed to George someone's objection that should George have been innocent, he would have written to Dilke immediately instead of delaying more than three years to offer up a defense.[141] But the matter was soon dropped. Soon after to his satisfaction Brown had concluded his part in the Hunt Brothers' affair and Hunt had "fixed upon Dilke as his arbitrator," Brown "went fishing" for Dilke. His lure was attractive, and before May 1826 Dilke had agreed to visit him in Italy. Brown wrote to Hunt "Dilke and his son will be here in Sept^r,—news that makes me wild; then I intend to go with him to Rome and see Severn...."[142] He wrote to Dilke of their plans to visit Rome and Severn, who, Brown said "has answered me in a sentence of joy on the occasion."[143] In the same letter Brown gave to Dilke the itemized account owed him by John Keats. The total was somewhat over £75, which later Dilke claimed erroneously included interest.[144] Brown here showed his continuing distrust of George: "The return of this money is as if I had *found* it, for I never much calculated on it and latterly not at all, notwithstanding what you wrote about Geo Keats."[145] In his next letter to Hunt, dated Oct. 29, 1826, from Florence, he spoke briefly of his "rambles" to Rome, Naples, and Paestum "with Dilke and Co." Not many details regarding the Dilkes' tour are preserved for posterity, and some of those which have been are confusing. But it appears that he left England near the end of May. Sir Charles wrote:

In 1826 Mr. Dilke took his son, who had left Westminster, being then sixteen, and in the highest position in the school, by Ghent, Brussels, Cologne, Munich, Augsburg, and Trent to Venice and thence to Florence. After seeing Bruges and Antwerp, they made their real start from Brussels in August, and posted in one carriage the whole way.[146]

By early September Dilke and Co. were with Brown in Florence, where he met Landor; Brown was pleased to relate: "It was amusing to see him and Dilke together, each by the side of his double; and, no doubt by sympathy, they seemed to take a liking for each other."[147] From Florence they proceeded to Rome to see Severn and Keats's tomb, about which Dilke wrote to Maria:

I have seen poor Keats' tomb, and the very charming little monument that Severn raised to him. Severn, then a poor young artist, who, though now comparatively successful, lives, as he himself told me, on half-a-crown a day, including his servant's wages, and at that time had little—but hope—raised this monument, and never would allow Brown to pay part of the expense of it. I always liked Severn, and shall like him the better as long as I live. You will readily believe me when I tell you I felt a great deal, though I had nerve to conceal it; Brown was brought to tears and walked off, but what was most strange, your boy cried a great deal, and was evidently much affected, though nothing was said by any one at all likely to affect him; indeed very little was said at all."[148]

From Rome to Naples, where apparently nothing much happened; from Naples back to Florence, where he left Wentworth in Brown's care, ostensibly for two years; Brown felt and recorded the compliment:

Dilke has left his son with me for two years; it was far from a pleasant parting, you may suppose when I tell you he always felt a cut in the heart at parting from any body,—"figurativi" what he must have felt as he bade good bye! and God bless you! to an only son for two years! I wonder he did it.[149]

He left Florence before October and proceeded back to England via Geneva, Paris, and Rouen, arriving in London early in December. "He reached his office on the day he had fixed, when he set out six months before, and 'having spent £11 less' than he intended."[150] During the time Wentworth stayed with Brown, Dilke (of course) sent him volumes of letters. Sir Charles quoted an extremely long one on the occasion of Wentworth's birthday (February 18):

My very dear Boy,
    When we cannot do what we wish, we must do what we can. If there be no great deal of deep thinking in this apothegm, there is a vast deal of truth. You will receive this letter on your birthday.

I would wish to meet you coming downstairs, or to welcome you at your first waking,—or myself to waken you with congratulations. To take you by the hand; to kiss your forhead; to give you my blessing; to wish you all possible happiness. This cannot be. All that I *can*, is to wish you happy; and to wish you may *deserve* to be happy, by being virtuous and good.[151]

Dilke clearly missed his son.

The Brown household had by now gotten almost out of hand; besides Wentworth, there was Carlino (who had left his Italian "family"[152] to come to live with his father), and there was also the unpredictable, trouble-prone, in-and-out boarder, Kirkup, who was just then "in" and had brought his mistress Maria with him; so that Brown, accustomed to living alone or at most sharing living expenses with one, found himself in a household of five. He wrote to Hunt about the unusual arrangement, but soon adverted to the impending confrontation between him and John Hunt. It is here that he first spoke of his intention of representing Hunt's side to the Arbitrators:

I think myself strong on all points, armour proof, and certain of victory. At the same time I am not vain enough to think it impossible I may commit some monstrous oversight or blunder in the statement, so I shall consult with Kirkup on it from first to last. I cannot imagine a better Arbitrator for you than Dilke. When he was here, I declined entering on the subject, lest it should be said that he commenced his office as a prejudiced judge.[153]

By July nothing had changed: not the impending confrontation, least of all the crowded household, so that it must have been a great relief to both Brown and Wentworth, and an exceedingly welcome development to Dilke, when after living with Brown eight months of the projected two years, Wentworth tucked under his arm that parcel representing Brown's painstaking efforts over the past four years[154] and set face for London.

After the successful conclusion of the Hunt business, Brown and Dilke continued to correspond frequently. The letters from Flor-

ence, according to Sir Charles, contain gossip mainly about Trelawney, Landor, and Kirkup. In April 1829 Brown related the
story, and his own part in it, of Landor's temporary banishment
from Tuscany under circumstances both ominous and comical and
undoubtedly contributed to Dilke's generally unflattering opinion
of Landor.[155]

It must have been something of perplexity, or at best disappointment, on Dilke's part, to open a letter sometime around Christmas
1829 and find Brown raising the old specter of George's guilt,
which Dilke had supposed to have been effectively laid some five
years earlier: "My dear Dilke, In answer to your favour of 31st
July 1824, or rather in second answer, for the first I sent on 6th
Septr 1824, I beg leave to inform you—but first I must wish you
a merry Christmas and a happy new year, the usual beef, ham,
turkey, plum pudding, mince pies, and a bowl of punch of my own
making;—ditto to wife.—" But the purpose of the letter, as Brown
stated, was to request the 1824 letter from George to Dilke, for
Brown wished to put it under scrutiny:

Fact is, your account of the business was, as I thought at the time,
though I was willing to take the best side, lame in the extreme. I
think his may be a better story, and therefore wish to see it. Besides, upon taking it into my head it is time to write Keats's life,
I read a packet of letters, in which I found a few things against your
statement, (if statement it may be called,) and a letter from Abbey,
addressed to Keats, upbraiding him for having given or lent, (no
matter which,) all his money to George. Then again, I have one of
Abbey's Accts Current with Keats, wherein there are two or three
matters which I cannot reconcile with what, you say, George asserts.
There are also taking them in their general tenour, documents much
against George. You will guess from this that I do not think George
has been calumniated, unknowingly by Keats, and afterwards by me,
in repetition. You will give me credit for wishing to see things in
the best view, if I can. Then, be not fearful that I will make a cruel
use of the letter from George; quite the contrary; all that I want is
authority for stating that Keats's generosity to Tom when under age,
and to George after 21, diminished his fortune, or rather finished it,—

or something to that effect,—I mean that it shall not be a stigma on George,—you understand me of course. . . . I only want George's own statement, word for word,—not, as you see, for any harsh purpose.[156]

In spite of Brown's repeated assertions that he would make no cruel use of George's letter, or that he wanted it for no "harsh purpose," Dilke did not believe him. Brown had written to Fanny Brawne requesting her permission to publish a section of a letter from Keats to her. In his letter Brown adverted to Hunt's account of Keats, showing him as a "whining, puling boy."

Leigh Hunt's account of him is worse than disappointing; I cannot bear it; it seems as if Hunt was so impressed by his illness, that he had utterly forgotten him in health. This is a dreadful mistake, because it is our duty to his memory to show the ruin his enemies had effected; and I will not spare them.[157]

Whether or not he did so, it was not necessary for Dilke to read that letter from Brown to Fanny to realize that in Brown's eyes George was an "enemy." But, as Stillinger suggests, Dilke probably had no other arguments at hand than those already presented in the 1824 defense. He should have had; in April 1825, George had told Dilke that "Mr. Abbey who had the management of our money concerns in a letter lately received expressed himself 'satisfied that my statement of the account between John and me was correct.' "[158] This would, of course, have nullified Brown's early claim that Abbey supported him in his argument with Dilke, but apparently Dilke either had forgotten or overlooked the sentence or else had considered it fruitless to try to change Brown's mind. Certainly, his high contention in his efforts to wrest nearly £3,000 belonging to Fanny Keats from the Jennings estate[159] would prevent any gossip or reminiscences with Abbey about the long-forgotten finances of the Keats brothers. In addition, George had already cause to regret the malicious rumors, as he deemed it, for he believed Brown had influenced Shelley to write in his preface to "Adonais":

I am given to understand that the wound which his sensitive spirit had received from the criticism of Endymion, was exasperated by the bitter sense of unrequited benefits; the poor fellow seems to have been hooted from the stage of life, no less by those on whom he had lavished his fortune and his care.[160]

To all the friends and members of the Keats circle those "on whom he had lavished his fortune and his care" could have meant only George, who wrote to Dilke that he considered the passage highly offensive:

There is a passage in Shelly's Adonais (preface) that is gall and wormwood to me, and seeing from Hunt's work that Brown and Shelly were acquainted I cannot but infer that for the sake of consistency he will repeat the wrong. Where did John get the fortune that he lavished upon me. I certainly promised to remit and should have done so had he owed me £10,000, and was justified by my prospects in thinking I should be able, it turned out that I was not able, on the contrary I was more miserably distressed than John, being as pennyless or more so and having a wife and child to partake of my miseries. I could at the time have exhibited a picture of distress that would have brought tears and forgiveness from John, the reasons why I did not are manifest, he had troubles enough and this would have capped them all. M^rs K can bear witness, how much I suffered from my inability to remit, taunted as I was by the goading letters of Haslam and Brown.[161]

In the summer of 1828 Georgiana and her eldest daughter[162] came to visit the Dilkes for the twofold purpose, as George said, "to see her mother and brothers from whom I robbed her in 1818, and to settle my business" (with Rice and Reynolds Co. and Abbey). While she was there, Charles Wylie, her brother who was assisting Dilke with George's money affairs, wrongly interpreted an account amounting to some £333 in stock as equal that amount in cash, when, in fact, its value was only 76 percent par. Dilke had advised George to draw cash on him, therefore, for about £225, the entire amount. Wylie's error is understandable, since he may not have been privy to the special relationship Dilke held for both Fanny Llanos and George, and was consequently unaware of the bookkeeping practices of Rice and Reynolds, which indeed, sometimes do appear lamentable. That company, keeping back £5 for services rendered, debited Fanny's estate for the £225 and credited Dilke £220 in behalf of George. Wylie, mistakenly thinking Dilke should have remitted £333 (the price of the stocks, not the cash), believed that Dilke still owed George something over £100 and "applied ... roughly" for it. Dilke was incensed not only at Wylie but at George for not refuting Wylie's claim. From the time that Wylie so applied (probably in the fall of 1828) until about the middle of December 1829, Dilke believed that George had participated in and authorized the deception. In the fall of 1829 Dilke wrote a letter protesting Wylie's unauthorized demand, and expostulated with George on the "impossibility of his being uninformed on every particular." There were three such "particulars": (1) Charles Wylie had evidently informed Dilke that he had written George of his own efforts in George's favor; (2) Dilke himself had earlier written to clarify the situation; (3) the Company of Rice and Reynolds would have certainly have sent the account. To these particulars George replied (1) he had received no letter from Wylie in more than two years; (2) Dilke's letter had certainly miscarried, for the most recent communication George had received from Dilke had been the £220 remittance itself; (3) the Rice and Reynolds Company had not written to him, nor should they, inasmuch as Dilke (as they believed) had apprised him of the details of the transaction. Thus George indeed was "uninformed on every particular," or so on November 14, 1829, he expressed himself to Dilke, who believed him, and thus the matter was cleared up.

By early January Dilke had answered Brown's initial letter and had apparently restated his July 1824 position that since Keats was unaware of his own state (George having intentionally misled him to prevent his becoming even more depressed), his complaints have no bearing on any inquiry into George's intent; that he, Dilke, was fully aware of such complaints against George, but as they were complaints in ignorance of his true financial situation, they carried no weight as evidence against George's actions; and finally, that in those complaints made during his extreme morbidity of mind in sickness and approaching death, we see not the real Keats but the false impression of a Keats having fallen somewhat from "his high feelings of generosity" manifested in health and good spirits. Dilke's later opinion of Brown's mindset on the "commercial kernel" may have originated upon receipt of Brown's answer of January 10(?) 1830, showing that he had thoroughly misunderstood Dilke's explanation of John Keats's "complaints":

...you must excuse me when I say I think you never rightly understood any thing of him but his poetry. How could you say that, after his illness, he sunk something from his high feelings of [g]enerosity? Why, from the moment he was taken ill, he had not [th]e means of proving his feelings of generosity to the amount of a penny.[163]

Dilke replied almost immediately, apparently to the effect that George's 1824 letter was not now to be found, that Brown had not the authority for stating that John's generosity to George finished his fortune, and that Brown ought not to accept any profits from the sale of his memoir in proof of his sole interest in advancing the fame of Keats.[164] To this letter Brown's answer of January 20, 1830, contained seven specific charges against George. But Dilke did not believe a word of Brown's charges: so confident was he of George's innocence that he dismissed all seven with the general observation that though ironically unknown to himself the *known* expenses of John surpassed his known income by some £300 or £400! Where else, therefore, could he have found the money but from George? It was, indeed a good question, one that Brown himself could not answer, but conversely, could not answer to Brown's charges.

Shortly after Dilke received the letter full of charges against George, he wrote a stinging one back to Brown, who replied with one even worse. The most telling sentiment in Brown's letter was a reference to Dilke's "enigmatical positiveness...": "I cannot recollect you ever gave up any one of your positive opinions, so that, if my memory serves me well, I ought not blindly to yield to any one of them, knowing you, like many men, to have been positive on the wrong side."[165]

The subsequent letters of Dilke and Brown became increasingly "frank," bordering on insults, with the result that their correspondence was broken off for two years. In 1833 Brown visited England and the two submitted their cases to Mr. William Dilke (Dilke's younger brother) for arbitration, who made copious notes but came apparently to no conclusion. To their credit, Dilke and Brown made up their quarrel and resumed correspondence; from Italy Brown sent to Dilke for insertion in the *Athenaeum* reviews of Italian novels,[166] a translation of a poem by Redi (bordering on bawdy),[167] and items about art and artists in Italy in ostensibly private letters, but from which Dilke extracted long columns for insertion in the *Athenaeum*.[168] Even after Brown arrived back in Plymouth, he was sending Dilke reports of the Plymouth *Athenaeum,* an institution featuring old and new artists; in one report in his jealously guarded and prestigious "Weekly Gossip" column, Dilke gave Brown a public compliment on his taste for Italian painting:

We are glad to hear from an old friend, and one whose eye has been trained and disciplined by a long residence in Italy, so good a report of the exhibition at the Plymouth Athenaeum. He makes special mention of pictures by Rembrandt and Annitole Carocci; of works by Reynolds, Wilson, Moreland, and Gainsborough; and of a collection of drawings by Lieut. Col. Smith, an amateur, he speaks in terms of high admiration. We like to hear of these provincial exhibitions, they are the best possible means to diffuse a knowledge and a love of art.[169]

But the friendship of nine and thirty years was finally shattered beyond repair by a series of unfortunate circumstances.

In the spring of 1835, whether for reasons of bad health, or for Carlino's education on English soil, or for the English soil itself,

Brown returned to England. For understandable reasons he had chosen not to live in London; for less understandable reasons he wished not to reside in the lovely agrarian community of Bedhampton, nor in the nearby metropolis (by comparison) of Chichester, now that Old Mr. Dilke, his "foster-father," had died. Between the choices of the "turmoil of a city"[170] and rural quietude he reached a kind of compromise first in the seaside town of Plymouth and then in his more permanent residence in nearby Laira Green, where "honest and happy human faces are to be had...at every turn."[171] There Brown enjoyed the best of two beloved worlds: country solitude and city art, in which he became and remained very active through his connection with the prestigious Plymouth Literary Institution. Almost immediately on his arrival he began giving lectures on Shakespeare's learning, Shakespeare's sonnets, Shakespeare's dramatic art, and on "the Intellectual History of Florence." The townspeople recognized his contribution by electing him curator of the library.[172]

In fact, Brown was just then engaged in two writing projects. One, conceived in 1830, was a book on Shakespeare's sonnets, which properly arranged, Brown affirmed, would reveal events and attitudes in Shakespeare's own life. When finished in mid-1838, it would be called *Shakespeare's Autobiographical Poems*. Landor had encouraged him, vowing that "No man ever understood Shakespear" as well as Brown himself.[173]

But another subject haunted Brown, one that had lain unfinished for six years. This was *Life of Keats,* and Brown, encouraged by Severn, resolved to complete it. *"The time has come,* AND I FEAR THE TIME MAY PASS,"[174] Severn proclaimed in large letters, confident, as he was, that Keats's poetry was generally highly valued: "his fame is a proud one."[175]

For the moment Brown was duly convinced, and so wrote to Hunt to announce his intentions and to request his (Hunt's) final letter to Severn. He confessed his pain at rearranging Keatsian materials, but resolved in spite of his pain "to fulfill [his] duty." Accordingly, he "boldly put down [his] name" for a forthcoming lecture at the Plymouth Institution. It was titled *The*

Life and Poems of John Keats. "Now that it is advertised, the card printed, the members looking forward to it, there is no retreating; it must be done."[176]

It was done, but not without difficulty: sometime after George Keats in 1830 received word of Brown's "threatened" *Life*, he had empowered Dilke to invoke an injunction against anyone's publishing any of Keats's unpublished poems, including, of course, those in Brown's possession.[177] Brown wrote to Severn in early July 1836 that an edition of Keats's already published poems may be reissued, but that any MSS poems were prohibited by George. "It was plainly told to me, if I attempted it, an injunction would be served."[178] Presumably only Dilke could have thus plainly told Brown; if so, it will be noted that his plain talk was delivered earlier by more than two months than his compliment to Brown in the Weekly Gossip Column.[179] By that compliment Dilke must have been trying to soothe the somewhat frazzled feelings of his old friend. It did not work. Two months after the public compliment Brown published in the *Plymouth, Devonport, and Stonehouse News* the MSS sonnet "If by dull rhymes."[180] In so doing he had called George's and hence Dilke's bluff. Dilke did not exercise his power of injunction, and thus Brown gained his point, but undoubtedly he gained it at the cost of Dilke's friendship. Whether the fault lay with Brown for openly defying Dilke's "threat," or with Dilke for threatening, the three-year effort to reestablish their friendship was wasted.

Brown again noted a change in Dilke's attitude. On a subsequent trip to London (summer 1838) Brown called on Dilke partly to discuss the unpublished Keats poems, partly out of "mere civility," and partly to advertise in the *Athenaeum* his forthcoming book, *Shakespeare's Autobiographical Poems.* Dilke, probably still piqued by what he regarded as Brown's foolish and taunting dare, showed his anger toward Brown. "He is dogmatical conceited, and rude."[181] He attributed the cause both to Dilke's "success" (with the *Athenaeum*) and to his jealousy of Brown himself, presumably of his literary powers.

On publication of his book, Brown was extremely disappointed in the *Athenaeum*'s less than favorable review. He had expected better treatment, not only for his belief in the merits of his book, but also on grounds that he had himself been a fairly frequent contributor to the *Athenaeum*'s pages. He called the review Dilke's "infamous treachery toward me."[182] Probably the review was not actually Dilke's, but Brown seemed to assume that it was, and Dilke, author or not, assumed responsibility for it.[183] Believing that Dilke had played him false, Brown wrote him a "declaration of war," protesting first, that Dilke's earlier behavior was all a part of a gross plan to insult Brown:

When in town I doubted that the behavior of Dilke, as he is subject to violent fits of ill temper. I doubt nothing now. It was all malice prepense. My fault has been in not lauding his literary talents, which was out of my power. I could praise his talents in obtaining a success, but no more. My conscience has undone me with him. Two days since I wrote him a declaration of war, because I would not be treacherous like himself; and I told him plainly he was generally regarded as a blockhead, quoting Charles Lamb's adjective,—for a particular sort of blockhead,—a dilkish blockhead. Thus during the winter I can, without remorse, draw him at full length in a novel. He is a capital character for one. Because I rarely show my teeth, he thought I was unable to bite.[184]

Dilke was accordingly drawn, though not quite at full-length nor not quite remorselessly. In *Walter Hazlebourn* the character representing him, Robert Wydel, is admitted to have some good points. The unfinished novel consists of 100 pages of closely written script, about eight of which are given over to a description of a Dilke temper tantrum.[185] According to Brown his lengthy description of Dilke's irrational and crude behavior was necessary so that the reader could be forewarned of what was to come. In the latter pages of the novel, therefore, he had intended to return to his unflattering portrayal of Robert Wydel for the purpose of completing his "full-length caricature." One wonders why he did not.[186]

In the meantime Brown had once again consigned his *Memoir of Keats* to futurity. He felt that in his "most plain, unvarnished

tale, and rather short...," he had done for his poet-friend all he
could under the circumstances and must wait for posterity to
complete the book he had begun. Now he was preparing to undertake yet another venture, this time a bold bid for opportunity for
his son Carlino; together they would embark for New Zealand,
where he had bought land and where he planned to take machinery
"from pins and needles up to a sawmill and steam-engine."[187] His
one remaining task before he embarked, however, was to find a
suitable biographer for Keats.

Such a biographer was found in Richard M. Milnes, a friend of
Severn, by whom Milnes was recommended. Together with his
Memoir, Brown handed over to an extremely grateful Milnes other
Keats memorabilia and departed England forever for what he
termed in ignorant and painful irony "the land of promise."

Sometime before April 1842, Severn secured from Milnes
Brown's *Memoir*. He had been busy too, preparing a paper on
Fresco Painting, which he submitted to the *Athenaeum*, and which
his old friend Dilke gratefully accepted. In a letter referred to but
not quoted by Sharp[188] he requests extra printed copies from Dilke
and makes his own position clear on the *Memoir*.

I am just now reading with pain, with anguish, a short Life of
Keats in Mss by Charles Brown, it is not fit for publication altho it
is *truth*, but it is not *all the truth*, nor the kind of truth—R. M. Milnes
who has all the papers of Brown's including the Mss tragedy, is to
produce something on the subject of Keats' life and works honorable
to all of us—for *I am distressed at the divisions of Keats friends
which at every turn are unjust & hurtful to his fame.*—Milnes I trust
will *unite* all these,—& as he is willing to produce a fine edition the
result must be fortunate.—I should like to write George Keats if you
could give his address, for we cannot publish some of Keats' finest
things without his permission.[189]

In his reply Dilke forwarded a dozen copies of the paper on Fresco,
thanked him for his intention to send a second, which he believed
"serviceable to the good cause." After stating that the printer would

return Severn's second Mss., Dilke adverted to the "painful subject":

> ... Your note touched on other matters to which I was unwilling to reply on the spur of the moment. I have no doubt Mr. Milnes will do justice to the subject:—whether a stranger can do justice to the man is a question open to consideration. I have never seen Brown's "Memoir," but the spirit of it was foreshadowed in his letter, and that led to a quarrel—the "be all and end all" of which was a refusal on my part to reply elaborately to sixteen pages of charges against George, conjured up out of the ambiguous givings-out of poor John, and George's letters, who had intentionally mystified his brother for the peace and quiet of his vexed and wearied spirit. You may say how could I know this—do I pretend to know more of Keats's affairs than Keats himself! Yes, I assuredly know more than all the Keats put together. How I acquired my knowledge would be a tedious story. It cost me years of anxiety, the benefit of which Miss Keats had and enjoys and even George benefited by it, the only one among them that affected to be a man of business, having given his guardian a receipt in full.[190]

To Dilke's reply that he had not seen Brown's memoir, Severn forwarded it immediately; Dilke again postponed attending to it till he could "defer no longer with propriety," and then wrote a totally condemnatory critique. His principle objection, which he said colored the whole memoir, was Brown's implication that he alone was the friend of Keats in England,[191] as Severn was his lone friend in Rome. "... In truth it is no memoir of Keats, but a memoir of Brown in his intercourse with Keats—or rather a dream on the subject.[192] ... Brown figures here as a sort of magnificent patron friend—an only friend indeed, except yourself. How is this? ... Was not John Reynolds, who knew him first and best a friend? To whom was Robin Hood addressed & why? ... Were not the Brawnes his friends? Was not James Rice his friend? The impression left by this memoir is altogether delusive."[193] With this together with some three pages of other criticisms Dilke returned the memoir to Severn. To the criticisms of the Memoir and also to Dilke's earlier letter regarding George Keats, Severn quickly replied:

> 3 Burlington Gardens
> May 20[194] [1842]

Dear Sir

In my first spare moment I beg to assure you that all your ideas of Keats gratify and satisfy me exceedingly, and I am not a little glad I mentioned the subject to you, as I am bent on a good life of him & a splendid edition of his works, and to this purpose as I come a stranger amongst you it behooves me to unite all the differences about him.—As regards George Keats I tell you candidly I never did understand the thing, nor could credit it. Your interpretation I can rely on, as I can understand it & as it agrees with the one idea I have had of George Keats—poor Brown will not interfere with our doings, and as he gave me the right of judging his memoir of Keats I shall on the first opportunity tell him I think it "clear out of the way" and that we must encourage Milnes to begin afresh, working up from Brown's material in distant and cool colours to set off the bright & gay.

If you could mention a leisure moment I would be glad to come & talk over these serious things, for serious I shall now consider them & not wait my own leisure.

If you knew the thousand[s] of fine [?] people who have known me as the f[d] of Keats at Rome & how much they wish the thing you would better understand my earnestness—so please tell me of any early moment and I will come to you—

Many thanks for correcting my 2nd paper on Fresco, 'tis what I wish—I have had 3 dozen copies & should be glad of the like as I am now deeply concerned in the subject.

> Your v[y] obliged
> J. Severn[195]

Charles Wylie[196] had not forwarded to Dilke the news of George's death in December 1841, and neither Dilke nor Severn could know of Brown's failing health in New Zealand, where, a few weeks later, he died. It is just as well, perhaps, that he never learned Severn's true opinion of his memoir nor of George Keats. For like Dilke, Brown was both noble and stubborn. It is to Severn's credit that he refused to risk Brown's enmity by unburdening himself on an issue where opinion could avail only to the alienation of a longstanding friendship.

During the years 1842–1848 Dilke occasionally aided Milnes in identification of places, names, and incidents in the life of Keats. By late 1846 he had not heard for certain though he presumed "there can be no doubt" that George died.[197] By 1848, incredibly enough, he could still do no more than presume, though he doggedly maintained his position as George's defender to the last. While uniformly all others of the Keats circle and friends on the periphery were ecstatic in their reception of Milnes's *Life of Keats*,[198] Dilke was somewhat less encouraging, though he confessed that he ran through the two "interesting" volumes "with eagerness and pleasure"; further, the pages wanted something of the vividness of Keats's ebullient personality, but as Milnes had done his "spiriting" kindly, his efforts should satisfy Keats's friends. Occasional errors would have moderate or little consequence; but on one subject Dilke was unsatisfied: Milnes had allowed to stand in the second volume Brown's "prejudice" that, justly or not, Keats suffered from his generosity to nameless others in many matters, about which, therefore, he was "careless." It was a remarkably different tone from the seven charges Brown had sent to Dilke eighteen years earlier, but Dilke knew, and knew that others would know, to what Brown was referring. Dilke determined that the error would not be repeated in the second edition:

I will not bore you with a Comment on Brown's delusion as shadowed forth in the 2nd volume—I am sure you meant to be not only just but kind. But poor George is, it appears, dead, and I am only the more anxious that the truth & the truth only should be told of him. You must equally desire it—and therefore, on the chance of a second edition, I will express a wish that you would, some leisure morning, put down in black & white, John's known & unavoidable expenditure, & then tell me what was the *possible* "remainder" in Dec[r] 1819 or

Jany 1820 from which George *could* have taken any thing. I waive all the advantage that might be taken of your considerate suggestions abt carelessness in money matters—Keats was neither careless nor careful but habitually *inexpensive.* Remember that *John* came of age in October 1816—Do his letters to Taylor abt "duns" & borrowings in May & July *1817* give hopes of a remainder in 1819, 20? I have too something to say about the division of Tom's property—but this sort of questioning on paper, would be wearisome and endless. Whenever therefore you are inclined for a talk on the subject I am at your command—[199]

The two reviews in the *Athenaeum,* the last of which was Dilke's,[200] were friendly. But Dilke's numerous notes in Milnes's *Life of Keats* evince what he considered Brown's penchant for assuming the role of magnanimous patron and father-confessor. One such instance of Brown's influence is to be found in a Milnes passage implying that Brown intended to follow Keats and remain with him in Italy. Opposite this passage Dilke wrote in vigorous denial: "This Mr Milnes must have stated on the authority of Brown and no other—What are the facts? Keats embarked in Sept^r *1820* & Brown was then in the River—Keats died Feby 1821 and Brown *started* for Italy in July or August 1822: fifteen or sixteen months after he was *dead*!"[201] Dilke, then, was less than pleased with Brown's influence over Milnes, particularly with the treatment of George. His total impression may have been prejudiced by the first statement in Milnes's preface:

It is now fifteen years ago that I met...Mr. Charles Brown, a retired Russia-merchant, with whose name I was already familiar as the generous protector and devoted friend of the poet Keats.[202]

The words "generous protector" irritated Dilke. He proceeded to write a great tribute to Brown, remarkable for its detachment and fairness in view of what had passed between them:

What Mr. Milnes means by a "generous protector" I know not—assuredly it had nothing to do with money. When John Keats died

Brown sent in an account to George for Board, Money lent, & *interest* amounting to about 72 pounds[203]—which by George's order I paid. Neither Mr Milnes nor his distinguished crack-brained friend of Fiesole [Walter Savage Landor] knew any thing about Brown—They were not sufficiently on an equality to penetrate the heart of his mystery. If it were to the purpose, I could here write down a character of Brown, that would be greatly to his honor—though there would be nothing in it ab^t the retired Russian Merchant or the generous protector. I saw him under all varieties of fortune, they under only one, of moderate, very moderate, independence. He was the most scrupulously honest man I ever knew—but wanted nobleness to lift this honesty out of the commercial kennel. He would have forgiven John what he owed him with all his heart—but had John been able and offered to pay, he would have charged interest, as he did George.[204] He could do generous things too but not after the fashion of the world. His sense of justice led him at times to do acts of generosity— at others of meanness—the latter was always noticed, the former over-looked—therefore amongst his early companions he had a character for anything rather than liberality—but he was liberal.[205]

A *Life* was finally produced and all the circle agreed that the belated publication was the important thing; it helped immeasurably to place Keats's name "among the English poets." But it would have been produced years earlier had either of the two principals herein discussed been willing to surrender materials to the other. George had legal ownership of the unpublished poems, it is true; but he did not possess the poems, nor without a legal battle was he or Dilke likely to obtain them. Had he been able to do so, many biographical questions concerning Keats's life might have been cleared up. Rollins, for example, believes that Dilke's incisive notes in the annotated copy show that "he could have done an infinitely better job than Milnes."[206]

Chapter Two

The Apprenticeship to an Ethnos of Literature

The Early Writings (to 1820)

Old English Plays. Dilke early evinced traits of the "Godwin perfectability man" that Keats had discerned. He was a Godwinian in 1815 when he wrote the Introduction to *Old English Plays* (6 vols.), and a Godwinian he remained throughout his life, though he would later depart from an important aspect of Godwin's teachings regarding the source of the "moral" impetus in society.[1] But even in 1815 before he had ever met Keats or presumably any of his circle, Dilke had broadened the Godwinian base to include a new and exciting approach to literature and society. At this point the notion was nebulous and ill-defined, but would be sharpened to clear focus in the years to come; his was essentially a Godwinian faith in the development and thrust of what can best be described as an *ethnos* of literature. In later years Dilke belonged to the newly formed Archaelogical Society, attended its meetings and occasionally exhibited artifacts both at the London and at the annual meetings of the prestigious British Association for the Advancement of Science (founded 1830) in other cities. He called himself, then and earlier in 1816, an "antiquarian," for that was as close as he could come to what is here termed an *ethnos* of literature. The Greek term *ethnikos* contains the germ of the idea "people-spirit," but its present English derivative, *ethnology*, contains also the idea of a study of a primitive people, which meaning was alien to what Dilke had in mind. His idea of an antiquary was one who was, to be sure, steeped in the traditions and lore of civilizations, but who in addition subscribed to the Godwinian ideal of the March of Intellect.[2] Thus the "ethnos of literature and art" intends to characterize not only the various nebulous notions of what Hazlitt in 1825 would refer to as "The Spirit of the Age," but more particularly, it focuses on Dilke's and others' twin concepts of (1) the productions of the people of a given culture and mindset (2) and their peculiar and distinctive character as it reveals itself in its literary and artistic movement from age to age.

Dilke believed that each age produced, indeed was informed by, its own particular genius and expressed itself in its own special artistic mode or genre. Once past, a given age of literary excellence could never regain its splendor, for the conditions contributing to its greatness and its special genius could never be duplicated. But society and the arts, especially literature, had a reciprocal relationship on one another: excellence and perfection in one would influence the mindset and tend toward improvement in the other. Given the right conditions for and in society, a new age with a new genius and a new genre would inevitably flower. Conversely, given the right conditions for and in art and literature, a societal attitude in keeping with the genius of the age would be forthcoming. Dilke's major effort of a lifetime was to do what he could to cause those reciprocal conditions to come about. The Introduction to *Old English Plays*, amounting to some twenty pages, is noteworthy for its clear indications as to how Dilke's mind was already constructing the beginning of a culturally-based literature. To be sure, this *ethnos* was to be refined here and there until its fruition in about 1837, when Dilke issued his finished version.[3] But here in the 1815 essay prefacing the *Old English Plays*, with becoming modesty and rather too many professions of his lack of experience, Dilke declared his *ethnos* manifesto—one of the earliest to appear anywhere in a literary context.

The 1815 Introduction is well written and forcefully argued. Aside from Dilke's unwieldy and convoluted prose, which fortunately he later outgrew, the essay itself shows some literary value; it is coherent, it contains a certain degree of systemization of argument, and the various phases of his essay lead naturally and unobtrusively one into another. It begins with the customary apology for its intrusion on the public's notice and proceeds to justify that intrusion with some comments on the scarcity of some plays and the apparent nonavailability of others. He offers then a better reason: second and even third-rate Elizabethan plays are often first-rate literature. On this declaration he launches into the main argument of his essay, which is to affirm the presence of a special kind of genius in the drama of the Elizabethan and Jacobean Ages. The nuances and ramifications of that special genius are what is here termed an "*ethnos* of literature."

He says in assigning that special genius to drama: "The drama of that age is not only deserving consideration for its superiority over every other of our own country, but particularly so as a *national* and *original* drama, *regulated by its own laws, and of course only to be estimated by them.*..."[4] Dilke believed that for this glorious distinction we are indebted to the Reformation and thus to the mindset and temper made manifest by it in literature:

In the chivalrous ages, that preceded that eventful period, literary honours, and, indeed literature itself, seem to have been held, as by prescriptive right, by the higher classes of society and the members of the religious houses; but at that great revolution of opinion the barriers were broken down, and all classes of society burst into the arena to contend without distinction. The translation of the Bible only, independently of the advantages derived by religion and pure morality, was of great and essential advantage; it opened to all the purest springs of knowledge, and wisdom, and poetry; and the dramatic writers of that age availed themselves of the advantages it held out: it must be evident to every man conversant in their writings, that it was their constant and undeviating study....[5]

What wonder, then, that the Elizabethan and Jacobean Ages spewed forth such magnificent poets. But there were other societal and religious influences than the Reformation and the Bible:

The Reformation, as to the purposes of poetry, would not perhaps have been attended with such consequences had it occurred at any other period: the age was singularly fitted for the full display of poetic genius: criticism was not then strong enough to wield its leaden mace; there then existed no established tribunals at which the poet might fear to be arraigned; there were then no acknowledged standards of excellence to which enthusiasm was to tame down its excursive spirit; the feeling and the sensibility of the poet alone regulated its course.[6]

Earlier in the essay Dilke had explained that the subsequent history of drama in England had been a sorry one. Shortly after the age of which he was speaking, the "gloomy...Interregnum" had imposed a puritanical fanaticism on society in general and on poets in particular and had prevented the "representation of their works by fine and imprisonment." Those principles in turn led to the artificial and diseased drama of Charles II's day:

In a great body of people, the puritanical principles, in which originated the severe ordinances of the usurpation, still existed in their full force, presenting an insurmountable objection to the countenancing of theatrical exhibitions: the players therefore became, in a much greater degree than usual, dependent on the protection of the great; and what congeniality could be expected between the uncontrolable wildness and unaffected simplicity of these old writers, their simple portraitures of nature, and passion; and the taste of a monarch and a court accustomed to the regular and inflated drama of the French school, with its unnatural and unimpassioned beings? And without withholding a sincere tribute of admiration justly due to many of the writers of Charles the Second's reign, it will scarcely be denied that they became of necessity the caterers to a diseased and unwholesome appetite. The gloomy bigotry of the interregnum stopped the course of dramatic literature; but the Restoration did what was infinitely worse, it poisoned the "pure well-head of poetry"; and from that period we have gradually descended to our present degraded and disgraceful level.[7]

Thus, the Elizabethan drama was the epitome of drama because the genius of the age manifested itself in dramatic forms. There can never be such another drama because there can never be another Elizabethan age. Thus was Dilke's first enunciation of an *ethnos* of literature. The view, fully developed and rigorously espoused by Dilke and a few others[8] in the expanding and influential era of the *Athenaeum*, would have far-reaching effects on literature and society.

The Champion.   Dilke evidently did not contribute a great deal to periodicals before he met Reynolds. Having been drawn into that society, however, he probably began in 1817 to submit modest résumés of plays to the theatrical section of the *Champion*, to which Reynolds also contributed. Even then, Dilke had credentials superior to those of most contributors, for as Keats said, he had already served his apprenticeship by editing old plays. In early 1818 he succeeded Keats nominally but Reynolds actually as Drama Reviewer for the *Champion*. That marked the beginning of his twelve-year period of apprenticeship in various magazines in preparation for his editorship of the *Athenaeum*.

Drama Criticism.   A passage in the *Athenaeum* in 1832 suggests that Dilke had known Editor John Scott and perhaps contributed various miscellania to his *Champion* since its early days in 1814–15. It is certain that after Reynolds had ceased to write for that journal in late 1817, Keats had served as drama critic for a week or so and then had turned the onerous job over to Dilke.[9] From internal evidence, chiefly of style and literary preference, we may judge that Dilke himself did not stay in that position more than six weeks, or until the later part of February. Nothing can be traced definitely to his hand before January 1818.

Dilke assumed the office of drama reviewer on January 11, 1818. He began by referring to the previous week's report (written by Keats) on the Drury Lane pantomime *Don Giovanni*, which both Keats and he agreed, was "wire-worn."[10] Many of his reviews during this six-week period are reminiscent of his earlier ethnological stances in the Introduction to *Old English Plays*.[11] He speaks, for example, "of the worst plays of the worst play-wrights of Charles II's time" and of the exquisite genius of Shakespeare, whom he was just then reading with his predecessor, and who, he affirms likewise with Jonson, is unapproachable in comparison even with other great poets precisely because he was "not for an age but for all time."[12] Later, in a passage reflecting Keats's dictim that poetry should "soothe the cares and lift the thoughts of man,"[13] Dilke shows an early literary stance that would not only resurface years later in the *Athenaeum*, but would become the very center of his system built on what he called "the humanizing influence of literature."[14]

People frequently "prattle" about the immoral tendency of the *Beggar's Opera*... and they can quote us grave authorities; but our contempt for the opinion would not be shaken, though they had "*five* justices' signatures" instead of *one*. The influence of the theatre is not direct, but collateral. It is neither by preaching virtue, nor bullying vice, that it is of service. It gains its end by making man happy in man's society: by humanizing our passions and rubbing off our discontent—the "thick scum" o'er life: it makes men better by making them happier.[15]

In what was probably intended to be his final bow to the readers of the Dramatic Review section, the notice of Henry H. Milman's *Fazio* of Covent Garden contains most of Dilke's philosophy of art at that time. It is the longest single review of his tenure, perhaps the longest in *Champion*'s history, and reads as if the author wished to say all that was left unsaid in previous issues. He opened the notice with a slap at those managers and "adaptors"— Dilke's bane as critic—that slash away at originals:

That the managers had a right to represent this play we have already admitted; that they had a right to alter and amend it, as the phrase runs, we cannot so readily concede. For instance, if some stone-mason should become possessed of Chantry's Sleeping Children, he would have an undoubted right to make an exhibition of them; but assuredly possession could not give him a right to take the chissel into his own hands, and having opened the eyes and levelled the dimples of the one, and substituted a head of his own for the head of the other, to exhibit it thus mutilated and disfigured, to the disgrace of the original sculptor. Now in what does a difference consist? —We do not assert that the managers have done all this:—the alterations are few, and not generally injudicious:—but we protest against their right to do it at all. The injustice, in this instance, is so gross and palpable, that we think the reader will readily admit it:—is it less so because the author cannot protest against it? Would it be less to mutilate the works of Phidias?—is it less to insult the memory of Shakespeare?—Yet this is unnoticed, because it is perpetually recurring:—and it will perpetually recur because it is unnoticed.[16]

"The fame of our poets is our inheritance!" cries Dilke, thus establishing another post in the as-yet-incomplete superstructure that was later to become his theory of literature. "The fame of our poets is our inheritance! We'd rather be connected in a tenth degree with one of them, we had rather claim them as our countrymen, than be the fag-end and salvage of all noble families in Europe."[17]

Dilke turned next to one of his favorite dramatic subjects, the distinctness of Elizabethan from all other dramas, particularly the Greek; adverting to his ethnos of literature theory-in-progress, he stated that both were suited perfectly to their ages and that suitability was exactly why we can term them "national" dramas.

Mr. Milman seems fully sensible of the excellence of, and intimately read in the old dramatic poets; but we do not think his estimate of them has been quite correct. He has endeavoured, he says, to revive "our old national drama with greater simplicity of plot." Mr. Milman is a Bachelor of Arts, and was probably just leaving college, and the Greek poets when he hazarded this. The fullness and intricacy of the ground-work of Shakespear, and the contemporary dramatists was not accidental, still less is it a defect, as Mr. Milman seems to imagine: it was in a great degree essential to the end they proposed, and was evidently sought after by many of them, Massinger in particular. The Greek poets have their excellence, but it is altogether distinct. The perfection of statuary is in the truth and beauty or dignity of a single object: the excellence of painting in bringing together innumerable and various objects into one harmonious and impressive whole:—this is the distinction between the Greek and English dramatists.[18]

But, says Dilke, because their ends and aims were different, so must the entire "groundwork..., superstructure..., jutting frieze, buttress,... and ornament" be necessarily different.

> The Greek drama is throughout simple, chaste, severe;—neither the writers nor spectators seem ever to have forgotten that it originated in a religious ceremony—and the language has always the sustained solemnity, and impressive energy of a moral discourse. Has this any resemblance to the dialogue of Shakespear or Beaumont and Fletcher, or Ford, or Massinger, or Deckar:—to unite the language of the one to the plot of the other, is to stick the rich tracery, and flowery ornaments of Henry the Seventh's chapel on the Acropolis at Athens. Here then Mr. Milman must have failed, because what he attempted was impracticable.[19]

After illustrating with examples the paucity of action in the play, Dilke moved on to discuss its language; he was pleased to observe that throughout the play the language smacked of something of the old dramatists. But not quite. In phraseology recalling his *Introduction to Old English Plays* (written three years earlier) he shows why. Although we are perpetually reminded of these old dramatists, the language does not signify the spirit:

> ...we are perpetually reminded of them; but not by a kindred spirit—not by one that would seem to have dined at the Mermaid and supped at the Devil: to have wandered with them into the fields of poetry and passion—to have drank from the same cup at the pure spring-head of poetry, and bathed with them in its waters, till he had become, "endued into the element"—but by the perpetual recurrence of ideas and phrases familiar to us "as household words." This may distinguish Mr. Milman from modern poets, as the armour of John of Gaunt would be distinguishable from a coat, waistcoate, and breeches: but a man will no more become an old poet by adopting their phraseology than the father of a race of kings by changing his habit.[20]

Foreshadowing a typical *Athenaeum* practice years later, he departed from the text to branch off into "a word or two on the subject of poetry generally." The word or two expanded into nearly an entire column; it is an adequate statement of his theory of literature at this stage of its development.

In the days of Elizabeth and James the 1st, poetry seems to us to have been in the prime and lustihood of life, "resembling strong youth in his middle age." There was a perpetual super-abundance of feeling, and poetry, and passion: the poets could, and did, squandor beauties on the most trifling and unimportant subjects:—perhaps the finest passage in Shakespeare is the death of Falstaff, and yet he could afford to let Dame Quickly make a jest of it. Poetry we must fear, is now in its old age, decrepit, imbecile, worn out; sans passion—sans feeling—sans enthusiasm—sans every thing. The little strength the poets have left they are obliged to make the most of; and perhaps the best is but the best economist. We fear there is the same necessity for this sneaking virtue in poetry as in the concerns of life. We have no feasts, and revels, and banquets, and masques, and pageants as of old;—the "Gentlemen of the Inns of Court" do not now expend the revenues of a democracy on "the King and Queen's Entertainment at Whitehall."[21]

In this passage are hints of the suitability of the poetry to the age, of the movement of the *ethnos*, as it were: the equating of something in the people with the productions of their artists and poets, thus making a peculiar and *national* identity of the poetry, defined and bound by their own rules and by no others (hence a *sovereign* morality and *ethnos*); and finally, a word on the benefits to be reaped in knowing cultural history and benefiting by its teachings. Many of the ingredients later comprising Dilke's theory of literature are here present; but they are yet far from his finished system.

Dilke concluded this review by devoting yet another column, the length of which, in spite of his reservations, he admits is a tribute to Milman's impact on him—focusing largely on its fault of substituting words for ideas: "Why Johnson's definition of network 'anything reticulated or discussed, at equal distances, with interstices between the intersections' is not worse" than several obscure passages which should have been "illustrated by action"—

not "narrated."[22] In spite of its faults, however, Dilke concluded by assuring his reader that the play suffers only in comparison with the great Elizabethan models, and is as far superior to most present day efforts as it is inferior to those models.

This was probably intended to be Dilke's final dramatic review for the *Champion*. Indeed, the lead notice in the Dramatic Review section for the following week (February 22) is a general discussion of the oratorios of the current season; neither the hand, the expertise, nor the ideas are Dilke's.[23] But a second column without title or apology is his, and its purpose is to explain "an opinion in our last article (February 15) ... not so clearly stated as we could have wished...."[24] That opinion was that the passage on the death of Falstaff is perhaps "the finest in Shakespeare." A friend (Keats, perhaps?) had "misunderstood," and if a friend may have been misled, what doubts may a stranger have? Dilke explained his "finest passage in Shakespeare":

The simplicity of Dame Quickly is like the philosophic jesting of the Fool in Lear. The death of Falstaff is told with such truth and simplicity that the scene is brought immediately before us. "After I saw him fumble with the sheets, and play with the flowers, and smile upon his finger's end, I knew there was but one way; for his nose was sharp as a pen and he babbled of green fields,"—His nose was as sharp as a pen: and this of Falstaff! the "horseback-breaker," the huge hill of flesh," to whom "eight yards of uneven ground was threescore and ten miles," who "larded the green earth as he walked along,"—and "he babbled of green fields!" He who had lived and rioted in the voluptuousness of cities, whose enjoyment centred in a cup of sack, over a sea-coal fire, in the Dolphin chamber, his breast unbuttoned, Tear-sheet on his knee, and all roaring at some unhallowed jest. He, Falstaff, "babbled of green fields!"—But the picture was not yet finished. "How now Sir John? quoth I, what, man! be of good cheer. So a cried out—God, God, God! three or four times." Poor Falstaff; this is too much! it carries you to the death bed itself.—We see at once his bodily and mental agony, and Shakespear felt the mind must not linger on it! Dame Quickly comes forward therefore, giving to the whole a finishing pathos, yet diverting the attention from what it dare not dwell on. Yet she does this with a *jest*![25]

There are both overt and covert resolutions to be found in this passage, observed Dilke. First of all, the jest "relieves the oppressiveness" of the death scene. Second, it signified the confidence of the genius in Shakespeare:

A man must be conscious of his sensibility, and equally assured that others are so, that in great grief should venture abroad without "the trappings and the suits of woe:"—a man's honesty, must be unquestioned and unquestionable who picks pockets for pastime:—and we think it a presumptive evidence of an immense power in a poet who ventures to relieve the oppressiveness of a death scene with a smile. Quickly, Bardolph, and the boy jest at it, say what you will. It is true that their jests, like a flood of tears, are equally the excess of sorrow and its relief, but this is only the confirmation of the presumed power. If a modern play writer describes a death scene, it must be mouthed out by some grave conceited personage, and ushered in by muffled drums and bell tolling. He would prose and prose and think it irreverent to break a jest within ten pages of it. It must stand out bare and naked.[26]

This review concluded Dilke's tenure as dramatic reviewer; the hand that replaced his was tamer, and in some respects less challenging; certainly, the new reviewer was less inclined to make bold assertions and was perhaps more reserved in both favorable and unfavorable commentary. But already his choice of favorites shows Dilke with a literary bias that, like most other facets about him, never changed; he was a child of his age.

Cunningham's *Remains of Nithsdale and Galloway Song.* This Romantic preference shows itself clearly in two reviews in the *Champion* of Cunningham's *Remains of Nithsdale and Galloway Song.*[27] Dilke's fundamental requirement of poetry—that it reflect the strong and sincere passions of the poet—seems everywhere exemplified in his review. Superlatives abound; passions are depicted in their extremes; in the three kinds of ballads depicted, the "sentimental," the "humorous," and the "Jacobite," the simple narratives and direct, straightforward diction give evidence of power and feeling honestly represented. Of the Jacobite authors he says "They seem to have felt bitterly, and to have expressed without fear of restraint every thing they felt. Nothing can exceed the contemptuous and cutting irony of some of these ballads." He proceeds to explain that now we can discuss the "several pretensions of King George and the pretender..." without becoming personally involved or arousing passions or prejudices in others. But that was not the case then when "butcheries of Glencoe, and the horrible persecution that every where followed the battle of Culloden, are evidence of the hatred that spurred on the one party, and were not likely to excite a kindlier feeling in their antagonists."[28]

The "humerous" selections, too, received from Dilke high praise, and, as in the "sentimental" and "Jacobite," ballads, were richly deserving of superlatives; here are some samples of his comments on the "humerous' poetry: "What humour can be more delicate than that of 'The Pawky Loon, the Miller?' what stolen love told more sweetly than the 'Grey Cock?': it is inimitable!—what more delightful than the pure and disinterested passion in 'Tibbie Fowler'? ... The reader will be delighted with Galloway Tom. Nothing can exceed the depth of knowledge and humor in the last stanza."[29] After quoting a rather lengthy passage representative of all three types of ballads, he concluded: "This song is full of the finest imagination:—'the powther of a pink' would have sounded sweetly, in *Midsummer Night's Dream* itself."[30] These sentiments show that Dilke was then (and ever remained) a Romantic; in later years he could rail superficially against some of the artifacts of progress that were or would have been applauded by the Romantic poets—artifacts such as steam engines and manufacturing centers. But the raillery sprang from a romantic love of nature and of natural ways. His theory of literature sounds comparatively modern, especially in the maturity of the cultural concepts that he seems almost to have taken to himself as a natural, rather than a reasoned course. But it was more of a faith in the inherent and innate ethical goodness of literature and art, in the emotional and intellectual capacity of the people to apprehend it and finally in the belief that *pathos* and *ethnos* are reciprocal and ultimately will be brought together in a harmonious and beautiful world where Truth is Beauty and Beauty is Truth. These notions are Romanticism in its deepest and finest ideals.

Bailey's *Sermon.* Dilke reviewed in the *Champion* his friend Bailey's pamphlet entitled "A Discourse Inscribed to the Memory of the Princess Charlotte Augusta" (Taylor and Hessey, publishers).[31] After his usual fashion, Dilke introduced first his topic and then used it as a point of departure to discuss one of his own favorite principles—hobbyhorses, Keats would have said. In this instance the hobbyhorse was the indeterminable nature of the origin of evil, to the problem attendant on which Dilke gave nearly an entire column. His position was much as one would expect Dilke's to be, and his conclusion was that such origin being indeterminable, churchmen should leave the question alone! Bailey, Dilke reports, at first chose rightly, and in the early part of his discourse touched on the subject sufficiently, concluding that the "light of nature" was inadequate; therefore he, Bailey, must trust his readers to revelation. Unfortunately, says Dilke, he did not persevere in this opinion, for before the conclusion Bailey has met with a gentleman " 'eminent for his talents which enables him to explain his meaning more fully,' and backed by his authority, and misled by his dreaming, he thrust himself out of the light of revelation, or rather the security of faith, into the obscurity of reason."[32] This gentleman, whoever he was, lamented Dilke, was not the man to unfold the mystery; for the mystery is still there after the unfolding. "But let us hear him," Dilke said:

"Satan's will was perfectly free to choose either good or evil; but he had *all* motive to choose good, but *no* motive to choose evil. Consequently the sin of rebellion sprang out of him—it had its *origo*, its first impulse in and from his own will. Hence Milton's allegory of sin springing out of the head of Satan is the image of a profound truth." If it be the image of a truth it is of a very profound truth indeed, and much too deep for us to fathom. Admit that sin did spring out of Satan's head: the question is *how it got into it?* Satan was a *created* being. Now to suppose that a created being could receive from a creator *all* wise *all* powerful, and *all* good the *power* of doing ill, is altogether contrary to *reason*. Vice, or what has capacity and power to become vicious, cannot be *understood* to proceed from the supreme being, without denying some one of his attributes; his power, his wisdom, or his goodness. To reason of a being acting in opposition to *all* motive, from *no* motive, is to abandon reason that we may go on reasoning. To believe *this* we must *revert to faith*: and what then? we are running in a circle:—we start from faith and return to it:—we may remove the objection further, but the objection will exist in full force.[33]

Dilke recapitulated his argument that the origin of evil "... is beyond human comprehension, and churchmen should not dabble with it." In the course of the review he does, however, give high praise to the other ideas in the tract, to the "amiable" author thereof, evidently "not only well read in the best of our divinity, but intimately conversant with our poets; a zealous lover of truth, with a poetical imagination, and an enthusiastic spirit." In addition, he singled out passages of great beauty and sweetness of imagination; one such passage he prefaced with these remarks:

It would be extreme injustice, after having so freely canvassed this writer's opinions, to close our review without allowing him to appear on points of a less abstract nature. Now, although we are decided enemies to that morbid philosophy of religion which is perpetually persuading us that positive evils are relative blessings; at least have no fancy, ourselves, to be "purified" by a fit of the stone or the gravel, and had rather agree with others that there is no such thing as positive evil, than write an essay on the good fortune of a dislocation or a fracture, we think the following, which avoids the extreme we allude to, and the methodists run into, inimitably beautiful.

Dilke quotes:

"Nations like individuals are purified by the humiliation of moral suffering. When the sun sets, the moon and stars are like serene thoughts; they stand as it were alone and visible to all eyes and their own consciousness, in the same space where they were but an hour before lost in the light of day."[34]

Other passages are as highly praised. Bailey, however, was not thoroughly pleased about the review and wrote to Taylor to say that for the sake of the book and for Dilke's own, he had "better have let it alone," for Dilke was "at best a Sceptic in his principles."[35] Undoubtedly, Dilke contributed a great deal more in those years, but such contributions cannot be assigned as his with anything more than guesses.

The London Years

Dilke's acquaintance with the *Champion*'s admirable and able editor, John Scott, may have proved to be much more important than were his contributions to that journal. It established him as one of that coterie of talented writers whose offerings were later to grace the pages of Scott's influential journal, the *London Magazine*. Scott drew around him a talented company of writers. Besides Dilke, there were John Clare, Charles Lamb, Leigh Hunt, Hartley Coleridge, J. H. Reynolds, Thomas De Quincey, Thomas Hood, William Hazlitt, Allan Cunningham, Barry Cornwall, T. N. Talfourd, Horace Smith, Charles Darley, Thomas L. Beddos, and many others only slightly less known. Not often have so many names of first rank in literature come before the public in a single enterprise. It merited the honor and respect of all men of letters.

"Thurma."   When Scott died of a wound sustained in a duel in March 1821, Taylor and Hessey, the publishers and friends of Keats, bought the *London*. With Taylor as editor, the magazine continued on at first in its sparkling and profitable ways. The editor wisely, for a time, retained the liberal but unobtrusive political stance which Scott had taken; and wisely, too, he entrusted a good bit of the "filler" and "rewrite" duties[36] to subeditor Thomas Hood and to his able assistant John Reynolds.[37] Dilke may have been contributing articles to the magazine from the first months, though none can be assigned definitely before September 1821. After Taylor became editor, however, Dilke contributed three articles over the signature "Thurma."[38] The first of these is entitled "The Antiquary," and is intended as a kind of character sketch—not an entirely flattering one—of a typical antiquary. The article is not significant except as an insight into Dilke's method of depicting character, which he does largely by illustration and example. His writing has become by this time more facile, more light and breezy than it is in the 1815 "Introduction," and though still sometimes subject to awkward, convoluted sentences, he often surprises the reader by a bold remark like "an antiquary is necessarily a high churchman and a Tory..." Most of the article is given over to a listing of the likes and prejudices of an old antiquary friend who in every way qualifies for the description given the "typical" antiquary in the first part. The old gentleman, a Mr. W—— from Winchester—undoubtedly a creation of Dilke's imagination—is something of a Sir Roger de Coverley and Uncle Toby in one. Dilke concluded the article with the observation that

"...affection, master of passion, swayed him to the mood of what is liked and loathed;" and so it does not only a simple antiquary, but all other people worth remembering: It is a clue to the whole mystery of the human mind; the text to Sterne's chapter on Hobby-horses; the soul of Wordsworth's poetry; the source of Hazlitt's power, –Rousseau's pathos,—Montaigne's knowledge; the foundation of Shakespeare's dramatic characters; and possibly the occasion of this first essay in the London by
Thurma.[39]

A second contribution over the signature Thurma is much more substantial. Ostensibly, it is a treatise on Westminster Abbey; much of the discussion is given over to a comparison between Greek and Roman architecture; but the article actually is a more or less-connected treatise of a phenomenological view of age and youth, of what constitutes greatness, of whether it or its opposite is really determinable, and finally of a few large philosophical hints on the unimportance of whether it is or not. He begins the article in a straightforward enough manner:

If I were to distinguish briefly between Greek and Gothic architecture, I would say the one appeals to the reason, and the other to the passions of men. It requires knowledge and judgment, therefore, to appreciate the excellence of Greek architecture; whereas Gothic architecture declares its own excellence by taking firm hold on the passions and imagination, while the will and the judgment are inactive, or overpowered.[40]

Elaborating on the primacy of the passions with respect to the enjoyment of the Gothic, Dilke affirms that "Wherever there is perception and sensation, an eye to see, and a capacity to feel, there is knowledge enough for Gothic architecture. Enter the west door of Westminster Abbey, and the mind is subdued in a moment. We make our bow to old superstitions, and have a respectful admiration of the first reverend absurdity that offers itself...."[41] Dilke proceeds to show why Burke's definition of the sublime is particularly applicable to the feeling one has on entering the true essence of the Gothic, which is Westminster Abbey: "the mind is so entirely filled with its object, that it cannot entertain any other, nor, by consequence, reason on that object which employs it."[42] Dilke then posed the obvious rhetorical question: "With all this admitted... is a Gothic cathedral finer than a Greek temple?"[43] and answered:

O no! It is another thing. There is no parallel, no similitude, no point of agreement whence we could begin comparison. Their purpose, aim, and excellence, are entirely distinct. Our admiration of Greek architecture grows with our growth; we have the vantage of it; we comprehend its simplicity, its unity, its excellence; and never expect to see it equalled. But Gothic architecture hath the vantage of us; our admiration cannot increase, for our knowledge does not; and we never think about any thing equalling it, for we never had any standard to measure it by.[44]

After a few comments on Gothic "proportion," or more accurately, the utter lack of it, Dilke moves closer to his real subject: a disquisition on phenomonology[45] as that study relates to age.

It has been well observed, that Gothic architecture is much older in our imagination than its actual chronology, or a Greek temple of three times its antiquity. The fact appears to be, that it is really older in our associations and feeling, *where alone antiquity exists at all.* This very Abbey is not only 500 years old, but there is nothing like it in existence, of less reverend antiquity. Greek temples are of yesterday. The lanthern of Demosthenes has sprung up under the new street act; and the Temple of the Winds is now building, I hear, in St. Pancras church: all our architecture is Greek, or a corruption bearing some palpable relation to it; it is as familiar to us as our household furniture, in which some ornament of it is usually distinguishable: we meet with a Greek portico, a Greek column, a Greek capital, or some part of Greek architecture, building, or just built, at every turning. With our feelings, therefore, a Greek temple is not necessarily associated with great antiquity; whereas a Gothic Cathedral is not only of very great age, but seems to have outlived the capabilities of the world.[46]

Dilke then touches on the relationship of the *ethnos*, the people-character of a thing, to art; and next, to the relationship of both to "old time"; he thus fixes another section to his superstructure of a theory of literature:

There can be nothing really old that is not separated from us by a long interval of varying manners, customs, habits, and opinions; there must be a chasm between us; a breaking off of all connexion and association between it and ourselves; it must be passed away, and Greek architecture is yet passing.

A chronological table will not decide the antiquity of a thing; that depends on a thousand other circumstances besides its age, and exists only in our individual feeling and opinions; an old book, an old author, an old statue, an old building, even an old man, are all of different ages to different people; a girl just entered on her teens looks forward to unmarried twenty as hopeless age.[47]

Thus one's individual view of a thing plays its small but important part in Dilke's later theory. It is essential that mankind be aware of his history, of himself, of what Keats termed the "grand march of intellect," of the meaningful significance of Glaucus's thousand years of servitude under the curse of Circe[48] and of the sick, blanched face of Moneta; and finally of a recognition of these symbols for what they are: they are Everyman, symbols of civilization, symbols of history of man, seen usually in Hobbesian terms. In *Leviathan* and in Yeats, this history-of-civilization figure was doomed past, present and future. The Romantics saw him differently: his past was indeed Hobbesian, but his future was not. At worst, he could, like Demogorgon, be shadowy and unpredictable. In any case, hints Dilke, if he should ultimately arrive at some apocalyptic vision, he ought to be aware of his triumph!

A third article written by "Thurma" adds nothing to Dilke's theory of aesthetics, but does afford some interesting information relative to his notions about people.[49] In an essay on pleasant and unpleasant people, he writes that often the pleasant fellow is shallow, undependable, and ultimately selfish, while the unpleasant person may be what he is because he recognizes the truth of the Hobbesian past hinted at in the previous essay. He is thus humane though dour, philanthropic though introverted, dependable friend to the last though critical. He does not gain many friends, though he is himself a reliable one.[50]

Letter to Lord John Russell.   Dilke was interested in politics as well as literature and wrote on the former subject as well. He regularly attended parliament sessions and undoubtedly sent digests of proceedings to periodicals as early as 1820. As Carlyle did later, Dilke in 1821 vigorously advocated the repeal of the Corn Laws. He addressed to Lord John Russell[51] a pamphlet in the form of a letter which Rodwell and Martin published under the title "The Source and Remedy of the National Difficulties, deduced from the Principles of Political Economy." In this pamphlet he remarks that he believes Lord Russell to be sincere and zealous in his public opinions and conduct and, because of his youth, not likely to have his understanding clouded by established theories. Having been convinced by one of Russell's essays that he was inclined to liberal principles, Dilke set forth certain arguments in favor of the laboring classes:

... the richest nations are those where the greatest revenue is raised;

as if the power of compelling men to labour twice as much at the mills of Gaza for the enjoyment of the Philistines, were the proof of anything but a tyranny or an ignorance twice as powerful.[52]

One consequence of the publication was that John Taylor, editor of the *London Magazine* after John Scott came increasingly to rely on Dilke as the political spokesman.

Political Reporting. Sir Charles would later characterize his grandfather as a "republican all his life," a radical in youth and a moderate republican in age, but a republican nevertheless. But if we may judge from Dilke's later commentaries on political subjects, both in the *Athenaeum* and in *Notes and Queries*, he became, if anything, more radical with age. Even during the 1820 to 1821 period of Scott's editorship on the *London* Dilke had probably ventured an opinion or two on politics as that science related to theories of Godwin and Malthus. Upon assuming the editorship, Taylor appointed a well-known barrister, Mr. Charles Phillips, to write and police the political offerings—though there is evidence to suggest that the offerings of Phillips himself needed policing.[53] Phillips had established a reputation for eloquent oratory and was often referred to as the "Demosthenes of Ireland," though these gifts are not readily apparent in the pages of the *London*.[54] Though his sympathies were liberal and spanned a broad range of political issues, his pet projects were those having to do with Irish interests. "Every month as long as Phillips wrote the abstract of public affairs he kept pounding away at some aspects of Ireland's troubles. . . ."[55] Especially did he denounce those personages both of public and ecclesiastical offices who preyed on the defenseless peasantry.

In the spring of 1823 a new hand can be recognized, bolder, more radical, and less disposed than was Phillips to sympathize with the Irish Catholic peasantry, though no more inclined to sympathy with their oppressors. The new bold hand was probably that of Dilke, now as in 1821 a pragmatic utilitarian concerned primarily with currently realizable methods of achieving needed reforms.[56]

Dilke's period of greatest activity with the *London Magazine* lasted about twenty months, from May 1823 through February or March 1825. It appears that in May and June 1823 both Phillips and Dilke contributed to the regular feature "Views of Public Affairs."[57] In May, Phillips continued his reportage on the Spanish struggle to retain her "constitutional" government, on the political immorality on the part of French Royalists in their efforts to destroy it, and on the bitter likelihood of their eventual success. Along with the "domestic affairs" section, Dilke was assigned the Irish question, a sign that Taylor felt that Phillips had become too personally embroiled in his fight for the advancement of the cause of the Catholic peasantry.[58]

By June 1823, Dilke's hand is detectable in other phases of the "View of Public Affairs." The topics chosen for discussion do not vary much from those reported under Phillips's reign; but there is a certain causticity, a distrust, even an occasional note of sarcasm slipping into reports of such areas as public taste in arts or politics, in the general level of intelligence and good will resident in the ministers of government, and even in the ability of reporters—such as himself—to discern men of real quality when confronted by them. As it had done for the preceding two years under Phillips, the Affairs of Spain Column continued to receive by far the most space, usually amounting to three or four pages until well into 1824. Of these pages, the childish inanities of King Ferdinand received a disproportionate share. In other respects the "Spanish news" became to Dilke increasingly more melancholy as the French Royalist government sent an army to intervene and ultimately to overthrow the Cortez, the constitutional government in power since 1821.[59]

Irish politics, Irish cupidity on the one hand, and Irish stupidity on the other were likewise subjects that regularly occupied two or more columns. According to Dilke the Catholic hierarchy held a fretful Catholic peasantry in awe by feeding them such bogus "miracles," usually perpetrated by one Prince Hohenlohe, as were utterly transparent on the face of things, but which for some unfathomable reason, the ignorant and "brutified" peasantry were disposed to believe.

The Catholics...are by no means outdone—quite the contrary, they have again called in the aid of Prince Hohenlohe, and he has performed another miracle *by post*!! This has taken place in the person of Mrs. Mary Stuart, an inmate in the Convent of Ranelagh, near Dublin—she was dumb and bedridden, and had received the priest's viaticum for her final journey, when Prince Hohenlohe interfered, and rendered the viaticum unnecessary, by setting her on her legs again, and restoring her tongue to its pristine activity. She has taken her oath, that she is quite well, notwithstanding that she was attended by no less than three doctors; and the most Reverend Doctor Murray, titular Archbishop in Dublin, has actually circulated a solemn pastoral letter, declaring the miracle to be complete in all its parts! It must not be forgotten, that this Doctor Murray is placed at the head of the Roman Catholic church in Ireland, and that the great body of the people look up to him almost with superstitious reverence. His word is law amongst the Catholic laity, and with this full consciousness about him he publishes this impudent juggle to the gaping rabble! Far better would it become the Catholic clergy of Ireland to forget their little selfish wordliness—to sacrifice the mammon wrung from the popular ignorance, and, by educating, enlightening, and *unbrutifying* their flocks, render them worthy of the liberty for which they supplicate.[60]

The falsehoods may in themselves be thought harmless enough, Dilke implied, but their effects belie their idle appearance: they are extremely dangerous not merely because they give currency and therefore a modicum of acceptance to falsehood itself, but also because they abet superstition and slavery to ignorance:

The only way to end those things is laugh at them. It is certainly amazing how the Irish priesthood can have the audacity to publish these solemn blasphemies in the 19th century. It behooves, however, those who seriously desire the political amelioration of their sect publicly to shake off all participation in such babooneries—if they do not, if they silently acquiesce in this priestcraft juggle, they may depend upon it, they will feel the effects of it next session. People will ask, and naturally, if even the relaxation afforded by Lord Wellesley has induced these monstrous results, what would not complete emancipation lead to. An acquiescence in such absurdities proves one of two things,—either an hypocracy inconsistent with religion, or a brutishness unfit for freedom.[61]

The means to remedy the Irish situation admitted of but one solution. It was the rock on which Dilke was to build a system of related ideas and ideals and perhaps even prejudices. Its name was "education." It was the only means of unbrutifying Ireland:

Mr. Peel pledged himself that the government would, in the selection of its members, seek no other object than that of giving the greatest efficacy to the commission, and satisfying the desires of the house for the improvement of the people of Ireland. Various opinions were expressed in the course of the debate, as to the necessity of extending the benefits of education in that country in such a way as would least interfere with the religious opinions of the people. Mr. J. Smith very truly, and very forcibly declared that "England could not go on long without a more intimate union with Ireland, and government must first give its inhabitants the means of education, then the means of employment, and lastly, a participation in the privileges of the Constitution." There cannot certainly be the least doubt, that the first step must be to *unbrutify* the people; at present they are as totally unfit for freedom, as a human eye would be for the full glare of the sun, immediately after the removal of a cataract; their minds must be gradually prepared for it.[62]

If accounts from Spain, France, and Ireland were bad, those from Greece were decidedly encouraging. Early in his tenure Dilke noticed the successful efforts of the Morea (the republican forces of Greece) against the Turks.

Letters from Constantinople announce, that the Greeks will not now negociate with the Porte, except on the basis of their entire independence. We trust sincerely that this may prove to be the fact, because it would clearly tend to show, that the Greeks were daily gaining a confidence in their cause, which must be dear to every friend of literature, religion, and liberty.[63]

In succeeding numbers he speaks of Greek successes and uncivilized Turks who shunned not to inflict multiple atrocities and who must therefore expect reprisals in return.[64] Such is the nature of that most inhuman of human inventions, war. Yet if the Greeks or Spanish peoples "will not fight for their freedom, they do not deserve to enjoy it.[65] In the meantime he gives all possible publicity to a report emanating from Greece, which "calls loudly on the British people to aid this most interesting of all struggles,—a call which every lover of freedom or literature must sincerely echo."[66] Dilke noted too the heroic efforts of Byron in that struggle: "Lord Byron has written a letter to the Greek Committee making a tender of his services, and pointing out in what way he thinks their cooperation may be made most effectual."[67] A few months later he proudly reports that Byron has been elected a member of the Missalonghi Council, that he has sold an estate in England to help defray the expenses of the war, and that the uncivilized Turks have threatened to decapitate him should he fall into their hands; Dilke allows that "he has certainly earned their hostility by the double provocation of chivalry and genius."[68] A few weeks later Dilke announces the melancholy news of his death.[69]

Other causes were espoused in the *London* by Dilke and Taylor, causes which later were to resurface in the *Athenaeum.* One such crusade concerned the abolition of slavery, a strong stand taken also by Scott and Taylor. Affairs in Jamaica offered plenty of scope and opportunity for Dilke to drive home slavery's inhumanity, so that after he became editor almost every issue contained something about the unsavory practices there.[70] He commented sardonically on the supposed "philanthropy" of half-measures to alleviate the sorrowful plight of the blacks; half-measures would never do; the good intentions of their sponsors were "doubtless humane" but "humanity and policy have been long opposed on the question of the slave trade."[71] He noted that "the proprietors [land-owners] complain that the withdrawal of all physical control has been recommended before the population had been prepared ... for ... any moral substitute." But, he asks, "Whose fault is that?"[72]

Another important cause echoed later in the *Athenaeum* had to do with reforming the criminal code in England, which the editors believed both too severe and too prejudicial against the lower classes. Particularly under Dilke's period of editorship, notices relating to heavy penalties imposed for minor crimes were quite common. The following is typical:

Several occurrences have taken place in our Courts of Law within the last month not altogether unworthy of notice. No less than eight indictments have been tried during the last Old Bailey sessions, against poor illiterate wretches charged with selling the Age of Reason. These men, or rather boys, seemed to consider themselves quite as martyrs, and were sentenced to six months, two years, and three years' imprisonment for *the same offence*. The Recorder alleged the difference of the defences as the reason for the difference of punishment![73]

He is pleased, too, to notice the light sentence for his friend John Hunt, who was fined £100 for publishing in the *Examiner* Byron's "libel" on George III in the "Vision of Judgment." Referring to what he considered a light sentence, Dilke comments: "The Kings' Bench have done themselves infinite credit by such a sentence. Justice adds much to its dignity, and loses nothing of its force by being tempered with mercy."[74] Dilke championed the efforts, as had Phillips and John Scott before him, of Sir James Macintosh, who had for several years offered bills to effect a reduction of penalties for crimes not involving death:

Sir James Macintosh has made another ineffectual attempt to introduce an amelioration of our criminal code. He prefaced a series of resolutions with an eloquent speech, and concluded by moving the first, namely, "that it is expedient to take away the punishment of death from larceny from houses, shops, and navigable rivers." This was opposed by Mr. Peel, in a speech of considerable length, and finally negatived by a majority of 86 to 76. Sir James then moved his entire series, merely, as he said, for the purpose of having them recorded on the journals of the house. There certainly never was a code which more required amendment and modification than the criminal code of England.[75]

Other parliamentary personages whom Dilke admired were Lord John Russell, whom he reports in favor of extending the suffrage,[76] and especially Mr. Hume, who presented bills in the House of Commons in favor of extending freedom of expression even to those holding "infidel opinions";[77] an amendment against the "principle of increasing a standing army (in time of peace)";[78] a bill to abolish the "degrading punishment of flogging in the army";[79] another bill in favor of extending rights of working men to form "combinations" (unions) "to raise their wages and regulate their hours of work."[80]

The Apprentice Editor. The evidence in the format of the magazine as well as the introduction of a "tamer" hand in the Lion's Head to meliorate Hood's traditionally sardonic comments indicates that Dilke assumed the editorship of the *London* with the beginning of Volume 9 (January 1824).[81] Since apparently both Dilke and Hood continued to write the Lion's Head—a feature somewhat analogous to a combination of the "Weekly Gossip" and the "To our correspondents"[82] columns in the *Athenaeum*—it is reasonable to suppose that both for a time continued to coedit the *London*. By March 1824, however, Hood's satirical but often funny commentaries on certain hapless correspondents have all but disappeared, to be replaced by Dilke's more "encouraging" dismissals. In addition, a notice in March 1824 of a policy change to emphasize reviews would indicate that Dilke was clearly at the helm:

In compliance with the request of several Correspondents, our readers will perceive that we have entered somewhat more fully into the Reviewing Department of our Magazine. "Amongst the endless variety of literary journals, many of them conducted with ability, some with impartiality, there are few," it is said, "which are properly

—Reviews. The two leading Works, under this denomination, are, for the most part, collections of Essays, and those chiefly political. The minor publications of the same class are but partially devoted to their professed object, and are rather—series of Extracts, than Reviews. Critiques, exclusively dedicated to one purpose—the due valuation of literary pretensions,—yet embracing all subjects; Reviews, having for their sole object, literature in the abstract, and as their chief end, the information of the public on the contemporary issue of the press, so that society shall not become the purchaser of folly nor the patron of vice, but the friend of genius, industry, and learning,— are still wanting." The London Magazine will endeavor to supply this deficiency.[83]

The following inclusion in the *Lion's Head* for the May issue is typically Dilke's:

By the extension of this present Number a *whole sheet* beyond its proper limits, in order to include some very important papers, we hope to please both our Readers and Contributors, while we relieve ourselves a little from that vast accumulation of materials, which scarcely leaves us room on our table to pen this notice.[84]

Dilke may have continued on intermittently as editor and political correspondent through Volume 10 (July–December 1824). In the August issue he again anticipates a favorite *Athenaeum* attention-getter: he departs from usual format to feature some event of great current importance.[85] In this instance he waived the roar of the Lion completely in order to call attention to a eulogy on Robert Burns and Lord Byron.[86]

In January 1825, Taylor handed the editorship of the magazine to Henry Southern, who bought it outright a few months later. Dilke's hand is still considerably evident in the View of Public Affairs Section in January, rather considerably less for the February issue, and not discernible at all in March or thereafter. Thus ended a major portion of Dilke's apprenticeship to successful editing to begin five years hence. Characteristically, he exited with something of a private joke:

The Admiralty have issued a new pattern for the naval uniform. The officers, who have however a stock of clothes on hand of the old pattern, are allowed till the 1st day of January 1826, to wear out their old wardrobe.[87]

Miscellaneous Writings

"Thomas Heywood's Plays." During his tenure with the *London* Dilke had been sending contributions to other magazines as well. Sir Charles, his grandson, tells us that he contributed to the *London Review* and to the *New Monthly Magazine*.[88] Charles Brown wrote from Italy that Galignani had reprinted some of Dilke's articles in the *Parisian Literary Gazette*.[89] As he was gradually withdrawing from service to the *London Magazine*, he contributed at least one article to the *Retrospective Review* in March 1825, titled "The Early Drama—Thomas Heywood's Plays."[90] In this article Dilke strives to sketch a general overview of Heywood's plays but to give detailed attention to several of his best ones. His general comments on Heywood are equivocal. The playwright is in the second rank behind such as Beaumont and Fletcher, Jonson, Marlowe (some of his favorites); and, of course, Shakespeare is yet an immeasurable distance ahead of those even in the first rank. One of Heywood's faults, Dilke says, is that his love for the unshakable, heroic type of character makes his characters superhuman—therefore nonhuman—resulting in a loss of useful moral instruction. For his culture-theory of literature Dilke is now insisting that the *pathos* part of his formula receive its due prominence so that the beneficial moral effects of literature be disseminated among mankind.

Heywood, like many of our old dramatists, deals in the extreme of character, which frequently amounts to heroism. His heroes are of unshakable purpose, of irresistible patience; men who will stand beneath the sword suspended by a single hair; and, with the power of motion, still resolutely bids the consequence. The point of honour is discriminated with the most subtle nicety; a vow is considered as registered in heaven; it is the sentence of fate, and must be equally inexorable. The spirit, however, is frequently sacrificed to the letter, and the good and the true are disregarded, to preserve a consistency with a supposed virtue—a sort of character better calculated to supply, from the passionate and deep internal conflicts which it occasions, affecting subjects for the state, than useful example or instruction for human happiness.[91]

Occasionally, however, Heywood chooses to represent superhuman kindness or virtue, and thus with his penchant for extremes, in the humanizing influence of these plays he is unsurpassed; such characters do in fact provide models for "useful" moral instruction:

> There is an inexpressible charm about those characters, a politeness founded on benevolence and the charities of life, a spirit of the good and kind which twines around our affections, which gives us an elevation above the infirmities which flesh is heir to, and identifies us with the nobleness of soul and strength of character which shed "a glory" round their heads.[92]

The "spirit of the good and kind" elevates the reader and allows him to identify with such nobleness of soul and strength of character. Elsewhere he criticizes Heywood's *Edward IV* as "a long tedious business," primarily because "we find so little to excite our feelings."[93] As hitherto noted, a stipulation of moral instruction in a work of art is that it be capable of arousing emotion. He is most enthusiastic over those plays containing a broken-hearted lover, a happy reunion, or any other situation replete with *pathos.* Accordingly, he feels Heywood's best play is *A Woman Killed with Kindness* and gives the following reasons for his choice:

> This is the most tearful of tragedies; the most touching in story; the most pathetic in detail; it raises, in the reader's breast "a sea of troubles," sympathy the most engrossing; a grief the most profound.[94]

Shelley had said in his "Defence of Poetry" that the great secret of moral instruction is an identification of ourselves with the beautiful that exists in others, that therefore to be truly good, a man must possess the power of empathy in great degree. Keats, too, had spoken of a going-out of his identity and of taking "part in the existence," and of "pick[ing] about the gravel" with the sparrow.[95] "The great instrument of moral good is the imagination" Shelley said, and Keats and Dilke, together with a host of other poets, echoed this central Romantic sentiment as a first principle. Dilke reiterates his emphasis on *pathos* by a final passage from Heywood, to which he appends this comment:

We are overwhelmed with the emotion of the unhappy sufferers, and are carried along in the stream of distress, incapable of resistance, and unconscious of anything but the scene before us.... The most phlegmatic in feeling, the most obtuse in understanding, cannot remain unaffected; it must emphatically come home to man's business and bosoms.[96]

Though he may have differed to some degree with Keats about the psychological comforts associated with "remaining content with half-knowledge," Dilke agreed fully with Keats and Shelley on the primacy of the imagination as the great moral force of Man's makeup and hence as the great promise in his destiny. They talked of it many times; the ability to surrender or annihilate one's self totally (so that the imagination may be absorbed totally in goodness and beauty) is what Keats implied by the phrase "negative capability." These passages show that Dilke's emphasis on empathy and *pathos* was not far different from what Keats had in mind. They must have been discussing this very subject, the now-famous "disquisition," on the walk home from the Christmas Pantomime in 1817.

Hone's *Everyday Book*. Dilke's known contributions between 1826 and 1830 are few; indeed it is not likely that he was especially active during that period. Very ill during the latter half of 1825, his father died in early 1826. Dilke must have had little time for writing during those trying times. In May 1826, he and Wentworth embarked on a six-month tour—Wentworth staying on with Brown for eight more months.[97] In early 1827 the arbitration business with Hunt must have taken a good deal of time, and he seems to have been perennially involved in straightening out George's and Fanny's finances. Nonetheless, there was some literary activity: a letter written in July 1825 to William Hone, publisher and bookseller at Ludgate Hill mentions some "accumulated trifles" sent to Hone's "little periodical" entitled *Ancient Mysteries.*[98]

Two of these or similar offerings seem to have made their way somewhat later into Hone's *The Every Day Book and Table Book* (1828). Both are signed "O.Z."[99] One is a copy of Keats's intended "last will and testament," though "the sages of Doctors' Commons refused to receive it as such, for reasons which to a lawyer would be perfectly satisfactory, however, the rest of the world might deem them deficient in cogency...."[100] The will itself concerns primarily the order of people whom apparently Keats wanted paid out of the proceeds of the sale of his published and unpublished books:

Now I wish _____[101] and you to be the first creditors—the rest is *in nubibus*—but, in case it should shower, pay ————[102] the few pounds I owe him.[103]

Dilke then assures the reader that in fact it did indeed "shower" from an unexpected source: the Court of Chancery; he affirmed, too, that the shower was "sufficiently copious" to discharge the debts alluded to in the will. So that "His friends have therefore the gratification of knowing that no pecuniary loss has been (or need have been) sustained, by any one of those with whom he was connected, either by friendship or otherwise. I am, Sir, &c. O.Z."[104]

Dilke's other contribution is a listing of the manner in which Roman emperors from 42 B.C to A.D. 343 died; the list is prefaced by a rhetorical question:

Does any man envy the situation of monarchs? Let him peruse the following statement, which particularizes the deaths of the *forty-seven* Roman emperors, from Julius Caesar to Constantine the Great;

only *thirteen* of whom encountered "the last enemy" in the ordinary course of nature:—[105]

This warning is followed by the list of emperors and their manners of death; the following is a sample:

B.C.
42. *Julius Caesar* was murdered by Brutus and others in the senate house.

A.D.
15. Augustus Caesar *died a natural death.*
39. *Tiberius* was smothered with pillows, at the instigation of Macro, the friend of Caligula.
42. *Caligula* was stabbed by Cherea and other conspirators, when retiring from the celebration of the Palatine games.
55. *Claudius* was poisoned by the artifice of his wife Aggrippina.
69. *Nero* in the midst of a general revolt was condemned to death by the senate. Upon hearing which he killed himself with a dagger.
69. *Sergius Galba* conspired against by Otho, by whose partisans he was beheaded.
70. *Otho* destroyed himself, to avoid further contest with his competitor Vitellius.
70. *Vitellius* was massacred by the populace, who threw his dead body into the Tiber.[106]

This cataloguing runs on for some two columns, at the end of which Dilke tartly comments:

Where did these events occur? Among the savage tribes of interior Africa, or the rude barbarians of modern Europe? No: but in Rome —imperial Rome—in her "high and palmy state," when she was mistress of the world, and held within her dominion all the science and literature of the earth could boast.[107]

From this set of circumstances he finds support for one of his favored themes which we have met before and will meet with greater force and frequency again: "Surely we may with reason doubt, whether the moral improvement of mankind invariably keeps pace with their intellectual advancement. O.Z."[108] Hence, his heavy stress on the "moral" aspect of the "March of Intellect" and his equally strong insistence on the primacy of art and literature in the advancement of that morality.

The Gem. One other contribution before 1830 must be noticed, for it is particularly important not only for insight into Dilke's developing theory of literature but because it may be the only piece of prose fiction that Dilke ever wrote. It is published in Thomas Hood's *The Gem*, a collection of literary miscellania, and is entitled "The Last Embarkation of the Doge of Venice."[109] The short story (thirty-three pages long) is based on history, a "historical short story," if there be such a thing, and its setting is literally the last embarkation of the last doge of Venice in May 1797, though Dilke gives no dates or historical background, apparently assuming the reader will be familiar with historical incidents in Venice thirty-two years earlier. He likewise assumed that the general reader would be aware that Venice had maintained its oligarchic form of government for centuries but that in recent years (i.e., pre-1797) power had threatened to slip away, mutterings were occasionally heard, and intrigue and suspicion were reportedly everywhere. But a chief glory of those declining years had been Venice's splendid art. Furthermore, Venice had achieved a reputation as the great pleasure city in Europe. The story's setting is in May 1797 when Napoleon was determined to destroy the oligarchy and was marching with his overwhelmingly superior forces on Venice; seeing the futility of opposing him, the Venetian government had already resolved to offer no resistance. Hence, the last embarkation of the doge of Venice[110] a few days before Napoleon arrived. As indicated, Dilke evidently assumed that the reader would be aware of the political and cultural history of Venice.

The story opens with the English protagonist, Lionel Stewart, writing a "promised" letter, presumably to someone in England, about the city of Venice and about his host, the Marquis Boucheron, who is a revolutionary dedicated to the overthrow of the present corrupt regime, but who is very conscious of and reverential toward Venice's great past. Stewart feels, too, that same reverence toward Venice's golden glorious past, as well as the dreamlike, quasi-real character of the place—or perhaps more accurately, he feels that two "realities" blend into one, the reality of "real life" and the reality of art and literature:

> Every thing at Venice is dreamlike; for what is more so than to walk on the Rialto, where Anthony spat on the Jew's gaberdine?—to stand where Othello addressed the assembled senate?—to lose yourself in search of old Priuli's palace? and for realities, go to St. Mark's of an evening; see its fine square in all its marble beauty; the domes and minarets of its old church; the barbaric gloom of the Doge's palace; its proud towering Campanile: look upon the famous Corinthian horses; and think of their emigration;—on the winged lion of the Piraeus;—walk in the illumination of its long line of Caffées—observe the variety of costume,—the thin veil covering the pale Venetian beauty;—the Turks with their beards, and caftans, and long pipes, and chess playing; the Greeks with the scull-caps, and richly laced jackets:—look on this and believe it real, and ever after put faith in the Thousand and one Tales.[111]

His host, however, represents the more mundane "real," as politics however idealistic must always be, but even his "reality" is tempered by, and perhaps is slightly contradicted by, his sensitive "racial" memory of the glorious past:

> The Marquis Boucheron, who has lost nothing of hope and enthusiasm, is everlastingly lecturing upon the present condition and past fame of Venice, is deep in political intrigue, talks and thinks like a Venetian, and feels the present degradation and shame of the republic bitterly.[112]

These two "realities"—the consciousness of the necessity of a progressive present and the equally powerful consciousness of the need to preserve the traditions of the past—these must somehow be successfully blended in modern man: The conflict ironically is reminiscent of the historical positions of Burke and Rousseau, and undoubtedly in his bias, Dilke's selection of an European and an Englishman to represent them was no fortuitous literary accident. Stewart understands the Marquis's dilemma, however, and shares in his idealism; but as an Englishman, he will have nothing to do with *active* politics of another country.[113] "I reverence his enthusiasm and participate in his hopes; but I will not inter-meddle."[114] At that point the Marquis enters and announces that the time is at hand: Napoleon advances and soon the corrupt regime will be overthrown: "If you desire to share in the glory of giving liberty to this long-abused people, you must determine now."[115] Stewart declines once more the offer, pleading his aversion to intrigue, his reluctance to interfere in tradition alien to his own birthright, but mainly of his uncertainty in the knowledge that those deposed would necessarily be replaced by anything better. Perhaps certain Venetians like Boucheron knew so; but he, an Englishman, did not.

They agreed then to suspend their differences temporarily in favor of adjourning in order to witness the "gallant mimicry," as the Marquis said, of the embarkation of the doge of Venice. Arriving there in a gondola amid hundreds of other witnesses to the pageant (for in Venice, Stewart had written, one does not walk; to do so would require premeditation; one rides in a gondola), the two present a contrast. Among myriads of banners, gondolas, waving pennants, and handkerchiefs, the Marquis is bored and unimpressed. Not so with Stewart, who was an Englishman with appropriate reverence for even a Venetian past, especially if that past was rich in cultural history:

"This," said Stewart, in half unconsciousness, "surpasses old poets and fables! It realises all the gallant triumphing of Cydnus, that tamed down the ambition of heroes and outweighed empires!"—"A child's bubble, and a pageant for women!" said Boucheron fiercely. "It is the old Argonauts in all their golden glories!" continued Stewart.— "An old fool, repeating old tales," was the commentary; but it fell silent on the ear of Stewart, whose attention was wholly occupied with the scene.[116]

To Stewart the ceremony was an affirmation of lasting and permanent values, an approving demonstration of western heritage; to Boucheron it was just that precise heritage, much as he reverenced it, that stood in the way of freedom. The remnants of that culture must not be allowed to oppose or oppress, most certainly not to prevent the new order soon to appear.

Having established the conflict of ideals represented by the two friends, Dilke proceeds with the story. There is no more theorizing about governments, no more musing on whether reverence for the past does or does not inhibit freedom for those in the present, and whether we now are in fact appropriately or inappropriately imposing our will and ways on people yet unborn. As the conflict presented itself at this point, it represented a choice between Godwinian optimism with its emphasis on moral improvement and moral regeneration and another ideal close to Keatsian aesthetics: the growing consciousness, since Burke, of the reverence for historical guidance and the obligation of the present to perpetuate the heroic ideals of the past—specifically, the Anglo-Saxon ideals of unquestioned and absolute loyalty, justice, and self-reliance.

Other than the pageantry, nothing of significance occurred at the ceremony, except at the precise moment of its conclusion a violent storm broke, as if nature were joining in the spectacle as yet another witness to the end of an era. But on returning to the shelter of their gondola, the Marquis noticed a letter lying on one of the seats; opening it he read:

"Wait at the gate of Saint Apostoli immediately after sun-down—I *must* see you!" Stewart, who had just then got a glimpse of the writing, caught it away, and colouring deeply, stammered out an apology, with the assurance that it was intended for him.[117]

When Stewart blushingly acknowledged that the missile was intended for him, the Marquis chided him on his supposed "horror of intrigue" and enjoyed himself immensely at Stewart's expense:

"I suspect," continued the Marquis, "this explains the mystery of your long stay in the Euganean hills, better then Petrarch's villa, and the southern scenery, and the wild pomegranates, and the clustering vines, and the dreamy fire-flies, with which your letters of apology were always prattling, like a boy poet." Stewart, who for a moment thoughtful, was now smiling at the volubility and returning good humor of his friend; and was content even to be the theme of raillery, so he might escape from the wire-worn theme of politics. "Very true, very true," was his answer, "and perhaps I have been to blame in concealing it; but there are subjects too delicate even for friendship. While my passion was hopeless, could I breathe it even in your ear? Since it ceased to be so, there were other reasons for concealment; but you shall soon know all."—"Heaven forbid!—what, all your sighings, and whisperings, and sonnetings, for I suppose Arqua was inspiration in this way! Tell me her name, and let me shake her hand and kiss her cheek, and I will do so cordially; though I can tell her she has spoilt a very promising fellow, for which I am half inclined to bite my lip at her." ...[118]

As the afternoon dragged on Stewart made preparations for his tryst at Saint Apostoli Church just after sundown. On his way there a strange coincidence occurred when another gondola roughly bumped his own and a shrill voice was heard, "Is this the way to Saint Apostoli?" Moments later there was another violent collision and the same shrill voice, "This is *not* the way to Saint Apostoli."[119] Before he could unravel the mystery the other gondola had hastened quickly away; though he could make nothing of it, he decided at length to pursue his original course to Saint Apostoli.

On arriving at that place, however, he was surprised by attackers, captured, and bound by who he first assumed were robbers. He soon found that he was mistaken, for he was taken before a venerable, mild-looking, gray-headed old man with gentle manners. The old gentleman would give no explanation for such behavior toward him, however, and contented himself, to the discontent of Stewart, with the promise "Tomorrow I shall be with you early."[120]

After half a night's bewilderment and effort to make sense of the incidents preceding his confinement, Stewart lay down on his cot and slept. Soon, however, he was startled awake by a light touch and gentle voice. It was—one is as surprised as was Stewart to learn—his wife! She had gained entrance to his cell with the aid of a shrill-voiced dwarf—the same who had tried to warn him earlier in the collision of the gondolas—who was a spy against the then-tottering government. In the brief moment they have together she explained that like the Marquis, her own father had been engaged in a conspiracy against the corrupt government; but though tottering, and though its existence was numbered by hours, the government, or what was left of it, was still in power; finding that the government had learned of her father's and the Marquis's plot against it, she had sent for Stewart to tell him to warn the Marquis. But the French approach had made those in power all the more cautious, and thinking he was the Marquis, they had mistakenly seized Stewart, who had come from the Marquis's palace. But the fact that he was detained in error did nothing to lessen his danger. She had therefore come to present him with a letter, which he was to produce on the morrow, to show that his detention was not unknown. "Attend, attend... there is but one chance for you; produce this letter, which will be proof that their unjust detention of you is known; I will have friends, powerful friends, attending. The Government dare not now move against any but in secret...."[121]

The next morning he was summoned in person by the gray-headed old man, who brought him before another august personage, a Senator, evidently sitting as judge of some sort. At first resolved to face his situation temperately and calmly, Stewart soon gave vent to his feelings and assumed a haughty and proud manner; this attitude was countered with a stern rebuff by the old gentleman, who thus showed he could be as firm as the occasion demanded:

... notwithstanding his situation Stewart could not but admire the grandeur of the head of the speaker, which lit up as he spoke, and seemed the living model of those forms which Venetian art has immortalized for ever, or till art itself shall perish.[122]

After a few more ineffective thrusts Stewart determined to produce his letter which seemed, as his wife had said, a sure guarantee of his freedom; throwing the letter on the table, he shouted, " 'Do not think your injustice is unknown, or will be unrevenged; there is proof!—though that grey-headed old man,' pointing to him as he stood with the door open, 'was no party in conveying it to me.'[123] But the ancient one did not respond as he expected; instead his only reaction was to give instructions: 'Let the other prisoner be brought in.' "[124] Stewart was then fearful, not for himself, but for the life of his friend, but his apprehension was increased twofold when the guards ushered in not the Marquis, but his wife! "You are convinced now," said the Senator, throwing the letter carelessly on the table, "that your situation is *not* known, and *cannot* be known."[125] In the ensuing interchange of accusation and denial, it appeared that indeed his wife was extremely culpable:

"You knew of the conspiracy," observed the Senator—"Vaguely and imperfectly [she said]. I was not a conspirator."—"They met at your father's palace."—"Would you have his daughter betray them:"—"You came here led by a traitor,"—"She was *betrayed* here," said Stewart.—"Not betrayed where she trusted. The poor wretch who was her blind guide, and dreamed that the power of Venice was in his hands, was himself a weak instrument in the hands of others. But that is passed; you know that you are *now* in our power; our absolute, uncontrollable power!"[126]

But when as all seemed hopeless, the old gray-headed senator said, "You ARE FREE." Venice, he explained, is above the mean political squabbling as to what faction shall or shall not rule. Venice belongs to that which is permanent, its art, its grace, its beauty: in short its cultural history; its politics at a given time is just that: temporal. True, he believed Stewart and his wife innocent "though erring." But innocent or not,

Venice laughs at the poor childish denunciations of its political dreamers. "If," said he,—with the impassioned earnestness of religion, and looking up to heaven,—"if power is to pass from its throne of ages—if strength and manhood are to trample on the parent that cherished their infancy—if memory and gratitude are to be erased from human record and human feeling—if Venice must fall—be it so!—but let it fall under open and undisguised wrong, and not in the shame of self-debasement; let her be stricken down by force, not prostrate herself before it.[127]

As to the "traitors," who had fled, perhaps been now triumphing in the security of Venice's enemies, the old Senator instructed the couple: "Go you and tell them, had we willed to have it so, there has not been one moment of time that we could not have clutched them; though laughing at our credulity, they were entangled in our toils; they live because we gave them life."[128]

Thus the import of the conclusion of the story, it would seem, is that the conflict between Rousseau's progress and Burke's tradition is partially resolved; in Godwin progress is temporal, but tradition and therefore heritage are unchanging and permanent, a Grecian urn, a value beyond emulation, beyond even reverence, being, as it is, part and parcel of our societal makeup. An individual's politics may change; his cultural heritage never will. Thus, there really is no conflict, since the two realities exist on different planes.[129]

Dilke reasoned that in his scheme of things Godwin had given, as Rousseau had not, adequate attention to Burke's emphasis on history and to the importance of a "moral force" in society. "We stand on the shoulders of our forefathers and see farther," Godwin had said, and believers in the march of intellect revered him for it. But Godwin had overlooked the specific fount of moral excellence attainable through good art and good literature particularly as Keats and Dilke repeatedly defined good art: that which soothes cares and lifts thoughts. It remained to Keats and particularly Dilke to articulate that which Godwin had slighted: the appropriate place for *pathos* in art and literature as a powerful moral force in society.

This didactic short story is in many ways Dilke's most nearly complete statement of his theory of literature. Though it is a message in all its applications to life, it applies specifically to literature. This bold assertion comes to fruition in the following trends during the first half of his sixteen-year tenure as editor and proprietor of the *Athenaeum.*

Chapter Three

Dilke and the *Athenaeum*

A decade of political and literary experience in the publishing world altered somewhat the earlier simplistic faith of the Godwin Methodist. In the years shortly after 1805 some of "Micawber's" (John Dickens's) optimistic enthusiasm may well have been contageous, especially if experienced daily in the Navy Pay office. After 1816, to one who spent uneasy hours observing and reporting on sessions of Parliament, or on the deeply ingrained superstitions of the Irish peasantry, or on the whims and fantasies of a Ferdinand, such faith and enthusiasm would in time prove painfully naive in a world where rarely anything good seemed to turn up. The optimism was still there; else there had been a shortlived *Athenaeum.* But what made the *Athenaeum* what it was, what in fact gave it an identity, was a guarded optimism which harbored a degree of apprehension and anxiety about the future course of society. Like Blake, whose poetry he loved but probably never really understood, and like Keats and Shelley, whose poetry (even Brown admitted) he both loved and understood, Dilke envisioned a kind of future societal millennium: but only under certain conditions. Some of these conditions were more crucial than others, but collectively they amounted to two general faiths or persuasions: (1) in a perfect trust in the rehabilitative powers of great art and (2) in a large, general embracing of the emerging liberal spirit and social consciousness in that young age of ideals and ideality. In the *Athenaeum* these conditions took the form of causes. There were numerous causes, from those transient and topical to those substantive and eternal. Some of the former causes history has long since forgotten. The squabbles with Pettigrew and the "anarcheologists," for example, occupied far more than their appropiate portion of space in the crowded pages of the journal;

94

and even the furor surrounding the cause of the reformers of the literary fund seems, in the light of its ultimate effect, frivolous: and would probably seem so had its outcome been otherwise. But throughout the years the admirable and consistent array of causes, the belief, sincere and impassioned, and trust in the ideal are everywhere evident during the years of Dilke's editorship. Always the intent of such causes is directed toward the eventual and lasting societal good (or what was believed good) and must elicit our admiration and our respect—perhaps also our gratitude.

The Struggling Years

The *Athenaeum* was about two years old when Dilke became seriously connected with it. The periodical had been launched on January 2, 1828. Editor James Silk Buckingham had announced in the prospectus an ambitious undertaking:

We shall endeavor ... first to lay a foundation of solid and useful knowledge, and on this to erect a superstructure of as much harmony, ornament, and beauty, as our own powers and the encouraging aid of those who approve the design, will enable us to construct. If the edifice so reared be worthy of the name we have chosen for it, and, like the Athenaeum of antiquity, should become the resort of the most distinguished philosophers, historians, orators, and poets of our day,—we shall endeavor so to arrange and illustrate their several compositions, that they may themselves be proud of the records of their fame, and that their admirers may deem them worthy of preservation among the permanent memorials of their times.[1]

If ever the *Athenaeum* became "the resort of the most distinguished philosophers, historians, orators, and poets of our day," it was not to Buckingham's credit. He simply had too many experiments going at one time to do justice to any of them. It is worth noting here that although Dilke would certainly have approved of the statements in this prospectus, there is no mention of his two favorite principles of art: the presence of great pathos and its relationship to the people—productions of the age. It is almost certain that Dilke had little or nothing to do with the *Athenaeum's* inception.

The optimistic promises in Buckingham's prospectus were never much realized in the next two years. Although the *Athenaeum* appeared reasonably prosperous and maintained a front of dignity and respectability from 1828 to 1830, it belied its appearance with its forced variations in price, its number of issues per month, its changes of proprietorship and editorship, and even its name. After only six months Buckingham sold his stock to Frederick Maurice, one of the Cambridge Apostles, and to others of his friends. The *Athenaeum* under the editorship of Maurice was probably financed by the Cambridge Apostles, under whose auspices the journal was by this time becoming just another organ of special interests. The editor and his associates were upright, conscientious, sincere men, devoted to the principles of fair play, but their affiliation with the Cambridge Apostles resulted in overt propaganda. As a consequence the *Athenaeum's* policies were right or wrong depending on its reader's sympathies. R. C. Trench, in sympathy with the aims of the new publication, wrote to a correspondent in 1828:

That paper, the *Athenaeum*, which by-the-by, is entirely written by Apostles, should it obtain an extensive circulation, is calculated to do much good. It is a paper not merely of principle, but what is almost equally important, of principles—certain fixed rules to which compositions are referred, and by which they are judged. In this it is superior, not merely to contemporary papers, but to the reviews of the highest pretension.[2]

The Cambridge Apostles were intelligent, devoted young men and included among their membership John Kemble, Alfred Tennyson, Arthur Hallam, and R. M. Milnes, who later wrote the *Life of Keats.* They dreamed of peaceful reform in the world mainly through the church. Maurice was one of the most active members in the society, had good intentions, and worked toward strict impartiality. But in spite of his determined efforts, the magazine was soon known to be published by men having like principles.

Early in 1830, the *Athenaeum and London Chronicle* once more changed its name to the *Athenaeum, and Weekly Review of English and Foreign Literature, Fine Arts and Works of Embellishment* and Holmes, the printer, became part-owner. By May 1829, Maurice had resigned and John Sterling had become editor, in which position he remained even after Holmes became a proprietor. The entire stock of the *Athenaeum* was reputed to have been offered for sale shortly thereafter for the embarrassingly low price of eighty pounds. Financially, it had not proved a success.

That the fortunes of the new magazine were in a perilous state was no secret to the British reading public. If it were to survive, something had to be done to rescue the *Athenaeum* from the oblivion into which it was rapidly sinking. According to Professor Marchand, something was done:

[In] the early months of 1830 it began to be apparent that some new blood had come into the management as well as the contributors' lists of the *Athenaeum*. There was more liveliness and satiric punch in some of the reviews. Increased attention was given to foreign literature, both in reviews and in correspondence from Vienna, Madrid, Naples, Rome, Florence, Munich, Berlin, and St. Petersburg, as well as Paris.[3]

Sterling had called in some of the old *London Magazine* crowd, among whom were Dilke, John Reynolds, Allan Cunningham, Charles Dance, perhaps also Thomas Hood and Charles Lamb. The "Prospectus of the New Series" for the issue of January 16, 1830, stated that the literary management would continue to be "under the direction of the parties who have hitherto conducted it," but that "a great accession of literary talent has been secured ... by engaging the aid of several eminent and popular authors."

It is difficult to say exactly how much influence Dilke exercised on the management in early 1830. That he may have had some voice by January is possible. At this time one of Dilke's favored practices—that of assigning specialists to review works in certain fields—was beginning to be evident, as the notice "To the Reader" which appeared in the issue for February 27, bears out:

The departments of the Fine Arts, the Sciences, and the Drama are all under the direction of separate individuals, distinguished by their attainments in the part allotted to them; and even in the Literary Reviews, the same classification has been carried into effect to a degree, it is supposed, hitherto unattempted.[4]

Then in June 1830, Dilke, Reynolds, Hood, Cunningham, and one or two others bought about three-fourths of the total shares, with Holmes retaining one-fourth. Of the new proprietors Dilke unquestionably had purchased the lion's share; furthermore, he later indicates in a letter to George Keats that the purchase was unpremeditated and abrupt:

You have heard it appears that I am Editor of a Periodical—This is true enough.—It originated in an after dinner talk—I embarked on the work without forethought, or preparation—I was told that the Athenaeum was for sale on Monday, bought it on Sunday, and brought it out on Saturday—[5]

The first year was a struggle and showed only a slight improvement in the fortunes of the magazine. Apparently its sale was slowly climbing, but so meagre as almost to escape notice. Dilke still had some money left from the estate of his father, who had died four years earlier, but his Navy Pay salary of something less than £400+ per annum[6] was by no means sufficient to absorb the steady losses that the magazine was incurring: "... the loss was enormous and the chances fearfully against me—when I took the Paper and long after the loss was not less than £30 a week!"[7] By Dilke's own estimate a "steady sale above 2,000" was necessary to break even financially.[8] The sale of the *Athenaeum* in the closing months of 1829 and early 1830 was far less than that.[9] Dilke records in his 1833 letter to George and elsewhere that one by one, new and old magazines were at this time sinking.[10] It was evident that unless something was done soon, the *Athenaeum* would go the way of those less fortunate contemporaries.

In mid July 1831, an "Address"—rare for the middle of the

year—appeared on the front page; in the interests of the "Moral improvement of society" the journal must seek a wider audience.

The Proprietors of the Athenaeum, from their own honest anxiety, and in compliance with the desire of busy well-informed persons, to extend as much as possible the diffusion of General Literature and Useful Knowledge, have resolved, that on and after *the first Saturday in August*, this paper shall be reduced in price from *eightpence* to FOURPENCE.[11]

Reynolds, Hood, and probably other part owners argued forcefully against the reduction; nevertheless, says Sir Charles, "The change was made...and with magnificent results."[12] On the second day after the price cut the circulation increased to six times its former sale, or to probably about 3000.[13] Six months later, in another "Address" containing the new year's prospectus, Dilke wrote concerning the success of his venture that the *Athenaeum* maintained a circulation greater than that of any other literary paper,[14] and a year later that the *Athenaeum*'s "success has been more rapid and complete than any in the history of periodical literature,"[15] that whereas two years earlier "a contemporary paper" (the *Literary Gazette*) boasted that it "enjoyed by *many thousands* the largest circulation of any purely literary paper, it could now no longer do so, that exact statement belonging exclusively to the proprietors of the *Athenaeum*."[16]

The "Inner Circle" Groups

Dilke allowed certain latitudes of opinion and therefore a moderate deal of freedom to his reviewers and contributors in matters of poetic preferences or taste. But not so regarding policy or matters controversial like religion or politics. Over these he exercised strict control, so that, as Elizabeth Barrett said, "Mr. Dilke *is* the *Athenaeum*," and even near the period of termination of Dilke's editorship in 1846, her husband-to-be acknowledged that Dilke still "shift[ed] the pea."[17] Of the more than 200 writers whom Dilke employed from time to time, fewer than a dozen formed the permanent inner circle that wrote the bulk of the week-to-week print. Actually, the "inner circle" was composed of two groups serving two different functions. The first group was primarily the "art" or "old friends" group from the *London* and included Rice and Reynolds, Thomas Hood (Reynolds's brother-in-law), Allan Cunningham, and George Darley, all of whom he knew intimately and some of whom he had seen almost constantly since the Keatsian days. Later (in 1833) Henry F. Chorley was hired to do the "drudgery" work but ultimately became music and fine arts critic.[18] Dilke allowed all these writers reasonable latitude because he had great confidence in their judgment, though, as we shall see, in the special area of drama, Darley's contributions were unfailingly accepted because his theories of literature and art were almost exactly those of Dilke. Certain "fringe" contributors materially assisted Dilke in both his "art" and "causes" crusades. For example, Bryan W. Procter sent the following missile.

> 25 Bedford Square
> Tuesday *or* Wednesday
> March, 1832

My Dear Sir,

I shall be happy to come dine with you, to meet—anybody. I shall be with you punctually—I shall knock with the last stroke of six—or so close behind that you shall think it is *seven* and say "My Dear, we *must* have dinner."

I send you two scraps of verse. One you must accept (notwithstanding it is good for little) upon the score of the subject—John Keats. It is a shame to scribble so badly on so good a theme, but it has been done some time—a long time—and I put my hand on it accidentally, I thought that you would tolerate it for the subject's sake. The other (a thought) is of better quality—although I will not say a vast deal further.

> Yours very truly,
> B. W. Procter[19]

The Keats "scrap"—a sonnet—was published, and the "better quality" one was rejected. Procter obviously knew the "grave editor" well.

The Arts Group. James Rice. Except for Chorley all of the "inner circle" art group were Keats's friends or Dilke's *London* acquaintances or both. Rice and Reynolds were both and shared with Dilke the ideal of Keats's "great end of poesy" so central to the art group philosophy: art must soothe the cares and lift the thoughts of man. We have seen that Reynolds was responsible for Dilke's and untimately Brown's introduction to Keats and later to John Scott, who presumably introduced them to the *Champion* and hence to the milieu of the periodicals and publishers—a kind of knowledge they put to use shortly afterwards in the publication of the *London* after Taylor. We recall too that in yet another venture Dilke and Reynolds joined forces when, together with Rice, they succeeded in wresting from Abbey monies belonging to Fanny and George Keats.[20]

Rice was brought in as an early contributor and shareholder in the *Athenaeum*. His contributions were at first plentiful with several notices appearing weekly.[21] They were normally humorous "fillers" and poems, for he submitted the longer reviews only occasionally. He was largely responsible also for frequent theatrical contributions before Charles Dance was employed. Both Dilke and Reynolds declared that Rice was "the noblest and best" of their early acquaintances, and both noted especially his excellent judgment, wide knowledge, and refined taste—unusual compliments from either man, each of whom was inclined for whatever purposes to be rather sparing in this respect. Rice's death late in 1832 was both a personal blow to them and a professional loss to the *Athenaeum*.

John Reynolds. When Dilke took control of the *Athenaeum* in June 1830, Reynolds was his principal contributor, an honor and a duty he surrendered only after he sold his shares in the enterprise to Dilke. Only to Reynolds would Dilke entrust a free hand to strike at the insidious puffing practices of Colburn and Bentley. Having both earlier served in the several capacities as reviewer, drama critic, gossip filler, political analyst, fine arts critic, "original papers" contributor, travel correspondent, science reporter, business manager, and even occasional writer of "specials," Dilke and Reynolds could have written the entire magazine by themselves. In the early years they virtually did.

Reynolds's contributions fell off sharply in the middle years of the decade, though he was still contributing occasionally in 1834. As Lady Morgan, Taylor, Hervey, Darley, and Chorley gradually usurped his position as head reviewer, Reynolds's name appears less and less in the Marked File. It is probable that he continued as occasional contributor up to 1838, by which time he had publishing interests of his own. The personal relationships over the years between Dilke and Reynolds may be inferred from their close private and public association to 1835. After that time their records are scanty, and some of what remains seems contradictory. Certainly they were on friendly terms with the Reynolds family through 1838, as evidenced in a letter from Maria to Jane Hood:

I had a kind note from Marianne [Reynolds's sister] last night, she having heard of my loss[22]—and in it she says—though mind hers is *dated Wednesday* that she has been daily expecting to hear from you fixing your day for coming—as she wishes it would be while they were at Camberwell—that their house is let—and the people anxious to come in. I shall write to them and say you intend [to arrive] on the 8...They are very well—but I fear not very comfortable—& I was sorry that we could not help them. Mr. Green[23] wrote for a small loan and only for a short time the other day—but we really had it not... Mrs. Reynolds [formerly Eliza Drewe] is very ill. I sent the day before yesterday—and your Brother wrote me word "that his poor patient was a shade better—she had been attacked with something like intestinal inflammation—and now so weak...that he can hardly hear her voice. Dr. Darling attends her—but her recovery he fears will be a work of time—and that he [Reynolds] is out of heart about it.

In the same letter Dilke includes a note to Hood which affirms that "JHR" has contributed a "leader" in favor "of Hill's Penny-Post."[24]

When the Marked File resumes in 1839, Reynold's name does not appear; nor is it at all in evidence for the remainder of Dilke's period as editor, though a Reynolds poem was published by the then-editor Hervey early in 1848.[25] An 1840 letter from Reynolds to his brother-in-law Thomas Hood in Ostend seems to suggest that Hood had a few weeks earlier[26] appealed to Reynolds to join in a "treaty" with respect to Dilke.[27] If so, this "treaty" may mark a cooling period. But it was apparently temporary, for the families are back on visiting terms in 1846, when largely due to Dilke's urging, Reynolds consented to relinquish his Keatsiana to Milnes.[28] In 1847 Reynolds went to live at the Isle of Wight, where in spite of his drinking weakness he earned the respect of the people of Newport in his capacity as clerk of city court. After 1847 there is no record that he would see old friends of other and better days, but Horace Smith lived at nearby Brighton, and to avoid the stresses of public life Dilke increasingly took lengthier and more frequent holidays. His favorite retreats were Brighton and the Isle of Wight. It is pleasant to think that old friends may have renewed acquaintances there.

When Reynolds died, Dilke wrote eulogies in the *Athenaeum* and later in *Notes and Queries.* In these publications Dilke called Reynolds "a man of genius," but added the melancholy qualification that he "wanted the devoted purpose and the sustaining power ... requisite to its development." As if this were not drawback enough, Dilke further affirms that his genius and his reluctant entry into his "dismal profession" were mutually incompatible. The only "true period of his literary life," Dilke wrote later, was in the early twenties with the *London*: These were fitting tributes to a man, Dilke said, who "not unworthily deserves a niche in the temple of fame."[29]

Thomas Hood. Thomas Hood was another of the old *London* crowd, indeed, served as a sub-editor under Taylor. As Reynolds's brother-in-law, Hood undoubtedly knew Dilke socially throughout the 1820s.[30] As we saw, Dilke contributed to his annual the *Gem* for 1829.[31] Their social acquaintance of the 1820s ripened into intimacy in the early 1830s and into a "best-friends" status in the period 1833 to 1840, when most of the time Hood was living abroad. During this period Maria would experience firsthand Hood's penchant for playing practical jokes on those close to him, a failing which poor Jane patiently endured for the twenty years of their married life. Sometime later he began unburdening himself to Dilke and Maria about insensitive relatives in the presence of Jane's severe and nearly fatal illness, still later from Coblenz about his own infirmities, about dishonest Germans, about the copyright question, about prospective visits to and from the Dilkes, about the scoundrelly behavior of the Belgians, about the even more scoundrelly behavior of his publisher, and still later about advice as to sales of the *Comic Annuals*, and *Up the Rhine*. On many occasions Dilke settled Hood's affairs as he had earlier for George and Fanny Keats and Fanny Lindo, who at least once served as messenger between Coblenz and Pimlico.[32] Like George, Hood was always grateful, and like George, he did not hesitate to say so: "Many many thanks for your letter, and the kind interest and trouble it evidences on my behalf. They are such as I might have expected from the best and last friend I saw in England, and the first I hope to meet again...."[33] The letters from Coblenz and Ostend are long, pages and pages of gossip and business and intimate chit-chat and sometimes painful revelation of a homesick soul longing for someone to talk to. But the Dilkes visited the Hoods twice during their five-year self-enforced exile:[34] in return, sometimes Jane, sometimes Hood came to England, where instead of staying with relatives at Little Briton, each preferred the company of friends at 9 Lower Grosvenor Street.[35] Letters and letters, long, detailed letters from abroad increasingly signified the craving for home and an intellectual companionship seemingly nowhere in evidence in Coblenz or Ostend. But though the Germans cheated him, and though the Belgians were indifferent, and though he was never in worse health, Hood managed to complete *Hood's Own* (1838) and *Up the Rhine* (1840), as well as the *Comic Annuals* (1835 through 1839), which were immensely popular and at least some of which his old friend Dilke reviewed.[36] Dilke said of *Up the Rhine*, for example, that it was superior to others of its class because it was

...a book in many points of view excellent, and above all for the large spirit of humane philosophy which pervades it. That the public will relish or apprehend it is more than I know—assuredly they will never penetrate its heart of hearts—but no matter if they read to laugh they may be wiser without knowing it.[37]

Partly because of homesickness, partly because of further difficulties with his publisher Baily, Hood returned permanently to England in 1840.[38] There the close friendship with the Dilkes continued, even after Hood succeeded Theodore Hook as editor of the rival *New Monthly* (1842), whose proprietors Dilke complimented on securing Hood as editor. By 1841 Hood had gained another friend and professional ally in Charles Dickens, long a friend of the Dilke family and now a tireless confederate with Dilke and Hood in the service of good causes. Because of his great respect for their talents, Dilke joined both in supporting cause after cause, which in Dickens's case, would continue for as long as Dilke lived. As for Hood, so thoroughly convinced was Dilke of his integrity that he allowed him to review books by Boz. Not even Reynolds was accorded the privilege of reviewing books written by friends.

Sometime after 1842 a coolness developed between Dilke and Hood. Possibly their mutually strained relationship with Reynolds may have been a factor, but, as Whitley suggests, "professional differences" is a possible cause. Possibly too, the degree of their alienation may be overestimated, for the supposed break between them is mentioned neither in *Memorials* or in *Papers of a Critic*. In fact, the major evidence for arguing such a break in the first place is that which may be inferred from certain of Hood's letters; but even assuming that such letters as are preserved accurately represent the feelings not only of their author—a sick man—but also those of their subject, one is mildly surprised to find that his only complaints against Dilke relate to his *Athenaeum* policies. There is hardly a hint from Hood of any permanent break in friendship; true, there is a paucity of letters to Dilke to support such a hint. But during the two years of apparent "coolness," at least some of the correspondence continued and the two met frequently under both social and professional auspices with other close friends, such as Dickens, who remained intimate with both. Add to that the most severe criticism that Hood makes of Dilke and the *Athenaeum* is one referring to "the big man in Wellington Street who sells Heavy Dry at 4^d a pot."[39] Thus, although Hood's increasing complaints of Dilke's rigid *Athenaeum* policies do suggest strongly some falling away from the best-friend status of a few years earlier, some evidence suggests that such a break may have been minor.[40]

Allan Cunningham.   Another most important contributor who was not known to the Keats circle but who was a regular for the *London* was Allan Cunningham. Like Reynolds, Rice, and Hood, he was one of the earlier holders of stock in the *Athenaeum* in its first years under Dilke's regime. Unlike those of Reynolds, however, which covered the entire range of periodical subject areas, Cunningham's contributions were more of the "original papers" type.[41] And though he did render occasional service in less spectacular departments such as theatricals and reviews, undoubtedly Cunningham's originals were an essential factor in the eventual success of the *Athenaeum.* His most important contributions were the *Living Artists Series*,[42] and the *Biographical and Critical History of the Literature of the Past Fifty Years*,[43] though series such as his first, "The Aldine Poets," were for obvious reasons more thorough. Marchand's opinion that in his efforts to do so much in so little space Cunningham tended to be superficial is no doubt well grounded, but this rather harsh judgment must be tempered with the realization that he was writing—and writing well—to a specific aim and audience. He was never superficial when dealing with specific works or specific authors.[44] Dilke and Cunningham remained close friends until the latter's death in 1842,[45] though his contributions fell off after 1838 and possibly before. His place was taken, however, by Peter Cunningham, "the worthy son of a worthy squire," who rendered scholarly and valuable service up to 1852.[46]

Henry F. Chorley.   By 1834 the vast efforts which Dilke and other friends had put into the *Athenaeum* were beginning to pay off, "... the labors of ... [which] nearly put me into the grave,"

Dilke told George Keats, but "It is comparative play. I can command assistance [now]..."[47] One of those who rendered most welcome assistance was Henry Fothergill Chorley, who came to town "to throw himself upon it, and see what he could make of it,"[48] according to Harriet Martineau. Actually, as a shy young man of twenty-six, he had come to London already having secured a job as "drudge" for the *Athenaeum* for a modest £50 for six months' service, which was raised to £65 for the second half of the year.[49] Chorley remained a full-time staff employee—until Hervey in 1846, the only one—of the *Athenaeum* nearly all his life, during which his stature improved and his fame as music critic spread. In time he would come to be "general reviewer" of books, "poetry, fiction, memoirs, drama, and almost everything else";[50] occasionally for brief periods he would substitute as editor and was disappointed that Dilke never appointed him as such. But knowing his man, Dilke saw that the highly respected music critic was too friendly and not thick-skinned enough to assume editorial responsibility of the *Athenaeum.*

As a critic of literature he was "something more," as Harriet Martineau said, than merely proficient. Over the years Dilke entrusted some important books and assignments to him because he had confidence in his judgment. As a reviewer his greatest virtue was his honesty, even though that virtue tended sometimes to be sicklied over with the pale cast of sympathy, especially in reviews of women's works. But it was an age when occasionally to err on the side of sympathy was perhaps in itself a virtue, and so Chorley was allowed a free hand at whatever he wished to turn it to. Undoubtedly he was responsible for more columns of print than any other person between the years 1834 and 1864.

But, save for his music criticism, which reportedly sold many issues of the *Athenaeum,*[51] Chorley lacked the imagination, the originality, and the liveliness of the other reviewers. He was perhaps the greatest English music critic of his age. But as a literary critic he could not begin to equal Reynolds, Cunningham, Hood, or especially Darley.

George Darley. "Why endeavor after a long poem?" Hunt

asked Keats, who in reply defended his plan of *Endymion* as affording "a little Region to wander in":[52] an unsatisfactory answer, even to Keats himself. He comes closer to his real intent, however, in the ensuing discussion about how only heroic poetry may challenge, may truly test, the mettle of the poet. This notion of grand design and high purpose as essential to great art was shared by Dilke. Only the greatest may experience the high flights of fancy or achieve those excellent and subtle productions of genius, but Shakespeare was not alone in their attainments. Too many moderns, however, want too homey fare, and will have nothing else. As we saw, Dilke was laboring this precise theme in his 1815 Introduction to *Old English Plays* and had continued to hammer away at it for two decades. An even more specific and particularized account of the notion of the "grand design" or the "Heroic mode" and its relationship to beauty appeared in the *Athenaeum* in 1836. This notice, however, was not Dilke's, but was from the pen of one who would come to sound more and more like Dilke in the next few years. He would echo Dilke not merely in ideas, but also in style, so that it is often difficult to distinguish between them. That person was George Darley, who evinces remarkably similar attitudes toward art, literature, and society to those of Dilke.

George Darley's connection with the *Athenaeum* lasted from 1834 to 1846, the year he died. Prior to this, he had known Dilke, it appears, for a number of years.[53] Marchand suggests that Procter may have requested that Dilke recruit Darley for the *Athenaeum*, but Cunningham, Reynolds, or Lamb could as likely have so recommended, indeed, had a third party been necessary. Darley and Dilke certainly knew each other from their *London* days and possibly before.

So nearly, in fact, did Darley approach Dilke both in style and content that such a true discerner as Thomas Hood was fooled as to the authorship of a very important review in 1836, a notice of Thomas Talfourd's *Ion*.[54] This review represents initially a manifesto, for it is almost wholly given over to a rationale on the genius of the Drama in the Elizabethan age as compared to the puny, fanciful flights of contemporary efforts: precisely the points Dilke repeatedly stressed.

On countless other occasions Darley seems to plumb the very center of Dilke's theory of art and society; the following is a case in point, and might have been written by Dilke himself:

... we have a belief that in the perpetual advance of any people from rudeness to refinement, each phase of its civilization is fitted to be the opening and working out of a certain intellectual vein,—that is, to the production of a certain literature. Thus, we conceive, heroic ballad, chronicle, drama, epic poem, oratory, history, etc. have each their appropriate era of production in the life of a nation, so that history, for example, will be as rare and difficult in the earlier unpolished times, as heroic ballad in the age of refinement.[55]

These sentiments clearly reflect those of Dilke in his 1815 Introduction to *Old English Plays*, in his 1818 Drama criticism in the *Champion*, in his Thomas Heywood article in the *Retrospective Review* in 1825, and later in numerous issues in the *Athenaeum*.

The Art Group was given a primary charge by Dilke: "to sooth the cares and lift the thoughts of man," as Keats explained in "Sleep and Poetry." In review after review the members of the Art Group consistently condemned, or at least regretted, any scenes of brutality or slavery or other sordid realism in fiction.[56] Such scenes depicting the downtrodden, the miserable, are actually harmful and bad literature, Dilke felt, for they spoil "the fairyland of fiction,... the humanizing influences of beautiful thoughts and graceful images."[57] However well intentioned, misery and want contribute nothing toward the soothing of cares and the lifting of thoughts. The job of poetry and fiction—i.e., literature—is "to extend human sympathies"[58] Dilke said, and one does this by *increasing* capacity for beautiful feeling and expression—not by crushing it by belaboring their opposite. Thus all "social-problem novelists"—even Boz—are consistently requested to brighten their workhouses and orphanages a bit.

The appropriate place for depicting degradation and miserable workhouses and starving orphans is in the "grave and calm pages of the advocate or the historian"; for such fare Dilke engaged the Causes Group.

The "Causes" Group: Hervey, Taylor, and the Morgans.

The other group, though occasionally swelled at any given time (depending on the nature of the "cause") to six or seven members, was basically a nucleus of four. Two of these personages were T. K. Hervey, a poet of modest pretensions who succeeded Dilke as editor in 1846, and W. Cooke Taylor, a Whig and broad-church liberal who chastised factories for their tendency to dehumanize but lauded the "factory system" (assembly-line efficiency and mass production) for its potential toward progress. To these workhorses of the 1830s and 1840s fell the primary responsibility for reviewing books dealing with the march of progress and an array of contemporary liberal causes. Like most members of the art group, they occasionally crossed job lines to review a book on some aspect of *belles lettres*. As literary critics, Hervey and Taylor have been called third rate, and the designation was probably close to accurate. They were excellent editorializers, however, in the service of such causes as cleanliness for the poor, of human treatment for prisoners, of improving conditions for factory workers, of alleviating the nuisance of smoke from factories—a project initiated by Dilke and Dickens—but mainly for the *Athenaeum*'s salient cause: the institution of some form of "national education," which Dilke saw as a ready instrument to lessen the great "moral" deficiency associated with poverty, and which at the same time offered the universal and classical remedy to ignorance. Such a "reform" would thus serve to advance Keats's notion of the "grand march of intellect," one of Dilke's favorite phrases now fifteen years later.

The other two members of the "causes" group were first-rate critics as well and must be listed among the "causes" group only because the bulk of their contributions was more cause-oriented than literary. They were Sir Charles and Lady Morgan, whose voluminous contributions to the *Athenaeum* render them among Dilke's most valuable assets. Sir Charles Morgan, who had already

earned a fine reputation as a careful scholar and a thorough and respected critic and philosopher, was something of an eighteenth-century rationalist imbued with nineteenth-century humanism. Taken together, Hervey, Taylor, and Sir Charles Morgan spewed forth good and bad philosophy enough to satisfy an army of editors. But philosophy good or bad was, as John Reynolds once complained, dry, ponderous stuff.

For what was acceptable as lively, agreeable, and imaginative articulation of prejudices, though philosophy it assuredly was not, Dilke relied on Lady Sydney Morgan, who if ever there was one, was herself a character right out of literature. She was "philosophic" only in the sense that she was a seeker after principles of things as a way of thinking; principle searching—she called it "raising systems"—seems to have been habitual with her. As such, she and her husband shared with Dilke those traces of eighteenth-century rationalism, whose proponents discovered, or believed they discovered, ready-made forms in nature; but also like Dilke and her husband, she was in the forefront of the age which applied this rationalist tendency to the romantic concept of a dynamic, unfolding march of intellect in civilization.[59]

Unlike her husband and Dilke, Lady Morgan tried after principles of everything—not just society. She may in fact be a strong contender for the title of first structuralist. She was certainly one of the first truly effective feminists.

As to the book reviews, a single example will suffice to show their ranges of interest as well as their productivity: according to the Marked File, within a brief period in late 1842 they reviewed the following books: *Treatise on Man; On Life and Death; The Art of Duelling; Milton et la Poesie Epique; English: or the Art of Composition; Pantology: Survey of Human Knowledge; Essay on the Art of Flying; Poetry for the Millions* (itself perhaps a tender rebuttal to Hervey's insistence on the moral benefits derived from "cleanliness for the millions"); *Simplicity of Living; Whist: Its History and Practice*; finally *The English Wife: A Manual of Home Duties*, which Lady Morgan treated just about as one would expect. All these reviews featured these elements in common: in

each there was very little in the way of review and very much of opinion *à la* Morgan; in each they looked for and undeviatingly found some underlying structure or principle, even though unrecognized by the author himself (as was usually the case); and each was examined from the viewpoint of its effect on history or culture. Their views were especially suited to Dilke's cultural-literary bias as well as to his manifold causes.

The first cause to which Dike felt he must address himself appeared immediately. Ironically it was of the minor variety, certainly of no magnificent pretensions, but extremely necessary as prerequisite to those which were. It concerned the defeat of the well-entrenched system, in all its manifestations, of puffery: the greatest single obstacle to any literary journal aspiring to fair criticism.

The Battle against Puffery.   For years through almost successive numbers Dilke and Reynolds waged an all-out fight against puffery. They would later be joined by Hervey. Every conceivable method, every resource was employed to its fullest extent in stamping out "this intolerable practice." The *Athenaeum* called attention to advertisements, notices, and sometimes reviews in other magazines of books that were not yet even published.

The battle with the dragon of puffery was carried on throughout the 1830s, though repeated assurances, always premature, that the monster was slain appeared from time to time in the pages of the *Athenaeum*. But by 1840 no reader of what was by then the nation's largest literary periodical could fail to be well informed concerning puffery. Dilke's stubborn perseverance was rewarded by an increasing trust in the respect for the *Athenaeum*. He was as successful in exposing bookselling malpractices as he could reasonably expect to be. By 1850 puffing was the exception rather than the rule; a paid advertisement was labelled as such; a dishonest critic found it increasingly difficult to gain a few pounds on the side. The public was puff-conscious, and puffs were therefore less influential with the public.[60]

It was not until well after the puffery battle had been engaged that Hervey and Taylor commenced their editorializing.[61] By this time the Morgans too had established themselves as regular con-

tributors in the service of liberal causes.[62] Once a cause became "established," Dilke habitually though not invariably assigned to the original sponsor of that cause subsequent related books. Thus the individuals in the "cause" group became identified with certain causes: Taylor on the plight of the poor; on the need for reeducation of the middle and upper classes; on the abolition of capital punishment; on the "improvement of morals" among the working classes; of the abolition of child labor in mines. Hervey chose as his own perhaps less spectacular but not less important projects, such, he reasoned, as could result in immediate practical benefits: on the nuisance of smoke pollution from factories (ably assisted by Dilke and Dickens); on the need for sewers in the city, seconded by the Morgans;[63] on prison reform; on juvenile delinquency; on "cleanliness for the million" (state support of public bathhouses); but also on such theoretical and less pragmatic issues as the elimination of various forms of superstition in the "undisciplined" mind; finally, on the questionable benefits of associations. The Morgans rendered valuable specific service to Dilke's favorite cause—state-supported education—and otherwise knew or recognized no boundaries in their enthusiasm for the creation of a new and better world through the medium of the early Victorian periodical press.

Health and Recreation. One of Dilke's and Hervey's longest and most effective crusades involved their efforts to improve the health as well as the recreation facilities of the British peoples. They were occasionally assisted in this effort by Sir Charles, himself an off-and-on practicing physician whenever his specific knowledge was needed. In the mid-1830s the *Athenaeum* gave notices more and more frequently to books about public health. The first extended treatment appeared in a "leader" in November 1836, written probably by Hervey or Sir Charles Morgan.[64] It was a review of A. J. B. Parent-Duchatelet's *The Public Health, or Memoirs on the Most Important Questions Connected with the Solubility of Cities &c.*, where the opinion was advanced that the most important step in the improvement of health was the establishment of an effective and powerful body to watch over it: a "Council of Heath," composed of community leaders.

This concern with public health is apparent likewise in Hervey's efforts to inculcate a sense of the need for cleanliness among the poor. In 1845 he reported on the proceedings of the Association for Promotion of Cleanliness Among the Poor and lauded efforts to establish public baths and washing centers in certain English cities. Its benefits were more than economic and physical; they were moral as well:

The moral results remain to be developed in a ratio which the figure [the number frequenting the bathhouses] cannot express; for although it is probable that, in the beginnings of this social experiment, the already existing sentiment of the cleanliness will take the *earliest* frequenters where they can thus practise the habit—yet, it is certain that many who may be led by other considerations (such as the influence of example) to the bath and the wash-house, will there *find* it—and so bring away, with the gift they went to seek a far higher thing than itself. The moral consequences, in return, will long continue to influence the increase of the figure—but ultimately leave it far behind—the one having a limit somewhere, and the other none.[65]

Later in the year, after bathhouses had been established in certain towns,[66] Hervey waxed even more sanguine about the incalculable moral benefits to mankind from merely being clean:

Where the Englishmen could pay the price of being clean, he has, for the most part, preferred the privacy of his own home; while the very poor, in whose destitute abodes even this elemental comfort was an impossible luxury, have flocked at once to the fountain of health and moral purification which benevolence has, at length, thought of providing for them. The result shows how much of human good is too often suffered to run to waste, for want of faith in its existence among the poor. The rich have a wholesome lesson, as well as the destitute, in this institution. The mind of society, as well as its bodies, is cleansed in these Baths and Washhouses.[67]

Shortly after he assumed editorship (1846), Hervey recalled the bathhouse experiment in an original paper, titled "Cleanliness

for the Million": "The success of the experiment has been beyond the expectations of its most enthusiastic prognostication." Its physical reward to the poor in terms of "curbing disease and preventing cholera or other epidemics is itself incalculable," and hence, well worth the expense of installing; but, Hervey repeated he was happiest in its promise for its "moral" rewards.

If the morality of the case, no less than the physical blessings it implies, could be impressively brought before that large public who give freely for the good which they think they understand, the rapid progress of this great social movement would be secured,—and some portion of that large fund which annually passes away, in a beneficent stream, to wash the Ethiop white, would be diverted to fill the Bath and Washhouses of the English poor.

We have so dwelt, in the *Athenaeum*, upon all the moral considerations which are involved in the promulgation of this new law of cleanliness, that we could only repeat ourselves if we sought here to enforce that part of the subject. We could but speak, again, of its encouragement of that sentiment of self-respect which, where it does not beget, must be begotten by, the desire for personal cleanliness; and of all the moral fruits that grow upon that gracious stem—self-respect. Three-fourths of the petty vices which degrade society—and swell, under their most unwholesome conditions, into the crimes which ravage it—would shrink away from the light of self-respect.[68]

Dilke and Sir Charles Morgan came occasionally to Hervey's health crusade. No doubt impressed by the superior systems in France and Italy during his stay there, Sir Charles wrote from time to time especially on the need for sewers. He believed that "sewerage and water supply form two of the most valuable blessings that a government can bestow upon society."[69] Dilke himself carried on a running battle with factory owners and city fathers about the nuisance of smoke from factories and steamboats. He chaired the Metropolitan Improvement Society (founded in January 1842).[70] In the Weekly Gossip column of August 1842 issue Dilke accorded the society a prominent place and summarizes its aims, projects and history. The most important object of the so-

ciety, he says, was that of inducing the city government to prepare
a comprehensive plan of improvement, complete with surveys and
timetables, resolution, and money to put them to good effect. Chief
among the interests for and of the metropolis was the abatement
of smoke from factories, though this nuisance was certainly not
the extent of the society's interest in health matters:

> ... they [the Committee] would desire to extend their exertions to
> every point tending to the health, comfort and well-being of this
> vast city. The Committee have already discussed the means of abating
> the nuisance arising from smoke and furnaces, not only in the case
> of the great factories and breweries, but of the river steamboats; and
> they observe, with satisfaction, that the Corporation of the City of
> London have, for some time past, been making active inquiries on
> the subject.[71]

Dilke proceeded to enumerate several other aims of the society,
among which were recommendations: to institute more stringent
building codes and generally to induce a revision of the Building Acts; to effect an improvement of "the overcrowded and ill-
drained neighborhoods of the poor" [*vide* Sir Charles Morgan's
interest in promoting sewers]; to provide better buildings for the
lower classes; to adopt all means available for checking the mor-
tality rates ranging in those poorer districts.[72] In addition, the committee "are anxious to impress the public mind with the fearful
consequences arising from the burial of the dead in crowded places,
and to encourage, as much as possible, cemeteries formed at a distance from the metropolis."[73]

Of far less urgency but ironically of far easier implementation was the resolution taken by the committee to effect a sane
policy of street numbering, which at that time appeared to be
hardly short of chaotic:

> Every one is not perhaps aware of the great public inconvenience
> from the total abandonment of this branch of the duties of munici-
> pal administration to individual caprice; in illustration of this,

however, it may be mentioned that in some streets there are sometimes five houses with the same number; and that in the commercial part of the metropolis alone, there are no fewer than twenty-eight King Streets, twenty Queen Streets, twenty-six Charles Streets, and twenty-three John Streets, with numerous other examples of a corresponding character.[74]

"Our own correspondent"[75] was pleased to report he had noted that Sir Robert Peel (the Prime Minister) had lately apprised the House of Commons of essentially the same information as the committee had made public. Dilke noted further that the committee expressed their sentiment that to render the efforts of the society more effective, "influence and funds...must be increased," and finally, that "we trust this hint shall be sufficient."[76]

Obviously, the society fostered a wide range of improvements. Soon, however, the *Athenaeum* began to give more space to and to take a larger interest in the problem of smoke pollution. During a period in late 1842 and early 1843 Dilke ran monthly notices of society meetings and reports in the Weekly Gossip column. In September 1842 he announced that the society had caused to be implemented legislation which ought to prove effective.

A circular letter has been addressed to public and private companies, drawing their attention to the various patented and other methods by which a nearly perfect combustion may be effected; and should the letter produce no satisfactory result, after the lapse of a few months for the trial of experiments, indictments will be preferred against the offending parties; and this notice is intended to apply not only to parties having fixed establishments, but to the proprietors of river steam-boats. The nuisance is, indeed all the more intolerable, from the notorious fact that it originates in mere ignorance or carelessness on the part of the stoker, and is a wrong done to the employer as well as to the public.[77]

Shortly afterwards he was pleased to report that Charles Dickens had been elected to the General Committee, that the society had indeed forwarded letters to the proprietors of "upwards of 400

furnaces," each letter drawing "their attention to the means for
abating the nuisance."[78] Unfortunately it must be acknowledged
that thus far such letters "appeared to have produced little effect"
and indeed that some had been treated with outright contempt,
but that the sub-committee were just now employed "in collecting
evidence, with a view to proceedings by indictment against the
offending parties."[79] However, not all responses had been negative. Dilke quotes in his Weekly Gossip column a letter from a
firm agreeing to accede to the committee's recommendations.
Finally, Dilke is again pleased with Sir Robert Peel's promise to
appoint a board to report officially on the whole question of
"Metropolitan Improvement."[80] In the following month Dilke
reported that such a commission had indeed been appointed and
that members of the commission apparently were high ranking
personages of sufficient power to force the project to successful
conclusion.[81]

In many ways these causes vigorously and frequently argued
were what sold papers. And in this milieu of rising liberal consciousness—and in an awareness and celebration of that consciousness—certainly more papers than the Athenaeum were sold. But
just as surely, the Athenaeum sold more than any other, and for
that sale Dilke could not have been more obliged to any man than
to Hervey, to whom in his gratitude he left for seven years nearly
total control of his journal.

W. Cooke Taylor's "causes" were less pragmatically, less specifically oriented than were those of Hervey. Taylor's were more
inclined to be philosophically based, to be concerned with universal
and permanent good. We remember that Dilke and his London
Magazine editor, John Taylor,[82] had drifted gradually toward a
kind of Benthamite pragmatism; in the intervening years Dilke
had not wandered far from that 1825 persuasion. Cooke Taylor
represented the non-pragmatic branch. Together their comple-
mentary positions gave to the Athenaeum a range of causes, broad
enough to insure that in each issue one or another such causes
would be prominently featured—usually in the "leader."

Morality and the Downtrodden. Assisted by Dilke, Taylor

hammered away incessantly on two themes: that the living and working conditions of the lower classes should and could be vastly improved, and that their moral instruction should be rigorously encouraged and perhaps even supervised. By "moral improvement" he meant not merely the inculcation of a sense of honor and self-respect, as Hervey, Dilke, and the Morgans meant, but prolonged and regular doctrinaire instruction, and the more the better. He advocated the "homely virtues," precisely those which every child knew and which common sense held requisite to any civilized society. To the argument that such simple fare might be found boring and repetitive to adult family breadwinners, Taylor replied with wondrous consistency that these homely virtues could always bear repeating.

Most of the books and parliamentary reports having to do with the economic or moral status of the middle classes were assigned for review to Taylor. In 1833 and 1834 he reviewed books on history, morality, wages, and education of the middle and working classes; here, as with the Morgans, the books served merely as a point of departure for Taylor's ideas.[83]

Prison and Penal Codes Reform. One of Taylor's favorite causes was the abolition of capital punishment. In the early days several notices had appeared in the *Athenaeum*, all rather tending toward such a position, but it was not until the second decade that he seized upon the cause as his own. In a review of a pamphlet in favor of its abolition, Taylor quotes from a Mr. Livingston of Louisiana: "the fear of death ... will rarely deter from the commission of great crimes ..."[84] and goes on to repudiate the supposed beneficial effects of public execution:

The brutalizing effect of public executions on the spectators is notorious; there is a strange morbid tendency in the human mind towards imitating deeds of horror. Volney relates that after "the reign of terror," it was not unusual to see children amusing themselves guillotining cats and chickens.

The discussion of morbid imitation naturally suggests the consideration of "homicidal monomania," of which a fearful instance was exhibited some years ago, when the captain of a vessel called seven or eight of his crew successively into his cabin, and murdered each as he entered. We have had before us the Reports of the physician to the Lunatic Asylum in which this man is now confined, and they establish beyond doubt that this horrible act was committed in a paroxysm of insanity produced by a functional derangement of the bodily system. It is at least possible that cases may have been handed over to the hangman which ought to have been referred to the physician.[85]

In his concluding remarks Taylor noted the committee's belief that the "public mind" was ready for the change and that although other issues had heretofore engrossed the attention of the press and the general public, "yet an opinion unfavorable to capital punishments has been silently diffused through the thinking portion of the community."[86]

Antilottery Campaign.   Dilke himself carried on a number of relatively minor crusades in the Weekly Gossip column. Though from time to time Reynolds, Hood, Rice, Hervey, the Morgans, or Cunningham would offer a helping hand, the small skirmishes were largely his own. The longest such small war, waged for nearly fifteen years, was against art patronage and art "unions." Dilke registered strong opposition to these two "sicknesses," as he called them, though he regarded them as closely related and though they were both popular with artists at the time. He inveighed against art patronage for the same reasons that he was against literary patronage: because it compromised the independence of the artist. Dilke claimed that the art "unions," so-called, were nothing more than lotteries, where prizes were awarded on the basis of a fortuitous draw of a number, and as a consequence good taste was sacrificed to luck. It was therefore difficult to say which of the two kinds of establishments, art patronage or art unions, had the most pernicious effect on art, for the results were all too similar in both: art of first rank becomes neglected while patrons advertise, puff, and inflate art of second or third rank all out of proportion to its importance. Of course, artists will always welcome patrons and gifts: but Dilke and Reynolds warned repeatedly against confusing the interests of art and of artists. "The great thing for Art is to bring it before the public—to awaken public attention—to give a relish for Art in the great body of the people— to rouse the energies of Art. . . ."[87] With tireless consistency Dilke adverted weekly to the twin perils that unfortunately seemed to be increasing in popularity with artists themselves. Little wonder; it is human nature to seek comfort and security, even in artists, who supposedly care less about these mundane matters than the rest of us sublunary types. But so far as patronage or gifts are appealing to artists, they are just so far detrimental to art. Dilke clarifies the *Athenaeum* stand in one of several manifestos on art in the early years:

Our very hasty visit last week, led us to speak highly of this Exhibition, and subsequent examination has confirmed our first impression. We are satisfied that no country in the world could produce such a collection of works, equal in number and excellence, the result of one year's labour of native artists: there are many admirable in every department. What, then becomes of the last twenty years' talk about want of patronage? It fortunately passed by unheeded; and we are, as a nation, pre-eminent in art. The truth is there is too much patronage—the Academy itself is all the worse for patronage: it is the only apology for one-half the academicians having found admission there. The Academy is a corporate and a chartered body—it grubs on the dark—it toad-eats the aristocracy. Who are the men invited to their annual festival? men eminent in literature—men of informed minds, and associates of the academicians in private life, the glory and boast of England?—No; but my Lord A and B; and other nonentities. This is the interchange between corporate art and patronage. There must be more life got into the academy; as we said once before we must rattle its old bones about. The *public* must, somehow or other, be allowed to take an interest in its proceedings. Had it not been for the annual Exhibition and the public press, we should have sunk below the Knellers and the Hudsons of our forefathers. If art is ever again to equal its old renown, Englishmen, not artists merely, must become co-equal in knowledge of art with the old merchants and traders in the free states of Italy: they must reverence art because they feel its high excellence; and this must be shown, not in the wealthy few, voting away miserable money wrung from the starving many, but in the voluntary subscription of many, consequent on their knowledge and their love of art.[88]

On this particular cause, the manifesto remained in effect until at least 1852, never varying much in its application from year to year.

The Anarcheologists.   Another lesser *Athenaeum* cause which Dilke espoused, perhaps because it affected a society to which he belonged, was the effort to unify two disparate factions of the Archeological Association.[89] In early 1845 its then presiding Secretary, Mr. Pettigrew, bolted the parent organization and established one of his own. Charges were levelled by both factions, insults exchanged, and letters from both sides aired in the pages of the *Athenaeum* over nearly a two-year period.[90]

The Society for the Diffusion of Useful Knowledge.   Still another minor cause, one of the few negative in spirit, was Dilke's denouncement of the Society for the Diffusion of Useful Knowledge. Dilke approved of the society's ideals, wherein so-called "useful" literature was made readily available to the lower classes through its agent of the "cheap" press, the *Penny Magazine*.[91] Accordingly, he had "subscribed his guinea" since the society's inception in 1826. For once it turned out that the *Athenaeum* and the *Literary Gazette* found themselves on the same side of an issue in demanding what became of the profits of the society, since invariably its yearly balance statements showed none. It was subsequently shown that Dilke's and Jerdan's[92] suspicions had been right. The profits from the sales of the *Penny Magazine* had for several years been going into the pockets of a few speculators. Charged the *Athenaeum*: "The whole expenses of the Society are defrayed by subscription—and the Society itself is maintained for the sole profit of certain interested parties, who POCKET THE ENTIRE PROFITS OF THE PUBLICATIONS!" In this connection Dilke frequently saw fit to castigate the Council of the London University (established in 1826 and operative in 1830) for misuse of subscription funds. To keep from bankruptcy, periodically the University Council would appeal for increased subscriptions. On one such occasion the council had buttered its appeal with a promise to consider instituting chairs in Civil Engineering. Dilke remarked that the council was surely rather tardy in so considering; that, in fact, such practical courses of study were prominent among the reasons why the proprietors projected the institution in the first place; further that the prospectus of the university had in 1826 promised such a chair; and that such pragmatic and useful studies were intended to complement "the old cloisteral and monkish institutions of the middle ages which were not suited to the intellectual wants of the nineteenth century."[94] Finally, Dilke could not refrain from noting that the Council of the University of London and the Society for the Diffusion of Knowledge were composed of virtually the same people.[95]

Antimesmerism. Another cause which surfaced continuously during and after Dilke's tenure as editor was the effort toward the eradication of superstition (or of what was deemed such) in its various forms from the public mind. One of the most publicized of these efforts involved a well-known altercation between the *Athenaeum* and Harriet Martineau,[96] who in late 1844 had contributed a series of papers on clairvoyance. To the final paper Dilke or Hervey affixed a statement in effect denying the validity of Miss Martineau's informant regarding a clairvoyant experience. Whereupon Miss Martineau wrote to the editor to protest inadequacies in his denial, only to be answered by assertions of further error.[97] The issue centered on the alleged clairvoyant experience of one young girl, "J" (Jane Arrowsmith), who under mesmeric influence had revealed during a seance her knowledge of a boy's death in a shipwreck supposedly prior to the report of his death to her neighborhood. Through many charges and countercharges, assertions and denials, it was established and ultimately agreed to by both factions that the shipwreck had been common knowledge in the town before the seance; but Miss Martineau claimed that the girl could not have so heard of the death of the boy before the wreck. When it was finally established that a messenger had indeed brought news of the shipwreck and the boy's death to the very house where "J" was staying, she still denied such knowledge. Miss Martineau felt that Dilke (or Hervey) was attacking her character. Dilke felt that Miss Martineau and hence the public were being "put on" by Miss "J." The controversy cropped up periodically from January to September and occupied in all some twenty-four columns,[98] with the only ultimate certainty being Miss Martineau's dislike and disdain of Dilke.

Hervey likewise reported in several issues on the rising fame of a Paris "Electric Girl," who appeared to have both "attractive" and "repellent" forces: she habitually demonstrated her "attractive" powers by showing bits of paper clinging to the fingers of her left hand, at the same time, her "repellent" forces were revealed at the moment she would attempt to sit in a chair, which apparently of its own volition, would suddenly retreat a few feet: attraction in her hands, repulsion in her posterior. Amidst the expected Parisian jokes, the Electric Girl nonetheless quickly gained audiences and fame; some of her believers attributed her powers to a double comet (Gambard's comet) then in the astronomical vicinity, but such powers remained when the comet did not. Finally, she was brought before a committee of the Paris Academy of Sciences, where, unfortunately, she was undone; her fingers were shown to be moist and her posterior was plainly seen to be bumping the chair backwards.[99]

That Dilke and Hervey felt strongly about the need to dethrone such imposters as "J," and the Electric Girl, and others of their stripe is clearly evident. Dilke once gave his reasons in a long comment debunking "the old quackeries," and those reasons are pretty much what one would expect from him: he feared that quackeries may be mistaken by the vulgar for science.

How the old quackeries and impostures come round and round again, after being laid by for awhile to rub off the rust of exposure!— Strangely enough, too, we live in days that expressly invite them. The age is at once positive and speculative. To the scientific marvels of the time themselves we may partly owe it that no superstition can offer itself too gross for acceptance. The sudden removal from the field of the familiar to that of the hitherto unknown—the conquest of new scientific ground—makes the vulgar (and "the vulgar," be it understood, includes classes who have no suspicion that they belong to the category),—credulous as to every silly rumor of the strange treasures which the latter may contain. The imposter sets himself up by the side of the philosopher. The march of science has the marauder on its track.[100]

Copyright.   Probably no cause was more frustrating to Dilke than that concerning international copyright. For many years he, Thomas Hood, and later Dickens strove to prod Parliament to enact a satisfactory copyright system capable of protecting authors everywhere from pirating booksellers. In some measure they succeeded. In 1838, following the examples of France and Germany, England passed an International Copyright Bill, the author of which credited Hood and his *Athenaeum* articles on copyright for service to the cause. But the truly great coup—that of Parliament's enacting legislation to prevent reprints of English books written and published by unscrupulous booksellers in other countries— never came off. Indeed, just how the English government could prevent piracy of English books by other countries was never quite made clear. But Dilke, Hood, Dickens, and others felt that Parliament could find ways to bring pressures and sanctions enough of various sorts against even nonparticipating governments—notably America—to render the piracy unprofitable.

The copyright issue intruded itself frequently in the pages of the *Athenaeum* during its early years. In April 1832 Dilke reported in the Weekly Gossip column the intent of several men of letters to bring forward a measure "to secure genius the fruits which it produces," and to insure that the produce of the minds are as much a possession for their owner as "land is the property of the person who purchases it."[101] He proceeds to explain that the present copyright law afforded protection to the author for a period of twenty-eight years, but that in the event of his death prior to such time, the claim to profits cannot be received or revenued for his descendants. Eventually, then, the bookseller will have all and the heirs will get nothing. Has the world ever witnessed a greater injustice to the memory of great men? ". . . The man of business secures his gains in gold or in land, and bequeaths his all to whom he pleases; while the man of genius, who embarks the capital of his intellect in either verse or prose, has only a short-lived lease of what is as much his own as land or houses can be."[102] But it would be several years before the *Athenaeum*'s and others' efforts would have much effect on Parliament.

The copyright clause received an unexpected boost when in 1835 the Reverend Timothy Flint contributed a long series of papers on American *belles lettres*. Flint was an articulate eulogist of American authors, but in many of his articles he warned that America could never have a first-rate literature as long as American publishers could pirate and sell an English book for virtually nothing.[103] The big gun in the copyright battle, however, was Hood's "Copyright and Copywrong" articles in the *Athenaeum.* At the time Hood commenced writing these articles, the learned Sergeant Talfourd was arguing in Parliament for more specific and effective copyright laws both on domestic and foreign levels. In his earlier articles Hood accordingly concentrated on publicizing the weakness of the present copyright laws as they existed in England, and while he acknowledged an urgent need for fair and just international copyright legislation, he felt that the English Parliament should first concern itself with English authors in England. "I need not point out the notorious examples of direct piracy at home, which have made the foreign offences comparatively venial."[104] His second paper was an appeal to Parliament for recognition of the financial plight of most authors: "Poverty is the badge of all our tribe. . . ."[105] An elaboration on this theme comprised most of the third and final paper in this series. It may appear odd that on very similar grounds for very similar reason Dilke chose to call for protection of writers where he chose to leave artists to shift for themselves; that, in effect, the best interests of literature and literary men were identical, but that the best interests of art and artists were not.[106] Yet, there was a certain difference, one wherein the desired end justified the equivocal or opposite means to it: in both cases, the end result, Dilke believed, was that both artist and author retained independence and freedom: "it is desirable, for the sake of literature and literary men, that they should have every chance of independence, rather than be compelled to look to extraneous sources for their support."[107]

In the June 3 issue, slightly more than a month after the first series, Dilke proudly reported that, in great part owing to Hood's articles, Sergeant Talfourd's arguments for extension of term for copyright and for an effective International copyright law had been cheered by nearly all members of Parliament; Talfourd had reminded them that England's greatness was much indebted to her authors, but the heirs and descendants of these authors were in many cases denied the benefits justly due them.

In the following year, an International Law of Copyright was duly passed; but soon it became evident that the *Athenaeum*'s jubilation had been by its own admission premature. Within as short a time as a year, the law proved to be ineffective, for, indeed, the American bookseller trade managed to get copies of virtually any book they desired and were free to publish its contents in any manner whatever, sometimes even in newspapers![108] The Belgian king, in fact, overtly encouraged such piracy.[109] Worse yet, the interior copyright laws of 1838 were little more than confirmation of the old law in effect for more than a century. Term of copyright was still twenty-eight years, and heirs and descendants "got nothing."

Before and after 1840, when he returned from the continent where he had lived for five years,[110] Hood continued to prod Parliament on any excuse and occasion that presented itself, but Parliament became more and more insensitive to prodding. In 1841, on the submission of a bill for a third time by Talfourd, Dilke reports its melancholy fate: "Mr. Serjeant Talfourd's Copyright Bill, as we ought perhaps to have noticed last week, has been contemptuously kicked out—no, shut out—of the House of Commons. The assembled wisdom would not even grant him permission to introduce it."[111] Dilke goes on to record that the *coup de grâce* was administered not by some Tory-minded, narrow, greedy, book-seller-interested Royalist, but by one who was himself a member of the liberal order and a *littérateur*: Lord Macauley, who, as Dilke noted, had already served something better than copyrights as an inheritance for his children.[112]

While the issue hung thus suspended in Parliament, Dilke soft-ened the tone for immediacy of action, though he did not cease his "friendly agitation," as he called it. Nearly two years later, he resumed his earlier vigorous approach and once again enlisted Hood's assistance in pushing for international copyright. Hood spelled out the terms clearly: protection alike (following France's good example) for English and for foreigners; no importation of books from any country not holding copyright to that book; no importation nor exportation to non-participating countries at all (Belgium, Switzerland, and presently America).[113] Beyond this specificity Hood could produce no new arguments, though he, as usual, made excellent and pleasant use of the old ones.

There were other allies: from time to time in the *New Monthly* Bulwer-Lytton emitted only a slightly less vociferous call for fairness to authors. As noted above, William Jerdan joined the battle in the good fight against offending publishers, though in this instance Colburn appeared not to have been one of the offending parties.[114]

Also about this time, Charles Dickens returned from his famous American tour, where he had hugely berated Americans for their thievery and where he had apparently aroused much attention but very limited sympathy. Just as he then united with Dilke in the cause for eliminating smoke pollution,[115] and as he would later lend his name and pen in the effort to effect re-forms in the administration of the Literary Fund,[116] Dickens sought to aid Dilke in whatever way he could to regain a favorable par-liamentary climate for reintroducing an International Copyright Bill. He wrote ostensibly private letters which Dilke inserted in the *Athenaeum*;[117] he wrote other private letters to Hood and Dilke discussing strategy; he wrote articles, gave speeches, and made other public appearances in behalf of the copyright cause. He agreed, probably owing to Dilke's prodding, to chair an "Association for the Protection of Literature," which held its first meeting May 17, 1843.[118] "Our own correspondent" duly reported on the enthusiasm of those present, and more important, of a simple, direct, but hopefully telling Resolution: "that the members would not knowingly either edit, print, or publish any work in which copyright exists, whether such copyright be vested *in a foreigner* or an Englishman, without the consent in writing of the author or publisher, or sell a copy of any pirated edition of such work."[119] Unfortunately, while "the justice of this Resolution was fully admitted," Messrs. Longmore, Murray, Spottiswoode, "and others"[120] pointed out that "there were difficulties which made it inexpedient to adopt so stringent a principle as a fundamental law of the Association." It was then resolved, at any rate, to lend all possible support to the then existing copyright law (of 1838).[121] As a final gesture of optimism, the members elected a committee whose primary duties were to study the shortcomings and defaults of the existing law and to make recommendations pertinent to putting teeth into it. An earlier aggregate including nine publishers and Bulwer, G. P. R. James, and Marryat had served on an earlier committee.[122] These three members were re-elected, together with the nine publishers, but this time the committee was enlarged by electing Dickens and Dilke.[123]

In the following year (1843) Dilke continued to insert in the *Athenaeum* pertinent notices of parliamentary and foreign developments concerning copyright. In February he exhorted writers and publishers to send its lists of their copyright holdings to all customs officers in the United Kingdom;[124] again, on April 1, nearly three columns are given to the abuses of the present copyright law.[125] In May he deprecates the inclusion of a preface to *The False Heir* by G. P. R. James, who recapitulates in it all the good he has done in the service of copyright. Dilke praises the author himself as a worthy mystery writer who does not need to resort to devices or announcements of high intent, for they are sure to be misinterpreted as self-serving.[126] But a curiously prophetic notice, prophetic in more ways than one, appeared in the September 2 issue. It was among the final notices which Dilke inserted in favor of International Copyright; thus, either he gave up the battle, or he changed his mind. It was likewise prophetic in that the argument adduced in favor of no-copyright was based on another of Dilke's favorite causes: the spread of knowledge. Finally, it was prophetic in that two generations later Dilke's grandson, whose beliefs and opinions were by himself universally and sometimes erroneously represented to be carbon copies of those of his grandfather,[127] opted in favor of the spread of knowledge and not in favor of copyright.[128]

A System of National Education.   Though in the middle years of the nineteenth century parliamentary action in behalf of a system of national education was little more productive than it was in instituting an effective International Copyright law, Dilke at least felt better about whatever progress was made. While he recognized the barriers to International Copyright as formidable, he could never understand why concerted efforts on the part of well-meaning men could not in a reasonable time produce a satisfactory law. But he recognized the barriers to National Education as more than merely formidable and was therefore content and reassured even with slow progress.

Aside from his lengthy battle against puffery, which was narrower in its scope and influence, the efforts to persuade English Parliament to establish a national system of education was Dilke's cause celebre. Even in the journal's early years Dilke was stressing the need for such a system, but it was not until 1835 that the cause was promoted to the top of the list of Dilke priorities, where it remained until the middle 1840s.[129]

Though Dilke carefully refrained from specificity either in its matter or manner (preferring, as he said, to leave details to experience and debate), he was rather clear in his own mind as to what the phrase "national education" should mean. First of all, it required that control of education be taken from the church, where it had previously reposed, and given to government. Next, it assumed that something like "normal" schools be set up for the purpose of training, of administering examinations to, and of certifying as competent their teachers and trainees in various specified areas of study. Third, it required that the government institute the necessary measures to reward those schools and their products. Finally, for the good of the nation, it must provide that this plan replace the present "no-system" of education, and that as speedily as possible.

It was this last specification that Dilke gave wide publicity: the *need* for a national system in the first place.[130] Repeatedly in notices having anything at all to do with the subject he commenced with some reference to need: "the first great requisite in England, is a national system of education . . . and that right speedily, or England will lose irrevocably her intellectual rank in the scale of nations."[131] "*A National System of Education is essential to the moral well-being of the country* . . . we believe such a system absolutely necessary to enable England to maintain its supremacy among civilized nations."[132] "There is no object of national policy which can be compared in importance with that of National Education."[133] Coupled with these assertions of need were Dilke's constant reminders that the present no-system was a thorough disgrace. "It is not denied that . . . public instruction in England is unworthy of our age and nation."[134] In his appeal to the public for support Dilke repeatedly emphasized the word *moral*. Though he had long "outgrown" Godwinism, or so he claimed, he preserved this very central element of Godwinian philosophy. The state had long shown "utter indifference to the moral education of the people,"[135] and whereas Dilke was conscious of the dangers inherent in the state's meddling with morality, he believed that well-intentioned, knowledgeable persons looking to the experiences of history, philosophy, literature—in short, culture,—could succeed in erecting "a standard of morality to which few, if any, would object."[136] However, the great aim of National Education, Dilke felt, was not merely to raise the standard of morality, desirable as such a consummation might be; rather, a general elevation of the standards of artistic taste, in conjunction with a similar increase in morality, would surely produce such a beautiful world as the world had not yet dreamed of. The instrument by which such an outcome may be realized was National Education. And though no one could guarantee its success, the incalculable benefits which ought to result surely made an effort to achieve them worth while.[137] If to our more sophisticated world-views a century and a half later Dilke's optimism seems naive, we must recall that some of the best minds of his and of later days shared his hopes.

We have seen that Dilke repeatedly insisted that the interests of good literature were often averse to those of booksellers. As long as money was to be made by catering to a depraved public taste, booksellers would always be found to pander to it. This was just another complication which led Dilke to insist that the question the English Parliament must settle was not one of education versus no education, but rather of good education versus a bad education. The pick-pocket and the purse snatcher who never had an hour of formal educational schooling were nevertheless well educated in their respective crafts: ". . . he who cannot write can fire a corn-rick. . . . It is too late to be inquiring whether education be useful or not; every human being is and must be educated:—the question is whether it be desirable to close schools which are dens of vice, and open others for teaching the duties of citizens and subjects."[138]

Nowhere was bad education more encouraged than in the public taste for bad literature. Trash was not merely nonconducive to raising the standard of taste, but was actually detrimental in that it served ultimately to sanction and perpetuate that which was inferior. Those booksellers whose prime object was making money rather than giving services to a worthy cause did little too improve the current deplorable state. "We have heard it argued," Dilke wrote, "that a certain quality [of inferior literature] . . . is required by the public."[139] So that it may be able to separate the bad from the good, booksellers do well to provide that "certain amount." But the public is being not merely provided: it is being surfeited, or perhaps even suffocated: "The public appetite is not only to be gratified, but its mind *nourished*; it grows by what it feeds on."[140] The influences of the book trade, he argued, is always on the side of the superficial learning—booksellers "look forward only to a quick sale" and not to immortality:

If the press were actuated only by the spirits of literary men, its productions would be widely different from what they really are. It would then exhibit a fair picture of the constantly increasing experience of mankind, whereas it is now chiefly employed in throwing tubs to that great whale, the public; the desire to keep large capitals in circulation giving rise to an activity in the book manufacture, not subservient, and perhaps even adverse, to the interests of civilization.[141]

Often Lady Morgan joined Dilke in hurling salvos at booksellers. Her previous experiences with Colburn may have had something to do with her attitude, but to her credit she was publicly more gentle with the trade than in her private correspondence. "The moment . . . that a demand for inferior books is felt, there is a rush of inferior spirits to supply the market; and there is more money to be made, by a bookseller, through a judicious publication of inferior and popular matter, than by printing the highest and the finest effusions of superior genius."[142] Such statements were basic to both Dilke's and the Morgans' oft-expressed sentiments that no amount of Parliamentary wrangling or poor law legislation will avail to lift the downtrodden out of their condition. Until the nation "shall have resolved to initiate a system of national education," the poor will provide a seedbed for vice, misery, and degradation of spirit. "Legislative enactments cannot alter human nature: if we do not plant good seed in the fallow ground, assuredly there will be a goodly crop of weeds."[143]

In the Weekly Gossip columns near the middle of the decade, Dilke was pleased to record that undoubtedly his own exertions in behalf of national education were in part responsible for the creation of just such a society as he had envisioned. This was the Central Society of Education, upon which the hopes and good wishes of all friends to national education were bestowed. The auspices under which the Central Society was created boded well for its future. It was an outgrowth of plans and meetings of many influential members of the British Association for the Advancement of Science.[144] In preparation for the meeting in Bristol of September 1836, where a large number of interested persons attended a special inauguration meeting, Dilke projected his hopes: "We fancy we see in this association of Catholics, protestants, dissenters, . . . of gentlemen from north, south, east and west, the germ of many local committees, all we trust to be found hereafter cooperating with a Central Committee, whose office it shall be to bring all the moral energy of this great country to bear upon Parliament, and force upon its consideration, as its first great duty, the education of the people."[145] The following week he could report the completion of the formation of the society, and in proof offered excerpts from its "Prospectus of the New Central Society of Education, Lord Denman, President." In a somewhat disappointed tone, however, one that the *Athenaeum* repeatedly sounded, Dilke reminded the society that it should forego details in favor of large designs and general education policy. He observed that it was for the "statistical societies [to] collect facts."[146]

By May of the following year the gentle reminder had escalated into a general complaint: the society was wasting its time in too much concern for detail and prescriptive local remedies. Dilke proposed that the council address itself to these three national issues: (1) that the council study ways to convince England of the *need* for national education; (2) that the council decide first *who* will be teachers: i.e., what will be their qualifications; (3) finally, that the council decide *what* ought to make an educated man and, once having decided, worry about *how*. These requisites once observed, Dilke would allow specificity concerning the "who" and "what" to the following extent: (1) all candidates to be admitted without religious preference; (2) all candidates to undertake a more or less fixed curriculum, with more or less uniform examinations to determine levels of competence; (3) all candidates to attend a "model school," for prospective teachers, where one may learn "the art of instruction itself"; (4) all candidates to pursue in addition "locally augmented arts and crafts" courses, including industrial classes.[147] Beyond these specifics, if such they were, societies and governmental agencies should not venture. It should be left to the collective wisdom of experience and local debate to work out details. "All that the government should bestow on the system is superintendence,—just as it provides that competent persons should alone dispense drugs...."[148] Indeed, said Dilke, the Central Society could not possibly execute the task it had set before itself: the formulation [planned even to embrace local detail] of a system of national education; for that task was and would and should remain the "work of the government and the country." Rather, "Let the Central Society rouse public opinion, and bring its force to bear upon both; let it collect the scattered energies that now often work in opposition to each other—let it show the nation its moral disease—let it make every man feel the want,—but let it not usurp the proper functions of the government and the legislature."[149] Still later, observing the provocation that the Central Society had stimulated among members of Parliament, among the public press, and often between these two, Dilke could not forebear reminding the society, "We told you so."[150] He was pleased to note, however, that the *Athenaeum*'s ten years' struggle, the expressed wishes of leading *belles lettres* figures in all England, and perhaps even the otherwise detrimental controversy provoked by the Central Society were at last proving fruitful. Lord Brougham had introduced in the House of Lords a bill to establish a system of national education.

By far the greatest obstacle to such a system was the fear by certain members of the established church that moral and religious training would certainly suffer as a result of throwing wide open the doors to universal education; for such a national policy would indeed mean that all creeds and religions must agree to the selection of Bible readings and Bible interpretations. This stipulation many members of important sects would by no means accept. Dilke quotes an Anglican clergyman, a Reverend F. B. Woodward, whose main objections were that the system was, first, "a direct check to the growth of protestantism" and secondly, that it was a "direct encouragement, and a legal establishment of Popery and Unitarianism," and finally, that "it was calculated to spread Infidelity [in religious matters] from one end of the country to the other."[151] Dilke replied to these objections by asserting that the object of National Education was to create "good citizens and good subjects"; as no one would venture to assert that he who does not profess the protestant religion must of necessity be a bad man and a bad citizen, and if, even Rev. Woodward admits, education of any kind tends to the perpetuation, growth, and "moral" justification of the system that fosters it, then it must follow that education must make some good Roman Catholics better and that in any event a good Roman Catholic is a better citizen and a better subject than a bad Roman Catholic. Here as elsewhere, however, Dilke was not eager to enter into controversy or contention with religious figures of any persuasion, far less those of the established church.[152] In fact, this was the prime reason for his cautious attitude toward the whole question of National Education. He realized that religious issues were not merely complicated but deeply emotional and hence deeply ingrained in the national character. And there could be no doubt that taken out of the control of the church, religious education would experience a leveling process, which, no doubt, would lessen the influence of specific dogmas. To offset this "loss" Dilke advocated heightened emphasis on "moral" teachings, or instruction in what amounted to creating "good citizens and good subjects" unconnected with specific denominations. He further realized, however, that because instruction in specific creeds would be demanded by the vast majority of the English public, not to mention the English clergy, such specific doctrine must of necessity be a part of and system of national education. Very well! Let us then agree on specific interdenominational Bible readings, but let the strictly religious influence in the schools stop at that. As to further specific training, he advocated what he called "parental responsibility," wherein such specific doctrines would be left to the discretion of parents at home.[153] Though they may seem tame now, Dilke felt acutely the radical tone of these suggestions, suited though they were to his private convictions.

Among the more important causes that Dilke espoused in the *Athenaeum*, the foregoing list is by no means exhaustive. Other causes would follow which would enhance Dilke's purpose of inducing a climate of opinion conducive to the spread of liberalism and of social awareness. As editor and proprietor of England's largest literary weekly, his influence in that enthusiastic age was enormous.

The March of Intellect. All the foregoing causes, from current topical measures like prevention of smoke nuisance through more permanent ones like alleviation of severe codes and conditions of various downtrodden to the enduring ones of national education were all grounded in a basic Dilkeian faith: the "march of intellect." Keats more than once alluded to Dilke's deep-seated conviction, calling him a "Godwin Methodist" and a "Godwin perfectability man";[154] the intervening years had not dimmed that optimism. In the early years of the *Athenaeum* Dilke alluded frequently to signs of the March of Intellect in England, Germany, Africa, Turkey, Egypt, Austria, Canada, as well as to gratifying omens from America.[155] As civilization's primary means of furthering that golden ideal, Dilke reminded his readers frequently of the high calling of the literary and art magazines. For example, in an extended welcoming message for 1833 summarizing the contents of the *Athenaeum* for the previous year, he declared, "We do not hesitate to express...the honest conviction, that the volume for 1832, now concluded, contains a full and fair record for the period, of all that was of permanent interest to the informed and marching mind of the age."[156] In another instance a reviewer, probably Dilke,[157] on H. C. Carey's *An Essay on Wages* (London: Longman and Co., 1835) was pleased to note that Carey had quoted copiously from earlier *Athenaeum* extracts and statistical tables, which was gratifying ... not merely in reference to ourselves" but more particularly because such quoting may be taken as evidence of the "extensive diffusion and consequent influence of [periodical] literature"; thus even with "all its vices and errors," periodical literature has "done as much to promote the intellectual brotherhood of nations, to bring the ends of the earth together, as the labours either of philosophers or statesmen."[158] A few weeks later Dilke again alludes to "the mighty forces" of his own and other like periodicals: "If literature have it humanizing influences—and who can doubt it?—what mighty engines, for the happiness and improvement of society, are at this moment in operation all over the world!"[159]

While Dilke occasionally complained of the dearth of good literature, he believed that gradually the combined efforts of men of letters were having their desired results: "Many circumstances ... confirm us in the gratifying belief that literature and the arts are spreading among us—that they are gradually pervading and refining the immense body of the middle class...."[160] One such instance in encouraging the growth of societies appears some weeks later: "A band of city musicians ⟨the Cecilian Society⟩ gave Handel's "Israel in Egypt" on Wednesday last, in a very creditable style. Some of the choruses went exceedingly well, and the band was better than might have been expected, it being, we are told, chiefly amateur. It would be superfluous to enter into a detailed notice of the performance, our wish being rather to commend and encourage the progress of these minor societies, as widely and intelligently diffusing a taste for the art among the middle classes, than to weary our readers by anatomizing well-known works, and pointing out inevitable faults."[161]

The decision to encourage amateurism may at first seem contradictory to Dilke's stated policy of striving after perfection. But in various places Dilke acknowledges that the *Athenaeum* reserved to its reviewing staff the right of a double standard. He speaks of his habit of applying "the Highest standard to the most aspiring works," but that others of less pretension, once established as such, would be admired and censured "as through a glass of courtesy."[162] In another context he affirms that the attempt to measure all the issue from the same standard "would be at once absurd and unjust."[163] Booksellers who meet the demands of the reading public are admittedly not "in advance of the age," but may be partially excused, at least, for "going along with it."[164]

There is something to be said for supplying "the wants of [their] customers," so long as they refrain from catering to prurient tastes. Thus, music societies, literary societies, art societies, institutions of all kinds must of necessity foster a certain amount of popular fare which will have its roots in amateurism. But just as surely, deeper study and wider acquaintance will foster interest in better music, better literature, better art. The key to raising the standard of taste in all art (in its broadest sense) is first to encourage and improve societies and other such groups everywhere. These associations tend to "awaken an interest in art in thousands" who hitherto considered it a luxury "reserved to the rich." Such an interest could not fail to diffuse a knowledge of art and thereby raise the standard of public judgment."[165] Through such models as may be found in periodical literature, these converts to art and society could not fail to be guided in a pursuit of excellence in what another noted critic some forty years later would term "a study of perfection."

Chapter Four

The Post - *Athenaeum* Years

The Daily News

Even before he had totally relinquished editorship of the *Athenaeum*, Dilke rather abruptly assumed yet a much greater responsibility than any he had hitherto undertaken. He contracted to serve for three years as managing editor of the *Daily News*, a liberal newspaper established in the early months of 1846. Charles Dickens was its first editor, and, like Dilke, had served apprenticeship as a Parliament reporter. But after three weeks of editorship, Dickens surmised correctly that he was ill-prepared for that office; on February 9, 1846, it passed into the hands of his friend John Forster, where it reposed in April when Dilke joined the staff and where it would continue to reside until mid-October, when Forster resigned. Dilke then succeeded to the editorship, a post which he held for the next two and a half stormy years.

Though he was exaggerating somewhat, Dilke wrote to George Keats in 1833, three years after gaining control of the *Athenaeum*: "I can command assistance [now]...it is comparative play."[1] The problems associated with editing the *Daily News* were never play, even comparatively. There were few who praised and many who criticized, often concerning matters over which Dilke could exercise little control: the chicanery of rival papers, the preferred treatment outside England accorded rival correspondents, the negative reception in England to the sole major liberal daily. More immediately, there were many proprietors to please, proprietors whose interests were not often identical and whose conceptions of policy were not always in agreement. In its early years the paper was constantly in serious financial difficulties, a bothersome fact attested by its frequent price fluctuations. But as editor Dilke had to bear the responsibility of these added burdens, which, as he said, he "cheerfully accepted." Soon after he became managing editor he cut the price of the paper from 5 to $2\frac{1}{2}^d$, thus repeating the formula that had proved successful with the *Athenaeum*. This time, however, the price had to be raised again to 3^d. Even so, as Sir Charles maintained, Dilke's measure had set a precedent which would prove to be a forerunner of the cheap daily press, a development Dilke would have been proud to witness had he lived long enough.

He discovered soon enough that being editor and chief proprietor (as of the *Athenaeum*) was one thing, but being merely editor was quite another. Richard Cobden, MP from West Riding was not a proprietor, but some of his influential friends were. He wrote often, and as often as not, his friendly advice was veiled complaint: "Your reporting staff is very inefficient. The speech of Mr. Charles Hood on Wednesday was shamefully reported— not a single '*cheer*' was reported I think, whereas the whole speech was most admirable and it was cheered very much throughout, and most loudly at its conclusion. Mr. Weir will tell you of the reporting of my speech last night. The latter part of it (the reporting) was well done, but the greater portion was the very worst specimen of reporting I ever saw. I am astonished how ingenuity could so entirely distort a speech."[2]

Likewise, Cobden's friend John Bright was often unhappy with *Daily News* policy and reporting. He was extremely chagrined, for instance, over an unflattering news article on Mr. Baptist Noel,[3] a Dissenter in great favor with the Manchester school. "The attack on Mr. Noel is coarse and untrue. It is calculated to annoy every one of the new subscribers. The Dissenters are in rapture ⟨over Mr. Noel's book⟩, and if you could not have praised it, you might have let it alone,"[4] Bright wrote in early January, and later on the same day: "The most violently Tory article that ever appeared in the *Standard* would not have astonished and confounded me more if I had read it in your columns, and would not I am persuaded have done you more harm with the intelligent and trustworthy portion of the liberals in the country."[5] Sir Charles reports, however, that Dilke was not swayed in this instance nor in any others by either Cobden's or Bright's complaints[6] and, as he had with the *Athenaeum*, kept the *Daily News* policies free from the influence of friends and foes alike.

That firm control was apparently what the paper needed in its early years. At the end of three years there were still problems of management, of solvency, of reporting, distributing, but the impetus and influence of Dilke's liberal but prudent guidance were felt on the fortunes of the paper long after he left it.[7]

Even before Dilke retired from public life in 1849, he had begun his more important studies largely but not exclusively into the lives and writings of the eighteenth-century figures. His more enduring studies were those of Junius, Pope, Wilkes, Burke and Swift, though other luminaries of that century came occasionally under his notice. Of these the Junius and Pope interests were by far the paramount ones and together comprised at least twelve of the fourteen of his active scholarship years, or until 1860.

Later Writings

Junius. Comparatively speaking, Dilke began his Junius studies early. In 1848, while he was still active in public life, he contributed an article to the *Athenaeum* challenging Mr. Britton's theory that Colonel Barre was Junius.[8] Britton, following the unknown editor of an edition of the Junius letters published in 1812 (though prepared by Dr. Good), added about one hundred letters to the sixty thought to have been written by Junius. From his collection Britton attempted to prove by analogy that Barre was Junius. Dilke introduced his argument against Britton by stating that it is "high time that the question as to the authenticity of the Letters first introduced into the edition of 1812 as those of Junius should be examined."[9] After quoting from the 1812 edition preface wherein Dr. Good "justifies" the additional one hundred letters on the basis of "a thorough knowledge of our author's style," Dilke claims that Dr. Good transferred just what he pleased into his collections as "the miscellaneous letters of

Junius," so that "The extent of his temerity passes all belief."[10]
For various reasons Dilke challenged the authenticity of certain
letters in Good's edition: some were not consistent with Junius's
known political views; some attacked personages of whom Junius
spoke well, while other letters lauded those whom Junius consistently attacked; some written under the signature of "Atticus" were
included, while others under the same signature were not; and
all the letters signed "C" Dilke held suspect because one of them
attacked Wilkes, with whom Junius was then on friendly terms.
As to Britton's knowledge of Junius's style, Dilke had this to say:

"...with all deference to Dr. Good, we have no absolute faith either
in his judgment or in our own,—seeing how blindly others have
stumbled. Every age has its style—its style of writing and of handwriting. As we said before, there have been some thirty different
persons fixed on as the writer of "Junius's Letters,"—thirty persons,
therefore, whose "style," (as well as handwriting) in the opinion
of some one or other, or of many, was the style of Junius. Twenty-
nine of those—good, confident critics—must have been wrongly
assigned—perhaps the whole thirty![11]

Since, as Dilke was first to demonstrate, the case for the Barre
authorship depended on the authenticity of those questionable
letters, Britton's argument was considerably weakened.

Another claimant sometime later, produced not for the first
time, was Macleane, sponsored by Sir David Brewster, who cites
as evidence an anecdote told by West, contemporary of Junius.
Hamilton, Governor of Pennsylvania, visited West on the morning that the first Junius letter appeared in the newspapers. After
reading carefully the letter, Hamilton declared it to have been written by Macleane, who was "a surgeon in Otway's Regiment." According to Hamilton, Macleane had violently attacked him in
Philadelphia newspapers for issues relative to disagreements on
administration. To prove his familiarity with Macleane's style,
Hamilton repeated several phrases that Macleane had used against
him. As another proof that Macleane was Junius, Brewster called

attention to a "Letter to a Brigadier-General"[12] supposed by Brewster to contain the style, temper, and thoughts of Junius and further supposed to have been written jointly by Barre and Macleane. Dilke quotes Brewster's argument that Macleane must be Junius:

"We have not been able to learn if Macleane was in any of the expeditions to North America, which were fitted out in 1757 or 1758; but we know [We do *not* know] that he accompanied the celebrated expedition in 1759, when Wolfe fell on the heights of Abraham, and the command of the British troops devolved upon Brigadier-General Townshend. Major Barré and his countryman Macleane shared in the dangers and honours of that eventful day.... Brigadier-General Townshend was unpopular in the army, and particularly obnoxious to Barré and Macleane, and the other friends of Wolfe.... Irritated by this selfish and ungenerous conduct, the friends of Wolfe, and who could they be but Barré or Macleane, drew up and published, in 1760, the celebrated Letter to a Brigadier-General, already mentioned, which so clearly resembles in its temper, and style, and sentiments, the Letters of Junius. If Junius, therefore, wrote this letter, all the arguments of Mr. Britton in favour of Barré's being the author of it, and therefore Junius, are equally applicable to Maclaine; and if we have proved that Barré could not be Junius, it follows that, under these assumptions, Macleane is entitled to that distinction."[13]

Brewster is further quoted in admitting that little is known of Macleane during his residence in America, but that he appears to have become a physician in Philadelphia and that a contemporary (a Mr. Prior) now living in Philadelphia informs Brewster of his grandfather's friendship with Macleane:

"A gentleman in Philadelphia mentions 'Dr. Laughlin Macleane and his lady as acquaintances of his grandfather, and visitors at his house sometime between 1761 and 1766'...Mr. Prior informs us, that when in Philadelphia Macleane acquired great medical reputation, followed by its common attendant, envy, from the less fortunate of his brethren.... In 1766, Macleane met Barry, the painter, at Paris."[14]

In a blustering, mildly sarcastic manner that Dilke always affected when someone made unwarranted inferences or was too careless about facts, Dilke began to chop away at the foundations of Brewster's argument:

> Now, not to delay or perplex the argument by asking questions however pertinent,—not even to comment on such extraordinary opinions as that no friend of Wolfe's, in a whole discontented army, could have written a pamphlet against Townshend save either Macleane or Barré, although Townshend himself accused and challenged another man for having written it or got it written—no, nor to correct obvious and palpable errors,—let us assume the above statement to be true; and then consider, where was the interval of "some years," between 1761 and 1766, during which Macleane practised as a physician at Philadelphia, exciting the envy of the profession,... according to the memoirs of the Pennsylvanian?—or, according to Sir David [Brewster], within even narrower limits—that is, between the peace of 1762 and 1766 when Barry met him in Paris.[15]

Dilke attempts here to discredit Brewster's authority, the Philadelphia gentleman, by affirming that Macleane could not have accomplished all he is said to have done. He points out, first of all, that it was in 1765, not 1766, that Barry met Macleane in Paris; further, on the authority of Parliamentary History, Dr. Musgrave met Macleane in Paris as early as 1764. Thus, instead of "some years," this interval of time in which Macleane was supposed to have made a fortune from his profession, returned to England, and visited France becomes "some months." Then Dilke thoroughly discredits the argument about the Hamilton identification by stating "on the authority of official records," that Macleane was never a surgeon of Otway's regiment.

What now becomes of the assertion of Governor Hamilton, that the letters of Junius were certainly written by that "d——d scoundrel," "the surgeon of Otway's regiment"? What is to become of the letter to a Brigadier-general—of the hatred to Townshend as a stimulating power—and of one-half of the other personal feelings which, like "the legacy," serve, we are told, to identify Macleane as Junius? If the identity of the pamphleteer and Junius be proved—if the pamphlet-writer must have served under Wolfe at Quebec—and if, as Sir David intimates, the pamphlet must have been written either by Barré or Macleane, we think Mr. Britton may reverse the conclusion at which Sir David arrives, and fairly say "it follows that, under these assumptions, Barré is entitled to that distinction." But as Mr. Britton, like the church-warden's wife, is but mortal, we think it well to remind him that these are "assumptions."[16]

Dilke's objections, he admitted, do not prove that Macleane was not Junius. In so "proving," Dilke calls attention to Parliamentary records to show that Macleane was employed as secretary to Shelburne and was an avowed supporter of the ministry. Junius was not. But there are even stronger objections to Macleane's candidacy. Dilke referred to old newspapers that reveal a quarrel between Wilkes and Macleane, who challenged Wilkes to a duel. At the same time, and for a long time thereafter, Junius carried on his "long ... friendly correspondence" with Wilkes.

Finally, Dilke produced another objection to the Macleane candidacy. He showed that at the very time that Macleane was writing "On the defense of the ministry on the subject of the Falkland Islands," Junius was attacking it. Thus, Dilke disposed of Macleane as a candidate for Junius on the grounds that he was for the most part on the side of the opposition, and was first friendly and subsequently antagonistic toward Wilkes, even challenging him to a duel, while Junius remained friendly.

In other articles of less importance appearing from time to time from 1849 to 1852, Dilke made further inquiries into the probabilities of authorship of various of Junius's letters. He pointed out the futility of analyzing handwriting and style to ascertain the work of Junius. In other articles he ridiculed theories that Chesterfield, Lyttleton, the Earl of Chatham (Pitt), and Temple were the author of these letters.

By far the most popular claimant in the first half of the nineteenth century was Sir Philip Francis, though Dilke placed little credence in this suggestion. This claim was substantiated by Francis's young wife and by the fact that Sir Philip himself never categorically denied authorship. He was a clerk in the War Office and could have gained reasonable access to government secrets had he so desired. On the publication of Wade's *History and Discovery of Junius* (1850), corroborating Taylor's *Junius Identified* (1812), Dilke reviews the opinion pronounced in favor of Sir Philip Francis:

Lord Campbell has recorded the opinion of the Queen's Bench; and Mr. Wade tells us, that an "eminent Judge of the Common Pleas, Sir Vicary Gibbs, affirmed after the perusal of Mr. Taylor's book, that if the case had been argued before him as a Judge in a trial for libel, he should have directed the jury to find Sir Philip Francis guilty." Exactly the same judgment is said to have been pronounced by Lord Ellenborough, and, Mr. Barker tells us, by Lord Erskine: and the review of "Junius Identified" in the *Edinburgh* having been attributed to Mackintosh, to Brougham, and to Macauley, three more Judges or ex-Judges are said to concur in the opinion pronounced by "Brother Gibbs."[17]

Dilke facetiously observes, however, that the judges pronounced these opinions without their wigs on and that there may be something in the wig. But upon separation of fact from theory, Dilke contended that Sir Philip's claim to Junius is not entitled to serious consideration. First, Dilke attacks the Lady Francis argument. It appeared that far from acknowledging his authorship to his wife, more than fifty years his junior, Sir Philip, according to Lady Francis, *"never avowed himself more than saying he knew what my opinion was, and never contradicting it."*[18] It was her belief, as she states, that "the secret of his attachment and marriage so late in life" was that, "like the wife of Midas, he wanted some one to whisper the secret to."[19] Whereupon Dilke digressed to favor the reader with a few choice remarks on connubial misfortune and unfulfilled marriage goals: "He never did whisper it ⟨the secret⟩ to her!" But it is clear that Francis, in his old age at least, wished to be known as Junius, though he denied it publicly. Lady Francis tells of his wedding present, an edition of Junius, and of his post-

humous gift, a copy of Taylor's *Junius Identified*, testifying that
the first gift after their marriage "... was an edition of Junius,
which he bid me take to my room and not let it be seen, or speak
on the subject"; and that "his manners and conversation on this
mysterious subject were such as to leave *me* not a shadow of doubt
on the fact of his being the author, *telling me circumstances that
none but Junius could know*."[20] Dilke regretted that while she
was in a communicative mood she did not relate to the public
even one of those circumstances. Wade stated further on Lady
Francis's authority that before he went to India, Sir Philip admitted
to George III that he was Junius. Dilke called attention to the
incongruity of the statements that Sir Philip told her he had
avowed himself to others, yet never so avowed himself to her. But
the story has been told and proved false before, for George III, according to Queen Charlotte, "did not know who wrote the letters
of Junius." Those facts Dilke mentioned to throw discredit on the
testimony of Lady Francis.

In a second notice, Dilke considered the evidence itself.[21] He
quoted Wade to summarize the three types of proof that Sir Philip
was Junius:

"First, the correspondence of dates and incidents in the Life of Sir
Philip with the dates and incidents in the publication of the Letters;
secondly, the correspondence between the style, sentiment, and ability of the Letters, &c.; and thirdly, the resemblance between the
handwriting."[22]

With the second and third "proofs" Dilke would not bother to
argue, pointing out that the authorship of some thirty other claimants has already been so "proved" on this basis. Dilke objected
further that not one fact has been adduced to link Francis with the
Grenville Party, to whom Junius, by universal agreement, was
friendly. To the assumption that Junius, and therefore Francis, was
known to the Grenville Party through Wilkes, Dilke answered
first that Junius did not correspond with Wilkes until his career
was nearly finished, and that furthermore, no connection with

Wilkes and Francis had yet been discovered. Dilke pointed out other improbabilities in the statement of the Franciscans: that Francis could not have been in France in 1761 or 1762, as they contend, except as a prisoner of war; that Taylor's argument is ridiculous that Sir Philip was Junius in his twenty-ninth to thirty-second year, the "time of life in which it has been often remarked men generally undertake the greatest designs of which they are capable."[23] Furthermore, says Taylor, Francis was in London during the ascendancy of Junius, but Dilke countered with "so were fifty thousand others."

Dilke picks other flaws in Taylor's argument. He proves that, contrary to Taylor's sources, Sir Philip was dismissed from the War Office after Junius ceased writing, thus nullifying the motives Taylor had ascribed to Junius. Finally, to conclude his argument against what Taylor calls "personal movements," Dilke summarizes Taylor's argument, listing his own objections in brackets:

Just as Francis moves Junius moves, *like substance like shadow.* If Francis is in the country Junius is away. [Junius's absence being most unwarrantably inferred from his silence,—and his silence from the dates affixed by Good and Woodfall to the private letters,—and the connexion of the two as "substance and shadow" is to be proved by very slight and very suspicious evidence tending to show that Francis was *once* absent when Junius was supposed to be silent.] If Francis is abroad, Junius is not heard of till his return. [Junius having closed his labours months before Francis is supposed to have gone abroad—and "Veteran" some time—and Francis having returned two months before Junius is supposed to be again heard of.] If Francis is aggrieved by abrupt dismissal from office, Junius suffers, and pours out the vials of his wrath against all the offending parties. [Even "Veteran" having emptied the last of his vials on the presumed offending parties before Francis was dismissed, if dismissed at all.] If Francis finally disappears from the scene to another hemisphere, Junius writes no more. [Junius having ceased to write for eighteen or twenty months before.][24]

Dilke next attacks the center of the Franciscan argument by

pointing out that Almon, in publishing the *Life of Chatham*, took Chatham's speeches from notes said to be those of Sir Philip. From evidence afforded only in his letters, these notes are said to be the same as those Junius must have taken. Thus, though neither Francis nor Junius was a member of Parliament, both frequented the galleries and "both took notes of the same speeches at the same time and in the same words."[25] Dilke admits that he does not know how Junius and Francis got their information, though he suggests the newspapers as one possibility. Taylor had anticipated this argument, however, and had stated that after long and laborious search, he had been unable to find any trace of one such speech, and must assume therefore that it had never been printed. Therefore, since Francis's notes of the speech are so similar to what Junius's must have been, judging from his letter on that speech, Francis must be Junius.

If the theory was fraught with minor difficulties Dilke elected graciously to overlook them. He would not question the allegation that Almon's notes of Chatham's speeches are purported to be notes by Francis; nor would he balk at Taylor's suggestion that Francis's notes are exactly the same as what Junius's "must have been." Instead, he chose to argue that Taylor met with his difficulty in finding printed copies not because copies of the speech were not printed, but because newspapers themselves were in 1850, seventy years later, not generally available. Then, after eight columns of comparison of Francis's notes with Junius's Letters, generally debunking Taylor's "ifs," Dilke utterly devastated the latter's entire argument by giving the readers "the benefit of a morning's labours": he produced an old newspaper account of the debate which Junius-Francis allegedly took in notes from the galleries!

There was no need to look further. The only connection between Francis and Junius had been broken. No closer than any other person within reach of the *North Briton Extraordinary* or the *London Evening Post* was Francis to Junius. Dilke closes by calling again for his "one fact."[26]

Dilke's own opinion of the identity of Junius is never set

forth in very positive language. But in a rather apologetic manner, he wrote in 1851 an article linking Junius with the Reverend William Mason, poet and court chaplain. Dilke describes Mason as a friend to Walpole:

a man of great ability,—a poet of high order, his "Elfrida," after many years, still lives in our recollection as a creation beautiful for its simplicity, tenderness, and sweetness,—a satirist whose pen was diamond-pointed,—a painter and a musician, theoretical and practical:—in brief, a man of highly cultivated taste and infinitely varied accomplishments, who excelled in everything that he cared to know or to do. . . .[27]

Dilke adduces proof that his political philosophy was that of Junius, that his friends were those of Junius, that his position of court chaplain gave him access to Parliamentary proceedings, and that his abilities were quite equal to the task. Furthermore, Boyd, whom many believed to have been the agent of Junius, told Mrs. Boyd that Junius was the author of the then-anonymous *Heroic Epistles*. This poem was subsequently proved to be Mason's. Dilke alludes next to a letter wherein Mason himself links Junius and the *Heroic Epistles*. He quotes further several passages from Mason's poems to show that both Mason and Junius hated and insulted the same personalities, especially the Scotch. In summary, Dilke's theory was without serious fault in that all parts fit perfectly, with none of the objections such as those to Macleane or Francis. But even Dilke himself was not convinced. After presenting a faultless argument, he debunked his own theory in a concluding paragraph:

Enough, in all conscience, of what may be thought an idle speculation. Our apology is, briefly, that such speculations are just now the fashion; that such coincidences are at least curious; and that in the case of Mason it is a physical possibility,—which is more than can be said in those of all claimants to the honour. . . . We will only add, that if the fox now uncovered does not give the reader a good

day's sport,—we have another which we lately ran to ground, and
which shall be unearthed for his amusement.[28]

That no other candidate appeared does not tend to strengthen
Dilke's argument or indicate that he became more convinced as
time passed. In fact, Dilke was never serious about settling the
identity of Junius: only of settling who he was not. The British
Museum contains a Dilke letter to some publisher who had evidently asked him to try to identify Junius; Dilke writes: "It is not
even in the remotest degree possible that the twelvemonth will
enable me to solve the Junius mystery—for many reasons, one
being all-sufficient: *I never was a hunter after Junius.*"[29]

Dilke's Junius studies had been interrupted by the most melancholy circumstances of the death of Maria, "with whom he had
lived in the most complete happiness for more than 40 years."[30]
After Maria's death in November 1850 Dilke suspended temporarily his scholarly activities and took several long trips on the
continent and in Ireland. On some of these he took his seven-
year-old grandson, who would later eulogize him in *Papers of a
Critic.* But gradually he "suffered himself to be lured back to his
'tub,' "[31] i.e., his library of 12,000 volumes, which Wentworth had
built for him at his own home on Sloan Street. Ultimately the
studies into the eigteenth century continued.

After 1853, however, he wrote infrequently on the Junius question.[32] His interests had gradually shifted to studies on John
Wilkes and Edmund Burke, both of which were outgrowths of
the Junius researches, as also were the less important but still
substantial studies on Grenville, Rockingham, and Walpole.[33]

Pope.   Though Junius studies continued periodically to sur-
face in the 1850s and after as did Burke and Wilkes studies, from
1854 Dilke's first scholarly concern—he himself implied a
stronger hold which amounted to an obsession—was that of Pope.
About this time, too, Hepworth Dixon had inherited from Hervey the editorship of the *Athenaeum,* which office he had held for
seven years. Since 1846, with his embroilment as editor of the
Daily News, then his travels after the death of Maria, Dilke had

been too busy to interfere much in the week-to-week affairs of his journal; with the advent of the Dixon term in 1853 he became once again active, and in frequent and pointed notes to Dixon made every bit as much nuisance of himself as had the proprietors of the *Daily News*[34] some years earlier. In particular did he despair of one of his favorite sections, the Fine Arts column. The following is a sample of his daily notes:

I wish to suggest that a vigilant eye may be kept on *Fine Arts flourishings*. The notice (p. 1011) of Lord Cardigan[35] is not in the tone of a high class journal & (same page) "almost the only good thing a pope ever did" [referring to Alexander Pope] is neither liberal nor true—is indeed foolish.[36]

Again, in quotation of nearly an entire letter:

11 Feby [1860][37]

My dear Sir

After I had despatched my letter of yesterday I took up the Athenaeum. I have not, as you know, for sometime read the Fine Arts criticism—simply because it worried & bothered me. Stimulated however by our censurer I turned to it once again, and I was I confess grieved & astonished at the justification which it offered for any amount of censure. The writer has I believe *an ideal* with which I do not agree & of the truth of which the public are not satisfied; but we want somebody who can *sympathise* with us—a many sided not a one sided or no sided critic. Tom Cribb on the Elgin Marbles & your critic on St. Pauls are of equal value to an ignorant people. I do not say that he is wrong; but if he be right, he is of no use; and I submit for your serious consideration that if all modern art be all bosh—that if from McDowell, Marochatti, Lough, Hurd and down to the forty three competitors for the Art Union prize, be all beneath criticism or all beneath praise, there can be no need of art-critics or art criticism. Art is dead & there we end.
The one-sided peeps out in the *anticipatory* notice of Holman Hunt.[38] This is not what I object to—but the want of all sympathy with art & artists to the public, and all I ask of you is to deliberately read over the Art criticism of last week & form your own opinion.[39]

And again, in rejecting a "totally unsatisfactory" contribution from an unknown correspondent: "I shall say nothing of the violations of taste, which are trifles compared to the positive offence in the paper. On these I have dwelt at length because if such an article could get into type, it might slip into the journal, & then woe betide us.

Who is the writer I cannot conjecture—but, if as I suppose a new man, I warn you never to trust him with such a subject again."[40]

Dilke could praise, however, as well as censure, when he thought that praise was merited: "Your comment on the trial was extremely judicious—I could not have objected to or added one word had I been present." The preponderance of this correspondence, however, dealt with neither praise nor censure: rather with policy, such as the following specimen illustrates; because it throws light not only on Dilke's continuation of the causes of the previous decades, but also gives indisputable evidence that, as Browning said, he still "shift[ed] the pea," the entire letter is quoted:

76 Sloane Street S.W.
Sunday Feb 16 [1862]

My dear Sir

There is a tone creeping into the Athenaeum on the subject of slavery which is very painful to me, & which I think you cannot approve, although it does not appear to have struck you. I first noticed it in the reference to the American dispute, but it came glaringly forward last in the review of Underhill.[41] I indeed expect that the writer must have planters' blood in him—or stronger still than blood, planters' interests. The very confident assertion with which the article opens, is I believe untrue. It may have a colour of truth from the writer's point of view, for he sees nothing but planters' interests—ships' commerce, sugars reports etc. but it is absolutely untrue, interference to the laboring people—How can it be proof of poverty & distress, that a working man can earn, as he says, enough in a day to maintain him for a week? It is to me proof only that he was compelled heretofore for the interest of the planter, to give six times more labor than he received wages for. In truth the writer's whole argument is a protest againt emancipation & free trade—points on which I thought the Athenaeum was clear & fixed for ever.

I, indeed, who have not been unobservant on the effect of emancipation have come to a wholly different conclusion. I believe the emancipated do labor—but it is for themselves & not for other people: that there is in consequence, a growing middle class quietly accumulating property—that there is less produce shipped to other nations because there is more retained & consumed at home.

Pray consider this subject. Nothing but its great interest could have induced me to write this letter.

Yours very truly
C. W. Dilke[42]

Dilke had, in the meantime, plunged almost exclusively into his Pope studies. His discovery and purchase in 1854 of the Caryll correspondence enabled him to correct many previous biographers' errors and add new facts concerning Pope's life. Although Dilke proved in 1854 that Pope had altered certain letters, had added to others, and had even constructed correspondences which in reality never existed, it was not until after a series of articles climaxing in 1860 that he was able to outline the strange and complicated history of the various surreptitious and authentic editions. In so doing, he was able to trace the even stranger and shadier dealings of Pope himself in these editions.

In one of his first articles on Pope in 1854, Dilke states the known history of the surreptitious editions of the letters; shows that Pope in the authorized editions misdirected, shortened, and added to certain letters; and corrects some mistakes of previous biographers concerning Pope's financial conditions.[43] Dilke's story of the pirated editions of the letters is simple enough; it became complicated only when the full extent of Pope's complicity in the matter was made known, but that discovery was not until 1860. Dilke could affirm in 1854 only that a Mr. Cromwell, one of Pope's correspondents, gave his letters to a Mrs. Thomas, who professed to admire Pope but whose admiration was found unequal to straitened circumstances when she sold Pope's letters to Curll, a bookseller. Upon their publication, Pope was indignant and wrote to correspondents to ask that his letters be returned. An anonymous writer offered Curll the memoirs of Pope from 1704 to 1734. Another anonymous figure "in masquerade costume, a clergyman's gown with a councellor's band," approached and delivered to Curll printed copies of this correspondence. Because he was instructed to do so, Curll advertised the publication as a collection of letters to and from a number of Earls and other important men. These, then, were letters of Peers printed without their consent, and their publication was considered a violation of Peers' privileges. Curll was summoned before the House of Lords and dismissed because no names of any Peers were found in the collection. Pope offered a reward of twenty guineas to anyone who could discover the person or persons that carried on those negotiations, and double that amount if it could be told under whose direction the party or parties acted. Dilke gave Pope's own story thus:

Pope's own version of the story, published at the time, was this,—that, alarmed by the indiscretion of Mr. Cromwell, he had collected his letters—that, as several of them served to revive past scenes of friendship, he was induced to preserve them, to add a few notes here and there, and some small pieces in prose and verse, and that to effect this "an amaneunsis or two were employed." The inference which Pope intended is obvious; yet Pope never called on these amanuenses, publicly or privately, to give evidence on the subject; he never even named them. In brief, Curll's strange story was never disproved; and Pope's story, still more strange, was never proved.[44]

It is obvious that in 1854 Dilke did not believe Pope's version about the amanuenses. In so disbelieving, he was not alone, for he states that nearly all who have inquired into the matter agree with Lintot's statement to Samuel Johnson: "Pope knew better than anybody else how Curll obtained the copies."[45] But no biographer had produced an iota of proof.

Subsequently, Pope announced that (owing to errors and omissions of the first pirated edition) it was necessary to publish a genuine collection of his letters. Carruthers, as well as Dilke somewhat later, pointed out that the pirated edition and the subsequent "authentic" edition, prepared by Pope himself, showed little differences; in short, the interpolations, omissions, and errors are precisely such as Pope desired. Dilke in 1854 did not undertake to disprove Pope's version, but he offered proof that Pope in the Curll and in his own editions had tampered with letters and had even fabricated correspondences that never existed.

He was able to do so because part of the Caryll papers contained Pope's original letters to Cromwell. By collating these originals with the "surreptitious" and "authentic" editions, Dilke was able to prove duplicity on Pope's part. Purporting to be addressed to Addison in both the pirated and "authentic" editions, a letter beginning "I am more joy'd at your return than I should be at that of the sun"[46] is in the original not directed to Addison at all, but to "the honorable J. C." (Caryll). Furthermore, Dilke pointed out significant omissions and interpolations within this single letter wherein Pope had "cooked" his own correspondence to indicate that he had sent other letters to Addison, when actually they were sent to Caryll. By changing names of personages and revising incidents, the letters were made to fit Addison instead of Caryll. Evidence of tampering was indisputable.

The evidence, too, that "Pope knew better than anybody else how Curll obtained the copies" is indicated but not yet proved. Dilke is "sorry for the consequence—sorry at the exposure of such duplicity—sorry for the want of sincerity, honesty and truthfulness of our little hero."[47]

Dilke's earlier outline in 1854 of the Curll publication was substantially correct. By 1860 he was able to construct in elaborate detail the whole history of the "surreptitious" edition and at the same time to produce incriminating evidence that could leave no doubt of Pope's complicity in the matter. Upon Curll's publication of the *Letters to Cromwell* in 1726 Pope had written to his correspondents to ask for his own letters. Some complied with this request, others did not, and some sent copies of the originals. Pope's own story was that an amanuensis was employed to copy the letters thus received from correspondents. "Obliging friends"

entreated Pope to publish his own edition of the letters "to prevent a worse." Pope declined, publicly, at least. On October 11,
1733, one "P. T." writes to Curll offering him a chance to publish some letters, anecdotes, in P.T.'s possession. On Curll's eager
response, P. T. sent anecdotes but no letters; however, he asked
Curll to print an advertisement, after which he should receive
the letters. Furthermore, the original letters were to be shown at
Curll's bookstore upon publication, a promise impossible to keep,
Dilke asserts, unless P. T. were Pope. Curll, too wary to accept
P. T.'s terms, would not advertise without the originals, and for
a time the matter was dropped. Out of the goodness of his heart,
so Curll allowed, he wrote to Pope explaining that a P. T. claimed
to have in his possession a large collection of Pope's letters. Pope
replied to this letter via the newspapers:

"Whereas E. C., [Edmund Curll] Bookseller, has written to Mr. P.
pretending that a person, the Initials of whose name are P. T., hath
offered him to print a large Collection of the said Mr. P_____'s letters,
to which E. C. requires an Answer. This is to certify that Mr. P_____
having never had, nor intending ever to have any private Correspondence with E. C. ⟨who had published Pope's letters to Cromwell⟩
gives his answer in this manner. That he knows no such person as
P. T.; that he thinks no man has any such Collection; that he
believes the whole a Forgery, and shall not trouble himself about it."[48]

Dilke calls attention to at least three interesting aspects of this
letter: the unfriendly tone, the false implication that Curll had
threatened to print the letters, and the subtle and disguised permission to do so in Pope's refusal to "trouble himself about it." Curll
was understandably irritated. Dilke surmises that left to himself,
Curll undoubtedly would have published in the newspapers the
plain truth and would have denied that there were any clandestine
negotiations with P. T. or that he had threatened to publish any of
Pope's letters or had the authority to do so. Thus, on the appearance
of such a statement from Curll, there could be no pretext for the
obliging friends to suggest that Pope publish a new edition of
letters "to prevent a worse."[49] But before Curll had an opportunity

to publish such a letter, he received one the next day from P. T., affirming that since the treaty had been broken off in 1733, P. T. had himself been persuaded to print the letters. As Dilke puts it, "Revenge is Sweet." Since the letters were already printed, Curll could be no more responsible for their publication than any other bookseller. Accordingly, on April 5, two days after Pope's advertisement, Curll's was published. Thus far, he had reacted just as Pope had wished. Still, Curll would not advertise the actual contents of the volume until he could see the originals. P. T., on the other hand, was anxious for Curll to commit himself in an advertisement before he would verify the contents. A second impasse was imminent. But shortly afterwards, a parson, or a person disguised as one, appeared at Curll's home with a few of the original letters and a promise to deliver the remainder after the advertisement. Dilke again identifies P. T. with Pope:

He ⟨Curll⟩ knew Pope's handwriting well—he had the originals of the Cromwell Letters still in his possession. Where, then, did the originals shown to Curll come from? They were avowedly in Pope's possession long after. But they must have been out of his possession and doing service on that memorable evening.[50]

Finally, on the arrival of a few printed copies of the letters, Curll issued the advertisement as directed: "Letters to and from certain lords."

At 2:00 P.M. the next day five cartons of books were delivered on horseback to Curll's home, but before a single bale could be opened, the entire lot was seized by officers from the House of Lords, and Curll was ordered to appear next morning to answer charges. After due examination, no such letters to Lords were found as evidence; Curll was released, together with the letters. It is questionable whether Curll ever realized that P. T. was actually Pope himself, though he should have; the fact is manifest to one having access to original manuscripts.

Except for censuring Pope for his duplicity in the publication of his own correspondence, Dilke defended Pope against false

charges leveled at him by earlier biographers. He sneers at Roscoe's suggestion that Pope carried on clandestine affairs with the
Blount sisters; he excuses Pope from any serious breach of propriety in his conduct with Lady Montagu. His most important defense of Pope is his refutation of the charge that the poet accepted
a 1,000-pound bribe from the Duchess of Marlboro to suppress
the "Character of Attosa," allegedly descriptive of her. The slan-
der, invented in part by Warton, was perpetuated by biographers
down through Carruthers, whose *Life of Pope* Dilke reviewed in
the *Athenaeum* in 1857.[51] He shows, first of all, that not until
1746 was there a bribe ever mentioned, and then only by an
anonymous person serving as amanuensis to Warton's publisher:
Dilke quotes the "anonymous" source:

"These verses are part of a poem entitled *Characters of Women.*
It is generally said, The D—ss gave Mr. P. 1,000 pounds to suppress
them: he took the money, yet the world sees the verses; but this
is not the first instance where Mr. P.'s practical virtue has fallen
very short of those pompous professions of it he makes in his
writings."[52]

After dealing appropriately with the tale-bearer, Dilke abstracts
the "It is generally said" portion to claim as Warton's authority.[53]
This was in 1857, and at this time Dilke could offer no final proof.
He could ask only if this disreputable fellow is to be credited on
his own admission of "no-authority" when the whole life of Pope
"gives the lie to it."[54] However, in 1860, after reviewing his argument in 1857, Dilke advances the startling intelligence that the
charge must be untrue because the "Character of Atossa" was not
meant for the Duchess of Marlboro at all. As one of his arguments
Dilke points out that the italicized portion of the first line in the
following quotation offers strong evidence that the "Character of
Atossa" was directed rather to the Duchess of Buckinghamshire
than to the Duchess of Marlboro; Dilke quotes a Pope letter printed
by Warburton:

"There was another *Character written of her Grace* [Buckingham-shire] by herself (with what help I know not), but she shewed it me in her blots, and pressed me, by all the adjurations of friendship, to give her my sincere opinion of it. I acted honestly and did so. She seemed to take it patiently, and upon many exceptions which I made, engaged me to take the whole, and to select out of it just as much as I judged might stand and return her the copy. I did so. *Immediately she picked a quarrel with me, and we never saw each other in five or six years.*"[55]

Dilke produces further evidence that the "Character of Atossa" was meant for the Duchess of Buckinghamshire rather than for the Duchess of Marlboro by showing that even after her death Pope spoke bitterly of the former; on the other hand, Pope and the latter were on friendly terms up to a year before his death. There is no record of any ill feeling between them after that.

Finally, as if further proof were needed, Dilke refers to a state-ment by Warburton, whom Pope assisted in the collection of materials for an edition of Pope works:

"The Duchess of Buckinghamshire would have had Mr. Pope to draw her husband's Character. But though he refused this office, yet in his Epistle on the Characters of Women, these lines,

> To heirs unknown descends th' unguarded store,
> Or wanders, heav'n-directed, to the poor,

—are supposed to mark her out in such a manner as not to be mistaken for another."[56]

These lines are from the "Character of Atossa"; Warburton une-quivocally names their reference to be the Duchess of Bucking-hamshire.

The remainder of the article is devoted to an examination of this couplet and its application to the two candidates. To the ques-tion "to which one does the couplet refer," Dilke replies that the Duchess of Buckinghamshire died a year before Pope, leaving no heirs, while the Duchess of Marlboro left at least twelve and was still alive at Pope's death. This by showing that the "Character of Atossa" was directed not to the Duchess of Marlboro but to the Duchess of Buckinghamshire, Dilke cleared Pope from charges of indiscretion which many early nineteenth-century biographers had erroneously imputed to him.

The Elwin-Murray Correspondence. Recent Pope and Junius scholars generally speak highly of Dilke's contributions. Professor George Sherburn, for example, offers testimony to Dilke's accuracy and diligence with respect to Pope studies, though his praise could with equal verity be applicable to Junius, and to a lesser extent to Burke, Wilkes, Walpole, and Swift.

The contributions of Dilke were chiefly concerned with the authenticity of various of Pope's correspondences, though his criticisms of biographical detail evince an incisiveness that may be the ideal and the despair of any biographer. That neither Spence nor Dilke should have written a life of Pope is a major catastrophe to this field of scholarship.[57]

But the value of his contribution to Pope studies, in particular, was well recognized by his more informed contemporaries as well. The Roskill-Dilke papers contain an interesting and substantial correspondence involving Dilke, Elwin, (co-author with Courthope of a Pope biography in 1870—still considered the standard edition) and John Murray (Elwin's publisher), starting in 1857 and continuing through 1862.

In May 1856 Dilke received from Pope scholar Whitwell Elwin a letter asking for his assistance in writing a *Life of Pope*, which he was then contemplating. Elwin's publisher and Dilke's friend, John Murray, was likewise engaged to some extent in assisting Elwin, but to what extent and in exactly what capacity is not clear. Murray had encouraged Elwin to seek Dilke's assistance. Dilke and Elwin had accordingly met at the house of John Forster (Dilke's and Dickens's friend and colleague),[58] where Dilke had given his conditional approval; Elwin wrote in late 1856:

When I had the gratification of meeting you at the house of our mutual friend Forster you were good enough to say that out of respect to Mr. Murray you would contribute the very valuable materials[59] in your possession to the new edition of Pope provided Peter Cunningham was not concerned in it.[60]

John Wilson Croker, who was at that time also writing a life of Pope, had engaged Peter Cunningham to assist him, "and got little assistance."[61] Shortly afterwards, on his deathbed Croker had elicited from publisher Murray a pledge that Cunningham would be continued in the editorship. Thus Dilke's sole condition could not be met as long as Cunningham had anything to do with the new edition. "As it was evident," Elwin wrote, "that no permanently standard edition of Pope could be published without your ⟨Dilke's⟩ assistance, this was a most unfortunate result, and I have never ceased to hope that means might be devised for overcoming the obstacle."[62] Owing to the exertions of Mr. Forster, the impasse was at length unblocked, and after two years the difficulties were resolved: Cunningham reluctantly agreed to renounce any claim to editorship or participation whatever in a Pope *Life* published by John Murray. Further he yielded up all the documents and materials formerly belonging to him and to Mr. Croker. With Dilke's assistance a definitive life could now be written.

Elwin had hoped "to establish a complete correspondence with you [Dilke] on the subject of Pope." He showed Dilke's letters to Murray, who was elated at the prospect of Dilke's assistance: "I cannot refrain from expressing to you at once my sense of your great kindness in placing at his and my disposal the very remarkable collection of the Caryll correspondence." Murray further expressed the desire that Dilke would allow Mr. Elwin to consult him "from time to time and to profit by Dilke's minute researches and investigations of the character of his author and the intricate story of his works."[63]

Shortly afterwards, by June 22, 1858, a regular correspondence was indeed established between Dilke and Elwin on the subject of Pope. Dilke sent a comment on his surprise at Croker's carelessness and inaccuracies in his arrangement of Pope letters. Elwin replied that he had intended to write Dilke a long letter wherein he would have mentioned certain peculiarities of Mr. Croker's character and habits that would surely have lessened Dilke's surprise. But he was pleased beyond measure to see firsthand the value of Dilke's assistance:

"Your comments show the minuteness of your investigations and the great value of your aid. Indeed, I feel more and more that without it no proper edition of Pope can be published, nor would I go forward in it unless I had the benefit of your assistance."[64] By February of the following year it became clear to Murray and Elwin that Dilke's contribution was too great merely to be fobbed off as "assistance" with the letters. Murray accordingly wrote that both he and Elwin were in agreement in their "admiration of what you have done for Pope's letters. You ought really to come forth as the announced Editor of this portion of the work and claim the credit which is your due for working out and solving the problems of "Pope as a correspondent!"[65] Besides that, said Murray, "it is not possible for Elwin to assume to himself the credit of another man's work"; so pleased was Murray with Dilke's finished product that he declared "I am prepared to go to press at once with the letters accompanied by your notes and comments."[66] Mr. Murray concluded with the hope that Dilke "would agree to having his name attached to the Letters section." And why not? The work was already done, the effort, time, and drudgery already expended, and expended in highly creditable form. Anyone except Dilke would have jumped at the opportunity. And it is difficult, even with all his "great modesty" and "reluctance to bring himself before the public," as Sir Charles put it, to understand why he did not. But Dilke declined the honor. A year later (January 4, 1860) Murray offered it again, and again Dilke declined it: "As to my assuming the office of Editor of the Letters, or even reviewing the old drudging labors, it is out of the question. As I told Mr. Elwin, three months since, I am willing to advise, consult on specific points, . . .—but my thoughts and reading have taken another direction—I am once again a free man—[67] I do not the less heartily wish you and him success."[68]

Elwin's Introduction to the *Life and Letters of Pope*. Elwin's first volume of *Life and Letters of Pope* was printed, though not published, in 1862. Shortly before the final printing Elwin sent the proofs to Dilke for his comments and advice. Dilke was anything but flattering:

You are a bold editor—all the better for the great publick—but a few critical readers may be less satisfied. You quote as authorities

> Page 1. Pope 1735
> 2. Pope
> 32. Pope 1735

These are all distinct publications—& the verses quoted p. 32 are found only in one issue or one edition. Thereafter you must refer to Cooper 1735. Now Pope acknowledged that he "connived at" that publication. Then there is another Pope 1735. How is the reader to distinguish between these *four* publications. Mr. Murray tells me that you intend a general Introduction. If you visit London *give me a morning*, when, with the volumes *before me*, I could explain the facts.[69]

In other respects Elwin's "editorial slashings" were not to Dilke's taste: of the many interesting and spontaneous of Pope's letters which Elwin might have chosen to feature, he selected those that Pope had published, and thus they were "poor stuff—characterless and without interest, because he *prepared* them. . . ."[70] Further, Dilke complained that Elwin's editing itself was in the same tone as the prepared letters. The general result was flat, with "every bit of colour . . . struck out . . . leaving out the voice of trumpet & hautboy . . . the fair-haired, the brown, the exciting, the frolic, etc. Mind, I do not say that you are wrong; but that your fashion is not to my taste. Pope's letters want all the colour possible."

Even so, shortly afterwards (March 18, 1862), Elwin was eager

to know Dilke's opinion of the first volume, complete with Introduction:

My dear Sir,
    I was about to call on you today; but I find that the printer has
not yet sent you the final leaves of the Introduction, and as I am
anxious to have the benefit of your judgment upon the whole I put
off my visit till to morrow (Wednesday) when I purpose to look
in upon you in the forenoon. If you are not at home you will, perhaps, kindly permit your servant to let me in that I may wait your
return. I also much want a view of some of your editions of Pope's
letters to enable me to complete a Biography of them. I shall be very
anxious to know your verdict.
                                    I am ever
                              Very sincerely yours
                                  W. Elwin[71]

What Dilke's actual verdict was is not known. But apparently he
was happy at least with the Introduction.[72]
    Swift.   In his refusal of the Murray-Elwin offer of editorship,
Dilke stated that his thoughts and reading had taken "another
direction." The "direction" was that of establishing the writings of
Jonathan Swift. It would be Dilke's last such literary interest.
    In one of his more important articles on Swift, Dilke suggests
that the *Miscellaneous Works of Dr. William Wagstaffe* was the
work of Swift.[73] He demonstrates the lack of authority for assuming the work to be that of a real Dr. Wagstaff,[74] an obscure
physician whose scant records indicate little trace of literary tendency. After a search in the British Museum, Dilke declares that
the only publication by the real Dr. Wagstaff is *A Letter to Dr.
Friend Showing the Danger and Uncertainty of Inoculating for
the Smallpox.*[75] On the other hand, the *Miscellaneous Works* were
collected, so states the memoir to the book, by Dr. Wagstaff's
"friend." Thus, not only was the writer of the memoir unknown,
but also the collector was anonymous. Dilke found the distinguish-
ing characteristics of the Wagstaffe *Miscellaneous Works* to be
attacks on Steele. Furthermore, the publisher of the *Miscellaneous*

Works was Morphew, Swift's publisher, and not Butler, who published Wagstaff's *Letter on Smallpox*. Additional evidence of Swift's authorship is afforded in a letter from Pope, who refers to the pamphlet *Dr. Andrew Tripe*, generally ascribed to Swift, as one of Dr. Wagstaffe's. Finally Dilke calls attention to the similarity of the pseudonym "William Wagstaffe" and "Isaac Bickerstaff" and other "Staffs" Swift and Steele were known to affect. To ascertain that Wagstaffe was truly one of the family of "Staffs," Dilke points out that Swift published his own *Polite Conversations* under the name of "Simon Wagstaff."[76]

This completes the summary of Dilke's major contributions in his later years. As the reader compares Dilke's earlier articles with these latter ones, a curious question presents itself: Why does Dilke concentrate on critical issues in the former periods and on more or less biographical issues in the latter? How do the latter further the ideals of the Grand March of Intellect through not merely a humane-conscious but a humane-historically conscious society? I believe the answer is that Dilke felt that an interest in the man ultimately led to the interest in his works. He often says as much:

Facts in the life of a great man, especially of a great poet, are the life itself,—his mind, manners, morals grow out of them; and the great and the humble, the wise and the unwise, are all more subject to such external influences than the pride of man is willing to allow.[77]

Thus, to understand the works, we must first understand the man. But we can understand neither unless we also understand the "external influences." This statement echoes those of Darley in the affirmation of the necessary first steps in a culturally conscious society.

The British Museum Catalogue. The causes propounded in the *Athenaeum* did not wither and die with the termination of Dilke's editorship in 1846, nor did Dilke cease to advance his views whenever the opportunity presented itself in the *Daily News*.

But after 1849 Dilke's causes had less to do with politics and
the Grand March of Intellect than with *belles lettres* and with
topical issues. Several causes after 1849 deserve special mention,
for Dilke expended much energy and time on them. Still, the
improvement of society through knowledge is implicit in one of
his more avid causes of this period. In that it contained no moral
or physical reforms of direct benefit to the downtrodden, Dilke's
crusade for a "classed catalogue" (as he called it) to the British
Museum holdings was somewhat unusual. Even so, he argued, the
indirect benefits of such a catalogue "upon society in general" and
especially on the "march of intellect" were incalculable. The "totally
inadequate," "patched-up," "burdensome" listing of books and
manuscripts in use at the British Museum had been compiled near
the beginning of the century. From 1830 the *Athenaeum* had
hinted at the need for revision and reform of the uneven and
illogical practices of cataloging. Its criticisms were leveled at three
shortcomings: (1) there needed to be one general listing in
alphabetical order, perhaps by "department," or "title," though
these were secondary considerations of implementation best left
to the discretion of the management officers of the British Museum;
(2) the catalogue then should be brought up to date; (3) there
needed to be a system of uniform and essential information taken
from the title page of each book.

Before 1850 these specific criticisms were never identified or
brought together in one article as such. But the impetus needed to
make reform of the cataloguing a genuine cause was the publication in April 1850 of the *Report of the Commissioners Appointed
to Inquire into the Constitution and Government of the British
Museum, With the Minutes of Evidence*, which dealt with the
multiple aspects of running a National Library, among them being the then-debatable question of providing a single uniform
catalogue.

In a series of five articles largely written by Peter Cunningham
and Dilke,[78] the *Report of the Commissioners* was taken severely
to task; the first article registered disappointment generally with
the commission's findings. But the final four articles concentrated

on the commissioners' negative report concerning a "classed catalogue." Cunningham berates the commissioners' report: "By their
decision the national treasures accumulated and maintained at heavy
cost, have been to a great extent sealed up for our generation,
and perhaps the next,—and to some extent for all generations
that shall consent to live under the law of this Commission. Their
recommendation in the matter of the Catalogue is one of the
heaviest blows dealt against the progress of literature for many
years past."[79] The issue was complicated by the fact that the
Keeper of Printed Books, Mr. Panizzi, was in favor of a long-term,
cumbersome (according to Dilke, Cunningham, Carlyle, Collier,
and others) "manuscript" (i.e., handwritten) catalogue which had
the effect of depriving this and future generations, the benefit of a
workable catalogue at all.[80]

In the following week's issue Cunningham meets Panizzi head-on
and virtually accuses him not merely of subverting the will of the
people but of possible complicity with the commissioners themselves:

The real question at issue is, whether the public shall have the practical Catalogue of the national books which they have so long demanded, without which the books are to great extent withdrawn
from their use, and for which their own money has been voted,—or
whether Mr. Panizzi shall be allowed with the funds so assigned,
under the original pretence of executing the first design, to do another
work, which will, there can be no doubt, yield to himself a large
amount of personal fame? It is Mr. Panizzi against the great body of
the students of England. Now, in the midst of a certain apparent
candour at every examination, inferring readiness to listen to complaints of magnitude and meaning, and to objections however trivial
or absurd—it is impossible for the readers of these Minutes not to
feel that there is in all the leading questions a seeking to put Mr.
Panizzi in the best possible light,—and under-current of endeavour to
lead the evidence to a prejudiced conclusion on the part of the
Commissioners.[81]

Later Cunningham points out that the *Athenaeum* had no quarrel with the general administration of Mr. Panizzi: "—We have no ground of quarrel with Mr. Panizzi irrespective of the Catalogue. He has been a useful servant of the Museum; has added largely and importantly to the riches of the Library, and has increased certain facilities afforded to readers. He is wrong on one point— on which we have no doubt, nevertheless, that he may think himself right—and this is, the Catalogue."[82]

Peter Cunningham and Lankester[83] carried on in this vein, quoting authorities and claiming that a classed or "finding" catalogue belonged to the people of England and was thus not a decision to be made by three or four individuals who supported Mr. Panizzi. In the fifth and concluding notice Dilke joined in the battle. He reviewed the salient points of the four preceding *Athenaeum* notices, including the panegyric on Panizzi as an administrator as well as the customary column of disappointment in his views on a "Classed Catalogue":

We hope now to take a final leave of this Report; but cannot enter on the statement of our own views in reference to it without first acknowledging that we have risen from its perusal with the highest respect for the learned librarians of the Museum. In the words of the Commissioners—this inquiry has "impressed us" with "a high opinion of the zeal, the assiduity, and the intelligence" of the officers, and the assistants,—Mr. Panizzi, Mr. Jones and Mr. Watts seem to us of a race of bibliographical giants; and the first of these commanded our admiration by the manly spirit in which he faced all difficulties and grappled with all opponents. With this tribute to the man from whom we have had occasion to differ so much and so often,—we proceed to those considerations to which we have already expressed our desire to draw public attention.[84]

Dilke goes on to assert that by this time the issues are clarified; the rubbish has been swept away by fervent and serious discussions on both sides by men of good will, the side-issues, however temporarily annoying, have been recognized as such, and the mass of nebulous opinion has crystalized into a few hard facts. The principals were getting at last to the core of the problem, and all participants must acknowledge that the final difficulty with any classed catalogue was that the library is in a constant state of growth; Mr. Panizzi and his supporters were right, as far as they went: a printed catalogue was necessarily obsolete the moment it was printed, necessitating therefore a continuous and repetitive listing, each time covering the same ground. But so it was with progress itself, and thus we must not shirk from the challenge of the future simply because the future comes flush upon us too full and too overwhelmingly. Fortunately we need not; there is a way, Dilke announces, and one Mr. Cooley[85] has shown it to us. It is called "stereotyping." Mr. Cooley is represented as being asked by one of the commissioners: "You have alluded to ... stereotyping: will you have the goodness to explain what the process is ... ?"[86] to which Mr. Cooley gave answer to this effect: Books are to be uniformly listed according to author, title, subject, or however else the librarian wished to arrange them in alphabetical order, and the essential contents of the title pages noted: then they are to be separated individually "*by means of metallic partitions* ... Or even supposing them *to be cast in one plate and afterwards cut asunder*, I believe that they would not cost so much as the doubly-transcribed titles in the written Catalogue" [referring to the present system].[87] By such a means each plate (representing one book) would be permanent, set for all time, and when new books were added there would be no necessity for interleaving or reprinting the whole catalogue; the only cost for a yearly new catalogue would be the plates of new books and the paper; the setting and casting for all save the new books is already done, and hence the cost may be minimal. Though it was indeed in that day a novel idea, it was one which was tried and found eminently practical. Of course, after the lapse of a century, we can see that the process itself marked a transition stage. But its proponents, had they lived long enough to see its outcome, would have reasons to be proud. "Stereotyping" was the forerunner of the modern card catalogue, though "stereotyping," or something like it, by cards, is the usual method of obtaining a book at the British Museum even today. And though he did not originate the idea, I believe that "Dilke of the *Athenaeum*" was the first to champion it.

In the latter part of the article Dilke makes a startling recommendation that not even Mr. Cooley had suggested, perhaps not even conceived. Indeed, it is likely that only a "Godwin perfectability man"[88] with an art ethnos bias would ever think of it at all. Dilke envisioned the huge undertaking of "stereotyping" not only the holdings of the British Museum, but of all books printed in English as merely a first step in the triumphant spread of literature and art to all parts of the world. All England, America, and other English speaking countries should indeed do their part for books written in English. But as England was thought by the English to be a leader of nations, especially in forward-looking and progressive ideas, let her prove her leadership and influence by persuading other nations and tongues to do the same canvassing and cataloguing of their books in their own language. And what would be the result? A Universal Catalogue, of course, which would further immeasurably the ideal of the brotherhood of nations. Thus, Panizzi's scheme of a stopgap manuscript listing of Books is unworthy of English aims and ideals—"unworthy of an age and a people who, in the proposed Exhibition of 1851, have held out the hand of fellowship to the whole world and acknowledged the intellectual brotherhood of nations."[89] Dilke adverts again to the "temper of the times" that would produce a Great Exhibition: "Never was there a period when so beneficial a project could have been entered on with such probability of success. The large and liberal spirit in which, as we noticed last week, the Governments of the world have welcomed the proposal of Prince Albert for a great World Exhibition, is an earnest of success:—and we hope that those with whom this great World Catalogue might so honourably originate will not be deterred by the fears of the timid, the doubts of the ignorant (or worse, of the learned) and the indolence of the indifferent or interested."[90] After a few specific suggestions on how such a catalogue may be formulated and of how nations may exalt in their cooperation in this great venture,

Dilke takes note of the opposition that such a suggestion is bound to create:

Here we conclude. We do not profess to have improvised a great scheme to which objections may not be raised by the super-subtle and the over-refined; but simply to have indicated a course which, in our opinion, would do honour to the nation, and help the peaceful world in its onward progress,—one which may easily be elaborated and perfected if those in authority be pleased to countenance it. The learned librarians of the Museum may have a good-humoured laugh at it; but they should remember that if the world has its ignorances, learned bibliographers have their prejudices,—and that a laugh will not settle the question one way or the other. They cannot laugh louder than did certain other officials when Mr. Hill proposed to reduce all postage charges to one uniform rate, and that rate one penny; yet that idea spread and strengthened, and has become "a great fact."[91]

Dilke did not conclude. He was back some weeks later writing in response to criticism of certain portions of his plan. One such criticism by a writer in *Gentleman's Magazine* had to do with the cost of the "stereotyped" plates. Dilke's reply shows that in the intervening weeks he had done some research on the project:

The cost of mounting the stereotype plates—which we assumed might be two or three times the cost of the plates themselves—would, it turns out, be nothing at all, or so little as not to be worth including in a rough estimate.... years since we printed in the *Athenaeum* a page of advertisements (see No. 753, p. 303) from a stereotype plate mounted on a block so arranged and prepared that any other stereotype plate might be mounted thereon;—and we have ordered the specimen to be removed to our Office in Wellington Street North, that all who are interested may satisfy themselves that the project is perfectly practicable and easy.[92]

He then turns to his second "impractical" suggestion (which, in fact, it was, notwithstanding the merits of the first one), the matter of the Universal Catalogue:

Suppose that only one nation should join us in the great project,—then only to that extent have we approached the universal Catalogue;—but allow us to add, that a Catalogue of all works published in the French and English languages and in the territories under the English and French Governments would be the noblest monument of the civilization of the age, and the noblest present which these great nations could offer to the world.[93]

It is clear that, aside from the practical advantages derived from such a catalogue, Dilke's dream was more in accord with his ethno-cultural and Godwinian biases: "the noblest monument of the civilization of the age."

Nor was this the last of Dilke's recommendations relative to the British Museum.[94] But of significance is the fact that he believed that the concept of a Universal Catalogue was an idea whose time, like that of the Great Exhibition,[95] had come.

Miscellaneous Writings. Scores of miscellaneous but significant Dilke articles on a broad range of topics found their way into the *Athenaeum.* In April 1850 he wrote on the history of the "Fourth Estate";[96] a year later he wrote a series of notices dealing with the "history and character"—in a word, an ethnological study—of the Parish of Hampshire, where he was born and to which he loved to return.[97] In February 1852 he wrote with approval on the proposed expansion of graduate representation on the Senate of the University of London, which he supported liberally in his late years.[98] Later on in the year he defended Peter Pindar from attacks by his old antagonist Jerdan.[99] Three extremely important articles, which in Dilke's ethnos-oriented mindset were related, appeared in May and November and December 1852. "Original papers," the first was titled "The Book Trades" and the second and third "Practical Art."[100] They had to do with the high cost of publishing and hence the dissemination of art and knowledge. Here his message was as ever: do not attempt to train artists to cater to an ignorant public; if the public be uneducated and nonresponsive, then face the fact that the *time* of the art is not come! First, educate the public by finding ways to let the public educate itself; it will then support, even demand the art (whatever it was) just as the Elizabethan public supported and demanded Elizabethan plays. Why? because their time had come and were, as he had argued nearly forty years earlier, attuned to their age.[101]

An extremely revealing notice as regards Dilke's views of art appeared in December 1855.[102] Here he protested against the Practices and Constitution of the Royal Academy of Art, though he was careful to avoid saying anything "against the personal honor or character of the Members of the Academy."[103] In the course of his discussion of the academy's "close borough system" (as in the case of its treatment of his friend Haydon), Dilke charged that the academy had done nothing since its inception to further the course of art; the reason was manifest: the academy was run by patrons whom the artists must please, and therefore to that extent they prostitute their art:

> In every act of its formal existence, it is influenced by any and every consideration, except honour for love of Art. Its President is avowedly chosen not because he is the great artist whom artists love to honour— would teach the public to honour,—but because he can make a speech or make a bow, and therefore welcome, after the established drawing room model, the patrons who condescend on occasions to visit the Academy or eat the Academy dinner. After this fashion it would be better represented by a gentleman-usher or a master of the ceremonies.[104]

As for the dinners themselves, one need only read the names of the guests to assure himself that the whole elaborate fete is but "a mere trading speculation," and a compliment to full purses. And while this may be good, in the short run, for artists, it is assuredly bad for art: "Such patrons and such patronage have the same influence as Art-Union patrons and patronage,—and what that is was shown years since in the *Athenaeum.* They tend inevitably to lower the aim, end, and character of Art. Every man who lives by Art must paint up or down to the taste of its patrons,—"[105] Do the artists want a patron? They may have one, and this one will be good for art and perhaps even for talented artists. It is the same patron which the *Athenaeum* has touted for these many years: it is an educated public! He closes with this charge to the spiritually defunct academy:

Let the Academy teach the *public*,—artists would have the benefit as well as others. Let their Professors give lectures to the *public*,— show to the *public* what there is in Art which tends to elevate and ennoble,—lecture to the *public* on the great works in our National and other Galleries, and show why they are admired, and are deserving of all admiration. In this way the public would learn to appreciate Art and the artist,—such, at least, as remained—would be forced to work *up* to his public, and we need not fear to come disgraced, as we have done, out of a European competition.[106]

His general criticism was that in the ongoing world of progress and change such "closed" societies tended rather to retard than stimulate progress in the arts.

Also in three notices in 1855 Dilke demonstrated his detailed knowledge of characters and politics during the early years of George III's reign.[107] In the following year he wrote on the *Emendations of Shakespeare* by Collier, whom the *Athenaeum* consistently supported.[108] Other sixteenth-, seventeenth-, and eighteenth-century studies of a "miscellaneous" nature appeared from this time to the 1860s, though nearly all have some tangential relevance to one or more of the "major" studies.[109]

   The Literary Fund.   Dilke's final "cause" was in some ways his most disappointing. He must have set great store in its importance or he would have abandoned it after a few years. As it was, he resolved to continue on despite disappointment and eroding support year after year, until at least 1862, when failing health and old age forced him to withdraw from the battle. It was the cause of Reform in the Literary Fund.

   In retrospect, the cause was surely not worth the time and effort expended on it. Dilke had long been a friend and member of the Literary Society, though his complaints against both the expenses and the management began as early as 1836, in which year he was elected a member of the General Committee and to which office he was reelected the following year,[110] and which post he held continuously until the late 1840s. In 1841 he certified to the distress of Thomas Hood, who must have embarrassed Dilke by first refusing then requesting the gift of £50 which the society conferred on him. But in the later 1840s his criticisms of the General Committee increased in scope, vigor, and frequency. In so criticising, he carried on his side of the small war singlehandedly, for it was not until nearly the middle of the following decade that others joined the battle. His complaints were voiced in the annual meetings and then were duly reported in the *Athenaeum*, so that by 1855 he had succeeded, according to K. J. Fielding,[111] in making himself "generally disliked." Such complaints, first and always, fell under two major headings: (1) the "General Committee" spent far too much money on its own "expenses" in proportion to the amount it donated to worthy but destitute and deserving individuals or their survivors, and (2) the committee itself was not merely illegal but had usurped the power reposed formerly and rightfully in its "parent" body, the "Council." Other minor complaints against the present policies and policymakers were voiced from time to time in the *Athenaeum* and in the meetings themselves.[112] Apparently Dilke's first truly serious blast at the Literary Fund was in 1850, though the *Athenaeum* barbs had gradually become more and more pointed from about 1846. In September 1849, for example, the *Athenaeum* featured a point-by-point comparison of the extravagant costs in administering the Literary Fund with the "thrifty and sensible" practices of a sister organization having the same objectives, the Artist's Benevolent Society. Printing, stationery, postage, salary, and meeting rooms for the former were about £500 per year, while the latter managed just as well on £93. The latter parceled out the week-to-week correspondence among its willing members, while the former hired a full-time secretary, who, for £200, as far as the *Athenaeum* could ascertain, did "virtually nothing."

Throughout the following year Dilke charged primarily through the "Weekly Gossip" column that the Literary Fund was governed by a clique, which was called the General Committee (and of which he, himself was a member), and that the general member-

ship were intentionally kept in the dark as to the proceedings of
the annual business meeting; that the General Committee was
largely composed of persons of rank and patronage, whereas it
ought to be of literary men "working in the interests of other
literary men"; and finally that the clique (i.e., the General Committee) had, against the express intent of the charter, usurped the
place of the other governing body, the Council, and had rendered
it useless. Commenting then on the illegality of the General Committee's election of officers, Dilke wrote: "The election of a President, Vice-Presidents, and a Council is under these circumstances a
mere mockery and delusion. The Council, for any practical or useful purpose, has no more existence after than before the election. It
never assembles,—has never met,—and great doubts are entertained
whether it is possible legally to summon a meeting: certain it is,
we believe, that it has no power to meet."[113]

   In 1855 Dilke's cause received some badly needed support from
the former rival editor of the *New Monthly*, Bulwer-Lytton, and
especially from his former colleagues on the *Daily News*, Dickens
and Forster. The preparations for the annual meeting on March
14, 1855, boded well for the "Reformers" (as they now called
themselves), who circulated a notice to those from whom they
expected support.[114] Wishing to take the opposition by surprise,
Dickens waited until the last minute before notifying Mr. Blewitt,
the secretary, of the reformers' intentions. The meeting opened
and the "ordinary business . . . [was] disposed of" when Dilke presented his motion:

That whereas during the ten years from 1844 to 1854 both inclusive
the cost of assisting 429 applicants to the Literary Fund amounted
to 5,094 £ . 10s. 1d. (exclusive of the lector's poundage, advertisements, and expenses attending the anniversary dinners), and whereas
the cost of assisting 559 applicants to the Artists' General Fund
within the same 10 years amounted to 904 £ . 17s. 1d. (and exclusive
of collector's poundage, advertisements, and expenses attending the
anniversary dinner): the meeting is of opinion that the expenses of
the managing the Literary Fund are unreasonable and enormous, and
that a great change must be made in the administration of its affairs.[115]

But the effort in 1855 barely failed of convincing the majority. In succeeding years the "reformers" fared progressively worse.

In 1858 they decided to hazard all: since early May 1857 they had been preparing for the onslaught, as shown by Dickens's letter to Forster:

I have gone over Dilke's memoranda and I think it quite right and necessary that these points should be stated. Nor do I see the least difficulty in the way of their introduction into the pamphlet.[116]

The pamphlet of which Dickens spoke is one which was published by the three principal Reformers and which bears their name. Published by Bradbury and Evans, its sixteen pages dealt primarily with the history of the Reformers' efforts over the past three years. It therefore represents in part an appeal for support or at least understanding. But a second purpose is evident: the perennial call to action:

—That the Literary Fund Society is a Society of abuse, because it is governed, in direct opposition to the evident and expressed intention of its Charter, by an irresponsible Committee; because it limits its proceedings, in direct opposition to the evident and expressed intentions of its Founder, to dealing with the followers of Literature as beggars only; and because its enormous annual expenditure will not bear comparison with the expenditure of any other similar institution on the face of the earth.[117]

In spite of a humorous speech by Dickens promising not merely brevity on his own part, but absolute silence from Mr. Dilke and Mr. Forster—until next year—the motion lost by an embarrassing 70 to 14 vote.

There would be no such vote next year. What the Reformers failed to accomplish by persuasion they attempted next year to effect by something akin to bribery. Dickens let it be known that "an anonymous benefactor was prepared to bequeath his valuable library and collection of manuscripts to the society, with an endowment of £10,000 to maintain them," if they would agree to certain changes in the constitution,[118] doubtless the heads of the 1855 Special Report. The negotiations between Dickens, Whitwell Elwin, and Dr. William Smith[119] on one side and the committee on the other were ultimately unavailing, though the ploy made the committee look bad in the public eye.[120]

The issue did not die immediately, though it may as well have. By 1860 Dilke had grown too old to carry on an active battle, and without his active support Dickens and Forster could only stand off afar and yell insults.[121] Even so, as the 1857 *Athenaeum* report of the general meeting and the 1858 pamphlet both attested, the committee was slowly but surely adopting some of the 1855 special recommendations: a literary man need not necessarily have written a book; the number of literary men on the committee had sharply increased; annual testimonials and investigations of the needy had given way to revokable annuities, as per the 1855 Special Committee Report. These reforms, the pamphlet pointed out, were never admitted by the committee until urged upon them by the pressure of the Reformers. But no matter; other reforms would surely come in the wake of further disclosure of abuses: "I enclose a copy of Dickens' speech at the Oct. Genl Ben^t Fund—It is excellent and will bode in favor of our twenty years old arguments and contrasts. Is it possible that the Lit^{ry} Fund can brazen on in defiance of such exposure?"[122]

Little is heard from any of the Reformers on this "abuse" after 1862. But in a small way, they had affected to a degree the course of literary men, and therefore of literature. They might have had a more profound impact had their campaign been more successful. As it was, they reaped perhaps as much as does any crusader for any cause, regardless of his success in it: they believed sincerely in the ultimate good of what they were doing.

Retirement: Numero 3.   Beyond 1860 Dilke's contributions to Literature were almost exclusively to his "useful little journal" which he had helped to found and to which he had contributed a sizeable number of notes.[123] After 1862, these became less and less frequent, especially after he removed himself from his son's home at 76 Sloan Street and went to a retreat southwest of London near

Farnam, Alice Holt. There, with encroaching blindness and damnable attacks of the "shakes," his literary interests necessarily gave way to others less taxing. There was first of all, gardening, which had been more than a passing interest since with Wentworth, Professor Lindley, and Joseph Paxton, he had established the *Agricultural Gazette* and the *Gardeners' Chronicle*; but mainly he was concerned to continue what he termed the furtherance of the great personal goal of his later years. This was the education of his grandson, which he relinquished in 1862 to the masters at Trinity Hall, Cambridge.[124] The education of his grandson had been one of Dilke's chief duties and pleasures. It had begun about 1851 after Maria's death and had continued on through that decade and into the next. Together they took trips through Ireland and Scotland and on the continent, they indulged in such historical sport as retracing the flight of Charles II, they visited cathedrals all over England to study primarily Norman architecture, and they rested from their travels in Dilke's beloved retreat at Bedhampton; and though he may be a trifle immodest, Sir Charles is not much exaggerating when he writes that because of the nearly constant procession of famous literary, artistic, and scientific personages to 76 Sloane Street, he had met and known "everyone worth knowing from 1850 to my death."[125] Numero Three's education—"and there has not often been such an education"—was enhanced by his grandfather's sense of close family bonds and his resolution—rightly or wrongly, wisely or not—to make Charlie into the mold that Wentworth apparently could never quite fit: the mold which the "Grand" conceived as the complete man—the image, probably of Dilke himself.[126] In large measure he was successful. How could he be otherwise, "devoted . . ." as he was "to the education of his grandson" and ". . . full of leisure, full of charm, full of experience, full of knowledge."[127] Again and again, Sir Charles remarks on Dilke's successful effort to imbue him with republican ideals. "And my grandfather's thoughts were my thoughts," he repeatedly affirms.[128] But such an education was incomplete with mere knowledge. True, "I must get knowledge . . . ," Keats cries out in his frustrated and stymied efforts to depict the Poet's office on how best to advance the march of intellect. "I must get . . . more knowl-edge,"[129] and undoubtedly Dilke was among the first to recommend the remedy. But even more important than knowledge was "moral" growth: what Dilke repeatedly asserted from 1815 on as a bounti-ful capacity for feeling, including the ability to respond to "beautiful thoughts and graceful images." Thus Dilke must shape character, must see that Charlie was a *good* boy, must instill in him especially a high sense of duty. His influence has been char-acterized as "ethical . . . rather than religious," and Sir Charles him-self later affirmed, "So far indeed as character can be molded in childhood, mine was fashioned by my grandfather."[130] After 1862, when Charles matriculated at Cambridge, the Grand demanded the right, in spite of failing sight, "of reading everything that relates to you and your concerns." Sir Charles did not disappoint him and seemed to atone for his father's less than distinguished record at the same college some thirty years earlier.[131] And though the Grand was not entirely pleased with the grandson's apparently overwhelming interest in sports, he came to accept even that as part of the discipline and deep-rooted tradition of Trinity Hall. But he was obviously more elated about competition of a more scholarly nature, which was becoming more and more frequent.

"Hurrah! hurrah! my dear grandson. Ninety-seven out of a hun-dred—eleven above the second 'man'—is a position that would satisfy a whole family of loving friends, even if they were all grandfathers."[132]

By 1864 Charles had advanced to the head of his class: typical is the Grand's jubilant report to Wentworth of the May College Law Examinations:

"June 3rd, 1864
"If you carried out your intention of going to and returning from Cambridge this day, you know, and all in Sloane Street know, that our noble fellow has again won the prize. But the weather may have deterred you, and on the possible chance I copy the results:
"1. Chas. Dilke, 570 marks. Prize
Shee,   440

What a blessing that boy has been to my old age! May God reward him! I feel for Shee! for he has laboured long and zealously. I wish there had been two prizes.

"Your affectionate father,
"C.W.D."[133]

In effect the intellectual, cultural, and spiritual guidance, the experience, the successes, and the mellowing of a Godwin-Methodist turned cultural optimist—all these values and ideals Dilke had poured into the "wide hollows" of his grandson's brain; he believed he had seen them take root. In that belief he had hopes of his greatest single victory. For unlike Keats's Moneta or Shelley's Demogorgon, or Yeats's slouching Beast or even his own earlier "great whale," Dilke's symbol for the marching mind, the thrust and development of civilization now became more than symbol; it became real. It must stand or fall on what kind of man Numero Three would be, and he believed that he had reason to hope for the best:

"Alice Holt,
"By Farnham, Surrey,
"*July 28th*, 1864.

"MY VERY DEAR GRANDSON,
"Your letters give me very great pleasure, not because they are kind and considerate, of which I had evidence enough long since, not because they flatter the vanity of the old man by asking his opinion, which few now regard, but because I see in them a gradual development of your own mind."[134]

Shortly, very shortly after that Numero Three received the most melancholy intelligence. The Grand was dying. Fearful of being too late he rushed to Alice Holt. He records in his diary:

My Father met me on the lawn: he was crying bitterly, and said— "He lives only to see you." I went upstairs and sat down by the sofa, on which lay the Grand., looking haggard, but still a noble wreck. I took his hand, and he began to talk of very trivial matters— of Cambridge everyday life—his favourite theme of old. He seemed to be testing his strength, for at last he said: "I shall be able to talk to-morrow; I may last some weeks; but were it not for the pang that all of you would feel, I should prefer that it should end at once. I have had a good time of it."

'He had been saying all that morning: "Is that a carriage I hear?" or "I shall live to see him."

'*Tuesday*.—When I went in to him, he sent away the others, and told me to look for an envelope and a key. I failed to find it, and fetched Morris, who after a careful search found the key, but no envelope. We had both passed over my last letter (August 6th), which lay on the table. He made us both leave the room, but recalled me directly, and when I entered had banknotes in his hand, which he must have taken from the envelope of my letter. (This involved rising.) He said: "I cannot live, I fear, to your birthday—I want to make you a present—I think I have heard you say that you should like a stop-watch—I have made careful inquiries as to the price—and have saved—as I believe—sufficient." He then gave me notes, and the key of a desk in London, in the secret drawer of which I should find the remaining money. He then gave me the disposition of his papers and manuscripts, directing that what I did not want should go to the British Museum. He then said: "I have nothing more to say but that you have fulfilled—my every hope—beyond all measure—and—I am deeply—grateful."

He died in my presence on Wednesday, 10th, at half-past one, in perfect peace.[135]

Dilke's hopes in Numero Three were at least partially realized; his rise to prominence in government was meteoric, and some biographers see the promise of his eventual entry into the very highest levels, perhaps even as a successor to Gladstone. But regretfully, his forced retirement from public life shattered the dream. He was at the center of a scandal when in 1885 he was cited as correspondent in a divorce case. Though he consistently and staunchly maintained it, he could never convince the public of his innocence. In quite another context, at least, one of Sir Charles's ideas was most assuredly not one of his grandfather's ideas. As an influential member of Parliament, he consistently championed many of Dilke's republican ideas; what was even more important to Romantic Dilke as a herald "in the forefront of the approaching age": and as a learned man imbued with the sense of cultural continuity, Sir Charles would write the promise of the Anglo Saxon race in *Greater Briton*. So far, well. But Dilke had feared Sir Charles's love for soldiering, and "he became troubled by his grandson's keen and excited following of all the reports from the Crimea. He had a terror of the boy's becoming a soldier, and 'used to do his best to point out the foolish side of war.' But this, as the passage already quoted shows, did not deter his pupil from beginning, while still a growing youth, detailed study of military matters."[136] Dilke's apprehension was well founded. Where Dilke had hoped to spread culture through the gentle but pervasive means of literature and art, the grandson in *Imperial Defence* (1898) elected to spread higher culture—specifically Anglo-Saxon culture and ideas—through the firmer, more persuasive means of military might.

What Dilke would have been proud to own as his greatest contribution to the world was stifled on the one hand by the ironic circumstance of scandal and on the other by a total misreading or misunderstanding or rejecting of the Grand's conception of the march of intellect and of his high priorities given to literature and art. This too is ironic in that while Dilke's contemporaries seemed, in theory, to side with him, history shows that governmental mindsets of a later age sided with the grandson: surely a regression in the march of intellect. It was a tragic regression from which we may only now, a tragic century later, be regaining some lost ground.

Conclusion

What, then, was Dilke's contribution? What of the *ethnos*, the ideal of progress by a people nurtured by the gentler graces of good literature and art? What of the ideal of discovering the genius of each age, and of focusing an entire national consciousness on the effort to produce the best which that genius had to offer? Of what Matthew Arnold years later would call the study of perfection?[137] What of the germination of ideas and of consensus or dissonance of sentiment as he chatted with his friend who copied out *Endymion*? Had these nightly chats and daily discussions of negative capability and the primacy of feeling in literature, of Hazlitt's *Gusto*, the future of America, and of the march of intellect anything to do with the conception of Moneta and Apollo, the central figures in the *Hyperion* poems? Most assuredly they did. And what of his later contributions, among which may be cited his political articles in the *London* and *Westminster*, but more particularly, his close scrutiny of nearly every opinion that went into his journal over a period of nearly thirty years?

If in some ways Dilke anticipated Matthew Arnold, in still other ways he echoed Keats. Aside from their common views regarding the implications in the face of Moneta, and on how best to "cure" its sickness, Dilke, Arnold, and Keats shared similar views on the nature and significance of beauty in art. Strangely enough, in an age of established Romantic sensibility, it was a nascent platonism[138] that helped to form an intellectual affinity among such diverse minds as those of Arnold, Dilke, Keats, Shelley, and of course Darley and Lady Morgan, all of whom and not just the latter, "raised systems";[139] and, most important, an affinity in that all affirmed that an admittedly amorphous, undefined but nonetheless existent reality informed great art and linked it to the people of the age for which it was produced.

We have noted that Dilke's *ethnos* stance, apparently independently arrived at, manifested itself early in his publishing career, even in his *Old English Plays*. From the first he felt more acutely and maintained more doggedly than did his contemporaries that the Elizabethan Drama and the Elizabethan Age were necessary to each other, reciprocal to each other, and in the unfolding continuity of some undefined *Zietgeist* possible only to each other. This conviction gains in clarity in his developing years, so that by 1829 he had so codified his views to incorporate them in a rather didactic message about the nature of art: Venice—and all it stands for, its art, its history, its past—will persevere in spite of its own corruption, in spite of Napoleon, or in spite of anything else; for its past, its history and its art *is* Venice.

Even here he was edging close to his mature and final position espousing an *ethnos* of literature. That position yet required one ingredient to make it viable. That ingredient was a system, a means to order the parts into a coherent whole. On the "raising" of such a system, Dilke's mature *ethnos* of art and literature came of age; it amounts to this: the greatness of an art form of any age is due not to one or two great artists, or to beneficient and happy circumstances, nor even to such a palpably fortunate thing as widespread interest in and support for art. No one thing nor, in fact, not even a catalog of things could be thus singled out as responsible for the finest productions of an age. Instead, all things work to modify or otherwise affect a deeper current, a developing *ethnos*, or set of principles, a kind of *Zeitgeist* which Dilke referred to as the "genius of the age"; so that his fully matured theory would allow Dilke to proclaim that "the drama is by me considered the natural form through which the genius of the [Elizabethan] age made itself manifest. The genius of a succeeding age can no more surround itself by the circumstances of the age of Elizabeth than a river can flow upwards to the spring-head...."[140] This genius was the archetype on a grand scale that Keats, Shelley, Darley, and Lady Morgan so reveled in, and included all these things, though they were ancillary to its developing thrust. They may color and roughly shape it, and be clarified by it, but they did not inform it, could never substantially alter it, nor change its inherent direction or course; for though impalpable and shifting, incapable of being physically touched or seen, its reality was manifest in every genius and in every work of genius of its age. It was a *noumenon*, an entity, a thing separate in itself which informed its age and was in turn defined by its age. In greater or less degree each age had its own special genius, and it was the function of the art and artists of each age to find and exploit that age's genius. Only then could that other great amorphous, shadowy entity, the March of Intellect, which Keats called the face of Moneta, and Shelley called Demogorgon and Yeats called a slouching Beast, and Hobbes and Darley and Dilke called Leviathan[141]—only then could that spirit march through one age to a better one. It was as close to a religion—indeed, it may even be called such—as Dilke ever came. But it is best described as an *ethnos* of art. It is indeed in many points anticipatory of Matthew Arnold's later and more renowned system of the same type. Both took the "study of perfection" as their medium and the creation of a better age as their end. Arnold had the power of his great name and fame, but Dilke had the *Athenaeum*. Marchand suggests that Dilke's efforts may have been more effective.[142]

If Roger Wallins's argument that the literary periodicals of that day were so far effective that not even the like of Dickens and other social problem novelists could equal their influence,[143] then Dilke's array of causes boldly and consistently espoused for a quarter-century in England's largest weekly literary periodical had to have a most telling effect. That influence alone, I believe, in spite of his insistence on anonymity, makes Dilke among the dozen or so most influential literary personages of his era.

Notes and References

Chapter One

1. Letter, C. W. Dilke, Sr., to Maria Dilke, July 4, 1813. In 1974 Capt. Stephen W. Roskill, CBE, a descendant of the Dilkes, made available to Churchill College, Cambridge, a considerable collection of papers relating to the Dilke, Enthoven, and Roskill families. Nearly all this correspondence and other data, portions of which I have drawn upon heavily, remain unpublished and is here quoted throughout by his permission, by that of Sir John Dilke, Bart., owner of copyright to Roskill-Dilke Collection, and by that of Miss Marion Stewart, Archivist at Churchill College. Letters and other memorabilia from this collection shall hereinafter be referred to as the Roskill-Dilke Papers.

2. Letters, C. W. Dilke, Sr., to Maria and Charles Dilke, May 18, 1817, and June 24, 1824 (Roskill-Dilke Papers); see also Joanna Richardson, "Some Dilke Papers," *TLS* (August 29, 1952); *DNB* states that Henry Flitcroft (1697–1769) rose from humble beginnings to become famous as an architect. He probably knew Wentworth Dilke Wentworth, Old Mr. Dilke's father, when both were employed at Kew Palace.

3. As distinct from the older family of Dilkes of Maxstoke Castle, of whom Sir Charles Dilke tartly comments: "They were Royalists and are Tories" (Roskill-Dilke Papers); correspondence between the two branches, though infrequent and formal, was always friendly.

4. Winifred Street Wentworth's burial is recorded in the Parish of St. George in Hanover Square on March 23, 1762; Sir Charles Dilke MP (1843–1911) wrote a memoir and published some writings of his grandfather Charles W. Dilke, the subject of this study, titled *Papers of a Critic* (see note 21), wherein he states that she was born in 1721; but a note from Dilke in Roskill-Dilke Papers indicates that according to her burial record, she was forty-five years old at her death in 1762; this would place her date of birth circa 1717. It must here be acknowledged that Sir Charles (1843–1911) was not always

the most careful scholar with respect to such details as dates, places, titles of works, etc., but though inclined to certain prejudices (such as his unfair bias against Fanny Brawne), he is generally trustworthy with respect to facts and opinions on a larger scale.

5. Admiralty Records, Vol. 7/813, in the Public Records Office, Chancery Lane, London (I am indebted to Mr. V. Reilly of the Naval Historical Library and to Mr. Edward E. [Bill] De Young for most of the information concerning the Dilkes' connection with the Navy Pay Office). Since Mr. Dilke's parents then lived in London (see note 4), I am inclined to think it likely that he was first employed there; later his widowed father accompanied him to (or joined him in) Bedhampton, where he was buried in 1781. The first mention of Mr. Dilke's connections with the Admiralty is in Vol. 7/813, when he became employed on March 26, 1761.

6. Ibid., Vol. 7/814; according to *DNB*, Edward Clark (1730–1796) was prebendary of Chichester from 1771 and author of ecclesiastical and military books.

7. To distinguish among these Dilkes, Charles Wentworth the first (1742–1826) is herein referred to as "Old Mr. Dilke" or "Mr. Dilke, Sr."; the second, the subject of this book (1789–1864), is referred to as "Dilke" and later "The Grand"; the third (1810–1869) is referred to as "Wentworth" or "Charlie"; the fourth (1843–1910) is referred to as "Sir Charles" or "Numero Three." The fifth does not appear in this study.

8. Joanna Richardson, *The Everlasting Spell* (London, 1963), p. 18.

9. The Salary and Pension Books in the Public Records Office show C. W. Dilke, Sr., as a clerk in Portsmouth Dockyards at a salary of £230 per annum. On May 21, 1800, however, he secured in London a position as "1st Clerk to superintend the making up of accounts at £495 per annum" (letter from V. Reilly, Head of Naval Historical Library, and Vol. 7/817, Public Records Office, Chancery Lane). Old Mr. Dilke continued in this position until he retired after 50 years service on April 16, 1811 and went to live in Chichester in 1814. Among the Roskill-Dilke Papers is a section containing in minute detail Old Mr. Dilke's yearly expenses, apparently down to the last shilling. These begin with the year 1801 (paralleling his move to London from Portsmouth) and end with the year 1814 (with that from 1807 missing), when he moved to

Chichester. These lists are hereinafter referred to as the Expenditure Lists; in addition, a far less detailed account of Old Mr. Dilke's yearly income from the years 1787–1799 is included among the Roskill-Dilke Papers, where it appears that his annual salary as Chief Clerk (circa £230) constituted slightly more than a third of his total income.

10. More likely, the Dilke and Brown families had long been friends.

11. Charles Brown, *Walter Hazlebourn* (unpublished), p. 15; permission to quote granted by F. O. Cole, Curator, Keats House, Hampstead.

12. Ibid.; this private tutoring in London was apparently expensive. Old Mr. Dilke's carefully detailed accounts of every expenditure from the years 1801–1814 inclusive (excepting 1807) show surprisingly high figures averaging about £45 a year for the education of his three children. This suggests that he may likewise have been paying for Brown's, a supposition supported by the fact that on Letitia's marriage in 1804, the education expenditures seem not to have been affected, and, in fact, jump to a peak of £57+ in 1805, the last year of Dilke's schooling. With Dilke in the Admiralty in 1806, however, the education expenditure in that and in succeeding years levels off to approximately £35–40 for William's schooling until his induction into the navy in late 1811.

13. Dilke joined the office as "extra clerk," at a salary of £75–5 per annum, on the same day that Charles Dickens's father, John Dickens (Micawber), was employed. By 1808 Dilke served as "Clerk V in the Navy Pay Office at £144–15–5d per annum" (Letter from V. Reilly). On April 5, 1815 he was promoted to fourth clerk at £200 p.a. (Vol. 7/819); on April 7, 1829, promoted to 2nd clerk, £93+ per qtr. (7/821).

14. In *Walter Hazlebourn* Brown gives seven pages to a description of a Dilke temper tantrum, which, Brown says, must be given detailed treatment for its illumination on Dilke's behavior in later life (pp. 36–42).

15. Ibid., p. 42. This fact of Brown's "history" is suspect: according to a letter to Jane Hood in 1838, Maria, born in 1790, and her younger brother John were apparently brought up by a guardian named Spenser. She could hardly have been a "milliner" at age fifteen. Brown's account of Dilke's marriage becomes even more

doubtful by the presence of an intriguing and mysterious entry in Old Mr. Dilke's List of Expenditures for 1806: "To prevent publishing of Bands [Bans]: £1–18–6." Finally Brown either was, or was about to be, in St. Petersburg at this time (see Richardson, *Everlasting Spell*, p. 19).

16. Old Mr. Dilke's List of Expenditures (Roskill-Dilke Papers); perhaps as a wedding gift, the young Dilkes were apparently treated to a house for which Old Mr. Dilke paid nearly a hundred pounds for repair in 1806. But by 1808 Dilke and Maria had moved to another house, for which from the years 1808–1811 Old Mr. Dilke paid the rent, averaging about £50 per annum (List of Expenditures, Roskill-Dilke Papers).

17. See Richardson, *Everlasting Spell*, pp. 18–19.

18. *Walter Hazlebourn*, p. 35. Brown was then writing a play (later acted in the Royal Theatre in Drury Lane) called *Narensky, or the Road to Yaroslaf*, for which he would receive £300 and a lifetime ticket of admission.

19. See Preface; see also Leslie A. Marchand, *The Athenaeum: A Mirror of Victorian Culture* (Durham, N. C., 1941), p. 51ff.

20. C. W. Dilke, ed., *Old English Plays, Being a Selection from the Early Dramatic Writers*, 6 vols. (London, 1814–1815); see p. 53ff. I have seen another title prefacing this work, printed by Whittingham and Rowland for John Martin, the publisher, and also bearing the date 1814–1815: *Continuation of Dodsley's Old English Plays*. Perhaps the second title is a reissue of the first with a different title page but otherwise using the same plates.

21. Sir Charles Dilke, ed., *Papers of a Critic* (London, 1875), 1:72.

22. Letter from William Dilke to Sir Charles Dilke, 1878 (Roskill-Dilke Papers).

23. See *Papers*, 1:1; see also Letter from Mr. Dilke to Maria, July 12, 1815 (Roskill-Dilke Papers). Other than in periodic announcements of the series in the "New Books" section, I cannot find that Gifford so encouraged Dilke anywhere in the *Quarterly*.

24. H. E. Rollins, ed., *The Keats Circle* (Cambridge, Mass., 1965), 2:177; hereinafter referred to as *KC*. The Dilke and Reynolds families maintained close professional and personal ties until the early 1840s and after.

25. Charles Brown, *Memoir of Keats*, quoted in *KC*, 2:57.

26. Dilke states that contrary to the impression left by Brown's

Memoir, Keats and Brown did not become "friendly and familiar" until "long after they had met and met often"; but they were *"drawn together* by force of circumstances and position" only because the Keats brothers were habitually "with me [Dilke] three times a week, often three times a day" (*KC*, 2:104ff.).

27. M. B. Forman, ed., *Letters of John Keats* (London, New York, Toronto, 1952), p. 42; hereinafter referred to as *Letters*.

28. Ibid., p. 75.

29. Ibid., p. 88.

30. Ibid., p. 87. In his previous letter to his brothers (January 5, 1818), Keats had said "Dilke is going to take the Champion— he has sent his farce to Covent Garden"; Keats had earlier taken over the *Champion* theatricals from Reynolds, who was at Exeter, and had apparently contributed only two notices, both appearing in the January 4 issue. Dilke probably wrote the drama criticism for the weeks from January 11–February 22 inclusive (see Chapter 2). I have been unable to find any trace of his farce.

31. *Papers*, 1:5.

32. Ibid.

33. *Letters*, pp. 213–15. In this letter to Dilke at Bedhampton, Keats asked "How goes it with Brown?" who may have been plying his familiar trade of unpaid head nurse; however, he may also have been visiting Old Mr. Dilke, then living in his own "mansion" in Chichester, about seven miles from Bedhampton.

34. Ibid.

35. Ibid., p. 230.

36. In Dilke's annotated copy of Richard M. Milnes's *Life, Letters and Literary Remains of John Keats* (1848), quoted in *Letters*, 216n; the last word in the citation should read "Scotland."

37. Till his death in New Zealand in 1842 Brown remained convinced that the heartless authors of these reviews were at least partly responsible for the "disease...on his mind" that eventually killed Keats; see discussion in this chapter.

38. *Letters*, p. 237.

39. *Letters*, p. 259. Following Lowell, most critics think Fanny and Keats became secretly engaged a week earlier, on Christmas Day.

40. *Papers*, 1:8.

41. The matter in italics is Keats's.

42. *Letters*, pp. 278-80.

43. Ibid., p. 295.

44. Ibid., p. 300.

45. Roskill-Dilke Papers; permission to quote granted by Marion Stewart, Archivist, Churchill College, Cambridge. The "dear Boys" were the Snook children, Henry and John, who were attending Mr. Lord's Academy in Tooting, Surrey; "Lord Sands" and the "Marquis of Carrots" visited Brown's home in Hampstead for at least a week (April 16) during which time they annoyed Keats (see *Letters*, p. 318ff.); Burridge Davenport, merchant, and his wife were neighbors in Hampstead on quite friendly terms with Brown and Keats (see Keats's letter to Mrs. Davenport about Tom's sickness, *Letters*, p. 243). I have been unable to identify Misses Jin, Fanny (probably Fanny Brawne), and most regrettably, Emma.

46. Ibid., pp. 319–20.

47. Ibid., p. 403; Maria, however, took a rather different view of Dilke's "mania"; she writes to her father-in-law: "Dilke makes the most delightful Father I ever saw" (*Papers*, 1:13). In later years Dilke hobbyhorses on the raising of children (ibid., pp. 74–75).

48. Ibid., p. 394.

49. Ibid., p. 364.

50. Undoubtedly Dilke on occasion was capable of showing amazing insensitivity toward the feelings of others. But if in the late stages of Keats's illness Dilke was blind to his coolness he may in this instance be excused. Keats sent his remembrances and probably wrote to him from Italy. In addition, Dilke was so constituted that he always trusted to the "reasonableness" in others and hence was always prone to over-sanguinity as to how his own "reasonable" advice may be received. It was a failing which he would never recognize in himself.

51. *Letters*, p. 234; later Dilke rejected the teachings of Godwin for their failure to allot to literature and art a position of importance commensurate with their role in the improvement of the "moral" march of civilization. Godwin had emphasized the "moral" aspect of society but had indeed slighted the part of the humanities, an oversight which later his son-in-law would try to remedy in "The Defense of Poetry."

52. See the "Chamber of Maiden Thought" letter to Reynolds, *Letters*, p. 143; see also Kenneth Muir, ed., *John Keats: A Reassessment* (Liverpool, 1958), pp. 102–22; also see my article "The

Glaucus Episode: An Interpretation of Book III of *Endymion*," *Keats-Shelley Journal*, 27 (1978):23–24.

53. *Letters*, pp. 425–26; for Keats's meaning of this phrase, see note 51. Dilke's inability to refrain from "trying at truths," to "remain content with half-knowledge," was the impetus that sparked Keats's theory of "negative capability," that state of mind best fitted for total immersion in and contemplation of beauty.

54. *Papers*, 1:14.

55. See below.

56. *Letters*, p. 478.

57. Ibid., pp. 485–87.

58. Ibid., p. 496.

59. Ibid., p. 503.

60. Ibid., p. 504.

61. Ibid., p. 453.

62. Ibid.

63. Leonidas M. Jones, ed., *The Letters of John Hamilton Reynolds* (Lincoln, Nebraska, 1973), p. 21.

64. *Papers*, 1:11; later Fanny and Jane Reynolds (Hood) became and remained close friends: see pp. 20–21.

65. Hyder E. Rollins, ed., *More Letters and Poems of the Keats Circle* (in *KC* 2), p. 20; hereinafter referred to as *More Letters*.

66. Joanna Richardson, *Fanny Brawne: A Biography* (New York, 1952), p. 31; Carlino wrote to Sir Charles in 1878: "My impression always was that the love was mostly on Keats's side!" (Roskill-Dilke Papers; permission to quote granted by Marion Stewart, Archivist, Churchill College, Cambridge.)

67. Not necessarily accurate, but see below.

68. *KC*, 2:338.

69. Letter July 3, 1819, Roskill-Dilke Papers; quoted by permission of Marion Stewart, Archivist, Churchill College, Cambridge.

70. *KC*, 1: xlvii.

71. Marchand (see n. 19) notes that in the British Museum copy of the *Athenaeum* someone has written across a page "Dilke was a notorious sexual whitewasher" (p. 51).

72. See a Dilke letter to Milnes (*KC*, 2:223).

73. *Letters*, p. 464.

74. See note 41; I incline, however, to date their engagement much later, perhaps as late as May 1819.

75. *Papers*, 1:11.

76. *Letters*, p. 496.

77. Fred Edgcombe, ed., *Letters from Fanny Brawne to Fanny Keats* (New York, 1937), p. 3.

78. *Letters*, p. 523.

79. Edgcombe, *Letters from F. B. to F. K.*, pp. 26–27.

80. Jack Stillinger, ed., *The Letters of Charles Armitage Brown* (Cambridge, Mass., 1966), p. 75.

81. Edgcombe, *Letters from F. B. to F. K.*, p. 30.

82. Ibid., pp. 48–49.

83. Richardson, *Fanny Brawne*, p. 113.

84. As evidenced in Jane Hood's letters; in 1825 Thomas Hood had married Reynolds's eldest sister Jane and in the same year had collaborated with Reynolds on the very successful *Odes and Addresses to Great People*.

85. Peter F. Morgan, ed., *The Letters of Thomas Hood* (Toronto, 1973), p. 219.

86. Ibid., p. 253.

87. Permission to quote granted by Geoffrey Langley, County Reference Librarian at Avon County Library.

88. An intriguing note to Frederick Ward, the assistant editor of *Hood's Magazine*, lists a Mrs. Lindon as a contributor in July 1844 (*Letters of Thomas Hood*, p. 621).

89. Roskill-Dilke Papers; text varies slightly from that in Richardson, pp. 166–67.

90. Marie Adami, *Fanny Keats* (London, 1937), p. 137.

91. Richardson, *Fanny Brawne*, pp. 176–77.

92. Roskill-Dilke Papers; quoted also in Richardson, *Fanny Brawne*, p. 137.

93. Keats's description of Dilke and Brown walking around their back yard at Wentworth Place (*Letters*, p. 296).

94. Richardson, *Fanny Brawne*, p. 137.

95. Dilke was particularly displeased with Llanos's "silly speculation" regarding bridle bits.

96. This was in 1824–26; at that time George was, of course, aware of Dilke's trusteeship, but did not know about Abbey's "villany" nor of the extent of Dilke's exertions in his sister's behalf.

97. *KC*, 1:398–99.

98. Ibid., pp. 316–17.

99. Dilke letter to George, March 1828 (quoted partially in Richardson, *Fanny Brawne*, p. 113). In this letter Dilke wrote "Mr. and Mrs. Llanos and their infant were well when we left town," showing that the Llanos' had returned from Paris by March; Adami estimated their return somewhat later, in June. (Permission to quote granted by Sir J. L. W. Cheyne, Curator of Keats-Shelley Memorial House, 26, Piazza di Spagna, Rome.)

100. Marie Adami, *Fanny Keats* (London, 1937), p. 133.

101. *More Letters* (in *KC*, 2), p. 60. Of course, the situation was made even more delicate by the fact that Rice was Reynolds's law partner.

102. *KC*, 2:9–10.

103. Adami, *Fanny Keats*, p. 134.

104. *More Letters* (in *KC*, 2), p. 71.

105. Probably Dr. Seoane, reviewer of Spanish books and friend of the Dilke and Lindon families.

106. Permission to quote granted by Geoffrey Langley, County Reference Librarian at Avon County Library.

107. Adami, *Fanny Keats*, p. 141.

108. Ibid., p. 142.

109. *KC*, 2:176.

110. Ibid., p. 251.

111. From letters from Jeffrey, Georgiana's second husband.

112. Portions of the letter from George are quoted herein by permission of Sir J. L. W. Cheyne, Curator, of the Keats-Shelley Memorial House in Rome (see note 99); the letter from Georgiana is in Keats House, Hampstead.

113. *KC*, 1:315.

114. *More Letters* (in *KC*, 2), p. 48.

115. *KC*, 1:316.

116. Ibid., pp. 318–19.

117. Ibid., p. 323.

118. Whom thereafter Keats thought a swindler (*Letters*, pp. 399, 424).

119. For representative views on the extent of George's culpability, see Richardson's *The Everlasting Spell*; Brown, *The Letters of Charles Armitage Brown*, ed., Jack Stillinger; and Robert Gittings's *The Keats Inheritance* (New York, 1965), who called the controversy

a "virtual disaster" because it prevented a contemporary from writing a *Life* (p. 2).

120. See Stillinger *Letters of C. A. Brown*, p. 72n.

121. See Chapter 1, note 119.

122. Stillinger, *Letters of C. A. Brown*, p. 416.

123. Ibid., p. 62.

124. Ibid., p. 66.

125. Ibid., p. 69.

126. Ibid., p. 67–68.

127. Carlino's mother was Abagail O'Donaghue, with whom Brown allegedly performed some kind of wedding ceremony but from whom he usually kept apart.

128. See Stillinger, *Letters of C. A. Brown*, p. 99.

129. Roskill-Dilke Papers; permission to quote granted by Miss Marion Stewart, Archivist at Churchill College, Cambridge. This confirms Dorothy Hewlett's date of Carlino's birth.

130. See Adami, *Fanny Keats*, p. 108.

131. *KC*, 1:276.

132. Ibid., pp. 277ff.

133. Dilke to Brown, in *Letters of C. A. Brown*, p. 162.

134. Ibid., p. 159.

135. Ibid., p. 160.

136. Ibid., p. 161.

137. Ibid., pp. 187–88.

138. Ibid., p. 172.

139. At the time of its establishment a third partner had bought an interest in the *Examiner* but sold it shortly thereafter.

140. Ibid., p. 218.

141. *KC*, 1:286.

142. Stillinger, *Letters of C. A. Brown*, p. 255.

143. Ibid., p. 249.

144. In Dilke's annotated copy of Milnes.

145. Stillinger, *Letters of C. A. Brown*, p. 250.

146. *Papers*, 1:17.

147. Stillinger, *Letters of C. A. Brown*, p. 262; in his annotated copy of Milnes, however, Dilke refers to Landor as Brown's "crack-brained friend of Fiosole."

148. *Papers*, 1:17.

149. Stillinger, *Letters of C. A. Brown*, p. 262.

150. *Papers*, 1:18; dated December 4, 1826, is a criss-crossed, scarcely legible letter to Dilke from John Snook, who writes: "Dear Charles: I am glad you have had a pleasant journey. and I congratulate you on your safe return." Permission to quote granted by Sir J. L. W. Cheyne, Curator of Keats-Shelley Memorial House, 26 Piazza di Spagna, Rome.

151. Ibid., p. 20.

152. A family named Gordini in Pisa.

153. Stillinger, *Letters of C. A. Brown*, p. 267; Seymour Kirkup, a painter, had met Brown before 1824 (see *Letters of C. A. Brown*, p. 150).

154. In his biography of his father Thornton Hunt reports that the offices of Brown and Dilke proved beneficial for Hunt.

155. See note 147 above.

156. Stillinger, *Letters of C. A. Brown*, pp. 292–93.

157. Ibid., p. 295.

158. *KC*, 1:285–86.

159. See Gittings, *Keats Inheritance*, pp. 52–53.

160. Preface to "Adonais."

161. *KC*, 1:328–29.

162. Dilke notes in his annotated copy of Milnes that "Georgiana came to stay with us and brought with her a daughter as wild as a red-indian."

163. Stillinger, *Letters of C. A. Brown*, p. 297.

164. Ibid., p. 301ff.

165. Ibid., pp. 313–14.

166. *Athenaeum*, August 10, 1833, pp. 525–26; *Ettore Fieramosca; o La Disfida di Barletta* [Ettore Fieramosca; or the Challenge of Barletta] *racconto, di Massimo D'azeglio*; ibid., October, 12, 1833 (pp. 680–81); *La Vittine del Raggiro e del Potere: Storia Lombarda* [The Victims of Strategy and Power: A Tale of Lombardy] by Dott-Francesco Ferragni, of Cremana (1833), which Brown roundly condemns for its amateurish writing and befuddled logic; these were straightforward types of reviews as far as *Athenaeum* practice went, largely consisting of a few observations about the subject in general, a few more concerning the novel's strengths and weaknesses, and concluding with the typical *Athenaeum* procedure of quoting at length illustrative passages. Dilke had therefore schooled Brown in *Athenaeum* policy.

167. Ibid., June 14, 1834, p. 433.

168. Ibid., March 29, 1834, p. 244; May 10, 1834, p. 357; and June 14, 1834, p. 454.

169. Ibid., August 13, 1836, p. 572; Brown had written Severn that he had himself exhibited at the Plymouth Institution: (a) Severn's miniature of Carlino; (b) Kirkup's portrait of Severn; (c) Brown's copies of Severn's miniature of Keats; (d) Severn's "deathbed sketch" of Keats; (e) Girametti's study for the cameo for Woodhouse (see *Letters of C. A. Brown*, p. 338).

170. Stillinger, *Letters of C. A. Brown*, p. 346.

171. Ibid., p. 337.

172. Richardson, *Everlasting Spell*, p. 84.

173. Stillinger, *Letters of C. A. Brown*, p. 324.

174. Ibid., p. 332.

175. Ibid., p. 333.

176. Ibid., p. 340.

177. Ibid., p. 343; just when George Keats sent to Dilke the document authorizing this power is uncertain; in a letter to Severn, Brown said that Dilke's power of injunction was in effect by the summer of 1835 (ibid.). Yet in October 1836, George reminds Dilke that no interchange of letters or information had taken place between them since 1833 (*KC*, 2:22). If this document was executed for the express purpose of preventing Brown's publication of the *Memoir*, it must have been sent to Dilke before summer 1832, the date George would have seen that it was not included in Galignani's *Poetical Works of Coleridge, Shelley, and Keats* (as he thought it would be). Dilke had from George, however, an earlier power of attorney, which apparently contained no specific restrictions on its application and therefore may have served whatever purposes Dilke wished to make of it.

178. Stillinger, *Letters of C. A. Brown*, p. 336.

179. See note 169 above.

180. October 15, 1836.

181. Stillinger, *Letters of C. A. Brown*, p. 347.

182. Ibid., p. 369.

183. Probably Dilke never was aware of the review prior to its appearance in print, for he was undoubtedly out of town on business for the British Association for the Advancement of Science (he was in 1838 elected to the General Committee) and had delegated editorial responsibility to T. K. Hervey, who edited

in Dilke's absence and was later editor from 1846–1853. The review has the style and favorite authorities of J. Payne Collier, to whom most of the Shakespeare reviews were usually assigned. But Dilke so identified with the *Athenaeum* and its contents that he would never have excused himself to Brown on these grounds. The 1838 volume of the Marked File set is one of those not marked (see Chapter 3, note 21). Later Dilke was an officer (Treasurer) in the Shakespeare Society formed in 1840.

184. Stillinger, *Letters of C. A. Brown*, p. 349.

185. Brown, *Walter Hazlebourn*, pp. 35–42.

186. One reason may be that Brown sent it to Hunt, who called it "ponderous stuff" (Richardson, *Everlasting Spell*, p. 92).

187. Stillinger, *Letters of C. A. Brown*, p. 409.

188. William Sharp, *Life of Joseph Severn* (New York, 1892), p. 199.

189. Roskill-Dilke Papers: quoted by permission of Marion Stewart, Archivist, Churchill College, Cambridge. This statement does not seem to accord with Sharp's "In the spring of 1841 a letter was received from George Keats waiving his legal rights" (p. 191). For dating of this letter see my article "Two Dilke Letters" in *Keats-Shelley Memorial Bulletin* 27 (1976):1–9.

190. Sharp, *Life of Joseph Severn*, p. 199.

191. *KC*, 2:104; George had earlier predicted that Brown would so imply (*KC*,1:328).

192. Ibid.

193. Ibid., p. 105.

194. See note 189 for date of this letter.

195. Roskill-Dilke Papers; permission to quote granted by Marion Stewart, Archivist at Churchill College, Cambridge. Severn continued to send occasional contributions to Dilke's journal through at least 1845; in 1859 he invited Dilke to share with him and Milnes the cost of a new monument to Keats. Later he told Dilke's grandson and biographer, Sir Charles Dilke ("Numero Three"), that "his excellent grandfather informed him that he used to take down his [Severn's] excellent miniature to 'See Keats.'"

196. With whom Dilke was not on especially good terms.

197. *KC*, 2:176; Milnes knew and should have informed Dilke of George's death from letters from John Jeffrey, Georgiana's second husband, who copied and sent to Milnes George's Keatsiana.

198. Published in early August 1848.

199. *KC*, 2:250–51.

200. *Athenaeum*, August 12 and 19, 1848, pp. 789–91, 824–27; according to the Marked File, Heraud, a prolific reviewer on diverse subjects, wrote the first (see Chapter 3, note 21).

201. In Dilke's annotated copy of Milnes's *Life of Keats*, now in Pierpont Morgan Library.

202. Richard M. Milnes, *Life, Letters and Literary Remains of John Keats* (London, 1848), p. 5.

203. Actually £ 75 + *without* interest, unless such interest was paid by separate draft; an unlikely circumstance (see Stillinger, *Letters of C. A. Brown*, pp. 250–51 for a reprint of this account).

204. Apparently an error; see note 203.

205. In Dilke's annotated copy of Milnes (see note 201).

206. *KC*, 1:lxxxv.

Chapter Two

1. See Preface.

2. Ibid.

3. Of course, Dilke repeatedly stressed parts of the ethnos in the *Athenaeum* years and after.

4. Dilke, *Old English Plays*, 1:x; Dilke's italics; see Chapter 1, note 20.

5. Ibid., p. xi.

6. Ibid., p. xii.

7. Ibid., p. viii.

8. Especially George Darley and Lady Morgan.

9. Reynolds had been a prolific contributor for the two years preceding January 1818, at which time he turned the Drama section over to Keats and Dilke and took a six-week vacation at Exeter. When he returned he contributed nothing more to the *Champion*. He was a regular contributor to the *London Magazine* under Scott and afterwards John Taylor. Keats wrote to George and Tom in early January 1818: "Dilke is going to take the Champion theatricals"; and again on January 23, "Dilke having taken the Champion theatricals was obliged to be in town" (*Letters*, pp. 75, 87).

10. *Champion*, January 11, 1818, p. 27; Dilke meant "wire-drawn,"

i.e., "drawn out to extreme tensity" (*OED*), which is the term Keats actually used. For another instance of Dilke's misuse of this word, see p. 90. Just after Christmas, 1817, Dilke, Keats, and Brown saw this pantomime, on their walk home from which Keats conceived his theory, with Dilke's stimulus, of negative capability (see *KC*, 1:193).

11. Ibid. For a listing of Dilke's contributions, see bibliography items January to February 22, 1818.

12. Ibid., p. 28.

13. "Sleep and Poetry," line 248.

14. *Athenaeum*, December 26, 1835, p. 968.

15. *Champion*, February 8, p. 90.

16. Ibid., February 15, 1818, p. 106.

17. Ibid.; for nearly identical phrase and sentiment see *Athenaeum*, Nov. 3, 1832, p. 705.

18. Ibid.

19. Ibid.

20. Ibid.

21. Ibid., pp. 106–7.

22. Ibid., p. 107.

23. Dilke wrote comfortably, freely, and prolifically about books, painting, Fine Arts in general (in the *Athenaeum*), and especially drama; but in all matters musical, he was notably nonproficient. I know of only one notice, perhaps never published, concerning anything musical: one undated commentary sent from Paris correcting some of Galignini's impressions on an orchestra's playing for a ceremony celebrating the opening of a public building (Roskill-Dilke Papers).

24. *Champion*, February 22, 1818, p. 122.

25. Ibid.

26. Ibid.

27. Allan Cunningham, *Remains of Nithsdale and Galloway Song* (London: Cadell and Davies, 1810); *Champion*, January 25, 1818, pp. 58–59, and February 1, 1818, pp. 74–75; these notices are attributed to Dilke because (1) of internal evidence of style and content, and (2) they are cited in an 1832 notice in the *Athenaeum*, April 28, 1832, p. 265, wherein biographical evidence affirms Dilke their author.

28. Ibid., p. 74.

29. Ibid.

30. Ibid., p. 75.

31. Ibid., March 22, 1818, p. 186; ascribed to Dilke on the authority of Bailey (see note 35 and also *KC*, 1:20).

32. Ibid.

33. Ibid.

34. Ibid., pp. 186–87.

35. Letter to Taylor, *KC*, 1:20; Dilke remained close friends with Bailey and wrote to Milnes (author of the *Life of Keats*) in 1848: "Bailey, whom you quietly in-urn abt. 1821, is yet living 'a prosperous gentleman' and senior Chaplain in Ceylon" (*KC*, 2:250). Subsequently in letters to Milnes Bailey more than once alludes to "my old friend Dilke," who, Bailey surmised rightly, had in the second review in the *Athenaeum* "brought me to life again" (*KC*, 2:261).

36. "Fillers": news items, announcements, and the like usually running less than twenty lines; "re-write" duties were standard operations on virtually all contributions.

37. The extent of whose contributions has only recently been realized (see Jones, *The Letters of John Hamilton Reynolds*, pp. xxiii–iv).

38. Sir Charles erroneously remembers the signature as "Thurusa," but he must have had these articles by "Thurma" in mind because he lists as Dilke's a passage quoted by Conder, who praises a description of Venice. The passage in question is from a short story entitled "The Last Embarkation of the Doge of Venice" in Hood's annual for 1829, the *Gem*; the story is signed "Thurma." I have therefore assigned all articles signed "Thurma" to Dilke. Peter Morgan suggests that Sir Charles's error was owing to the fact that his listing of the contributions of Dilke, whose handwriting was as lamentable as that of his grandson, was taken from his Mss. See also note 109.

39. *London Magazine*, September 1821, p. 256.

40. Ibid., December 1821, p. 651.

41. Ibid.

42. Ibid.

43. Ibid.

44. Ibid., pp. 651-52.

45. Dilke does not use the term, though the *OED* shows it in general use in the 1840s.

46. Ibid., p. 652.

47. Ibid.

48. See my "The Glaucus Episode: An Interpretation of Book III of *Endymion*," *KSJ* 27 (1978):23–24.
49. *London Magazine*, February 1822, p. 126.
50. Ibid.
51. Who a decade later led the crusade in Parliament to repeal the Corn Laws; Joanna Richardson ("Some Dilke Papers," *TLS*, August 29, 1952) has seen this pamphlet among some private papers now apparently lost.
52. Quoted in *Papers*, 1:14–15.
53. See *KC*, 2:442–43.
54. Josephine Bauer, *London Magazine* (Copenhagen, 1953), suggests that one reason may be owing to Taylor's blue pencil, which "tethered his flights" (p. 121).
55. Ibid., p. 135.
56. Bauer believes that Dilke relieved Phillips entirely, but I see, or think I see, occasional stylistic features that are not Dilke's.
57. The "View of Public Affairs" was a regular feature of the *London* and averaged twelve to sixteen columns, most of which were concerned with foreign affairs. Aside from that afforded by ideas and positions known to be Dilke's, other kinds of internal evidence suggest Dilke's hand: (1) though a common practice of that period, Dilke was more consistent than were most writers in tying group nouns with plural verbs; thus, "the committee believe," "the association have," "the council are of the opinion," etc. This practice he never varied, even throughout the *Athenaeum* period and after. (2) At this period he had not completely overcome his earlier tendency to slip occasionally into a convoluted, jerky style, typically marked by such a sentence pattern as this: "The alleged purposes for the collection of the large sum to which, in a very short time, this must amount, are, redress of the grievances..." (*London Magazine*, January 1825, p. 132). Again, in the same article: "The truth seems to be, the Irish Government have suffered the Catholic Association to such a pitch that they now tremble for the consequences. The measure they have resorted to, to awe, or to check it, is, however, most imbecile, if not mischevious" (ibid., p. 133). Dilke only rarely regressed into these stylistic absurdities by the time he became editor of the *Athenaeum* and came more and more to emulate the powerful writing of his old friend George Darley. By 1836 even his knowledgeable friend and critic Thomas Hood was unable to distinguish between

them (see Morgan, *Letters of Thomas Hood*, p. 260, where Hood wrongly ascribes Darley's review of Thomas Talfourd's *Ion* to Dilke).

58. *London Magazine*, May 1823, p. 594.

59. In issues May through December 1823.

60. Ibid., September 1823, p. 338; see also August 1823 (p. 226) and January 1824 (p. 108).

61. Ibid., January 1824, p. 108.

62. Ibid., May 1824, p. 571.

63. Ibid., June 1823, p. 697.

64. Ibid., September, 1823, p. 336.

65. Ibid., August 1823, p. 223.

66. Ibid., October 1823, p. 450.

67. Ibid., July 1823, p. 106; Dilke probably received his information on the activities of Byron from Brown and Hunt in Italy, who, however, were not just then on the best of terms with Byron; nevertheless, they would have known from mutual friends (such as Trelawney and Mary Shelley) of Byron's whereabouts and correspondence.

68. Ibid., March 1824, p. 323.

69. Ibid., June 1824, p. 679.

70. See, for example, January 1824, p. 105; June 1824, p. 643; August 1824, p. 213.

71. Ibid., January 1824, p. 106.

72. Ibid.

73. Ibid., July 1824, p. 106; see Chapter 3 for Dilke's *Athenaeum* crusade for prison reform; in 1836 Parliament passed legislation alleviating many of the most severe codes.

74. Ibid., p. 107.

75. Ibid., June 1823, pp. 697–98.

76. Ibid., April 1824, p. 437.

77. Ibid., August 1823, p. 225; see also ibid., February 1825, pp. 303–4.

78. Ibid., March 1824, p. 236; Dilke distrusted the political power reposed in armies. It was on this major issue where the grandson departed from the Grand (though never acknowledged by Numero Three, who, much to Dilke's dismay, loved to play with toy soldiers). More and more, Sir Charles abandoned the principles of furthering the March of Intellect through an ethnos of art in favor of spreading "Greater Briton" to include all the world by means of what he termed *Imperial Defense* [1892]): i.e., by force of arms.

79. Ibid., April 1824, p. 437.

80. Ibid., March 1824, p. 326; in the *Athenaeum* Dilke strongly supported workingman's rights.

81. Hood was almost merciless, for example, with the rejected offerings of his correspondents. However, perhaps the gradual curtailment of his saucy pen was partly responsible for the growing opinion that the magazine was becoming "tame"; but that opinion was likewise frequently heard when Taylor was editor and Hood at his satirical best. Bauer thinks that Hood ceased his association with the magazine somewhat earlier, on the basis of a "singularly violent" letter against Hessey, which Bauer thought was written in 1824. Morgan, *Letters of Thomas Hood*, shows, however, that the letter was written in May 1825 (p. 65).

82. See also Sir Charles Dilke, *Papers* 1:16, who puts Dilke's editorship somewhat later. A feature modeled after the "tamer" announcements in the *London*.

83. Ibid., March 1824, p. 227; later in the *Athenaeum*, Dilke "put the strength [of the magazine] in the reviews." I have been unable to locate the source from which Dilke is quoting, but the style, tone, and direction sound remarkably like Dilke himself.

84. Ibid., May 1824, p. 451.

85. For example, Dilke would regularly give over whole *Athenaeum* issues to the proceedings of the British Association of the Advancement of Science, meetings of which he usually attended (he was made a member of the General Committee in 1838).

86. Probably by Cunningham.

87. Ibid., February 1825, p. 303.

88. *Papers*, 1:15.

89. Ibid.; in 1822 Galignani was editor of the *Paris and Monthly Review of British and Continental Literature*, continued in 1823 as *Galignani's Magazine and Paris Monthly Review*. These holdings in the British Museum were destroyed during World War II. Sometime between August 22 and October 27, 1823 Dilke "articulated in the *New Monthly*" for the first time (*Letters of C. A. Brown*; letter to Richards). I have not been able to identify positively any of Dilke's contributions to *NMM*.

90. "The Early Drama: Thomas Heywood *Heywood's Plays*," *Retrospective Review* 11, Part 1 (1825):127–55; ascribed to Dilke because (1) Sir Charles names the magazine and month; (2) this is

the only article in this issue related in any way to Dilke's interests and expertise; (3) this is precisely in the area of his expertise; (4) his style, tone, and habits of writing are everywhere evident.

91. Ibid., p. 128.

92. Ibid., pp. 127–28.

93. Ibid., p. 127.

94. Ibid., 154–55.

95. *Letters*, p. 68.

96. Dilke, "The Early Drama," pp. 154–55; the final phrase is part of Hazlitt's definition of poetry in "On Poetry in General," taken in turn from the Dedication of Bacon's *Essays*.

97. See pp. 36–40.

98. Letter from Dilke to William Hone, British Museum, Dilke Collection, Addendum 40856, file 17; Hone was a friend to other members of the Keats Circle besides Dilke, and is occasionally mentioned in the letters of Keats as a liberal but destitute bookseller. Dilke probably wrote his obituary (the Marked File shows the eulogy as unsigned) in the *Athenaeum* (November 12, 1842, p. 972), where his life is described as "one of unsuccessful struggle."

99. Admittedly highly dubious, Dilke's signature O.Z. could mean "opposite Z"; for Z was by now known to be Lockhart, who Keats, Bailey, Dilke and a few other friends were confident had written the damaging *Blackwood*'s article on *Endymion*; Bailey believed (rightly as it turned out) that Lockhart had tricked him into revealing information on Keats which had been used against him. O.Z. is here ascribed to Dilke because (1) he is one of three persons who could possibly know of the Court of Chancery "shower." (2) The other two, Rice and Reynolds, though acting as George's attorneys, were not so well informed on this matter as he. (3) O.Z.'s second contribution is suitable to interests like Dilke's but neither to temperament nor other known interests of Rice or Reynolds. (4) The second contribution would be a very appropriate "trifle" submitted to Hone's 1825 "little periodical": *Ancient Mysteries*.

100. William Hone, *The Everyday Book and Table Book*, 3 Part 2 (1828), Col. 430.

101. John Taylor's copy reprinted in *Letters of Keats*, ed. Rollins, has the name "Brown" inserted here.

102. Taylor's copy reads "My Taylor" (for Mr. Taylor?).

103. Hone, *Everyday Book*, Col. 430; Taylor's copy varies slightly from that given here.

104. Ibid. The Court of Chancery funds were not discovered until 1823 (see Gittings, *Keats Inheritance*, p. 39ff).

105. Hone, *Everyday Book*, Col. 395.

106. Ibid.

107. Ibid., Col. 397.

108. Ibid.

109. In Thomas Hood's *Gem*, 1829, pp. 217–49; ascribed to Dilke because (1) it is consonant with his known views; (2) it is signed "Thurma"; (3) Sir Charles notes in *Papers*, 1:23–24 that in his *Popular Description of Italy* (London: Duncan and Tegg, [1834], pp. 147–53), Josiah Conder quotes a long passage from Dilke's writings; that long passage is the first four and one-half pages of this story.

110. The doge was Lodovico Manin, who abdicated on May 12, 1797. In the following October Napoleon handed Venice over to Austria.

111. C. W. Dilke, "The Last Embarkation," in Thomas Hood's *Gem* (1828), pp. 220–21.

112. Ibid.

113. Stewart's position echoes those of the *London* four years earlier when Dilke was writing the "View of Public Affairs" section. He fiercely denounced the French for their incursion into Spain and for helping to overthrow the Cortez and to restore the monarchy (see *London*, May 1823, p. 594; August 1823, pp. 219–23); see also his high praise for the Monroe Doctrine, February 1824, pp. 215–18: "a philosophical state paper," he called it, which history would prove to rank with the most important of government documents.

114. Dilke, "The Last Embarkation," pp. 221–22.

115. Ibid., p. 222.

116. Ibid., pp. 226–27.

117. Ibid., p. 228.

118. Ibid., pp. 228–29.

119. Ibid., pp. 231–32.

120. Ibid., p. 236.

121. Ibid., p. 239.

122. Ibid., p. 245.

123. Ibid., p. 246.
124. Ibid.
125. Ibid., pp. 246–47.
126. Ibid., pp. 247–48.
127. Ibid., p. 248.
128. Ibid.
129. As a piece of didactic moralizing on an ethnology of art, the story make its points well enough. As a piece of literature, it is often amateurish.

Chapter Three

1. *Athenaeum*, January 2, 1828, p. 2.
2. Quoted in Marchand, pp. 10–11.
3. Ibid., p. 24.
4. *Athenaeum*, February 27, 1830, p. 127.
5. *KC*, 2:7.
6. See note 13, Chapter 1.
7. *KC*, 2:8.
8. *Athenaeum*, October 29, 1831, p. 707.
9. Marchand conjectures that it may not at this time have been over 1,000 (p. 24). However, see John C. Francis, *A Literary Chronicle of Half a Century* (London, 1888), who speaks of a "declining [circulation] of about 4000" (1:88). Here and elsewhere, Francis, the son of Dilke's printer, tends to exaggerate the circulation. A writer in the *Liverpool Journal* (September 7, 1833, p. 286), whom Dilke calls a "kind friend ... though unknown," but possessing "some skill and much knowledge," puts the figure at under 500. (*Athenaeum*, September 14, 1833, p. 622).
10. See *KC*, 2:7–8.
11. *Athenaeum*, July 16, 1831, p. 449.
12. *Papers*, 1:26.
13. John C. Francis puts the figure at 24,000 (see above note 9).
14. *Athenaeum*, January 7, 1832, p. 1. According to the "kind friend" (see note 9) in the *Liverpool Journal*, circulation leveled off at 15,000.
15. Ibid., January 5, 1833, p.1.
16. Ibid. Though the *Athenaeum* was healthy and flourishing

throughout the decade, Dilke was paying old debts incurred in its early years. Mrs. Gaskell, on what authority it is difficult to imagine, wrote that " £ 14,000 was absolutely sunk by Mr. Dilke" on the *Athenaeum* (*The Letters of Mrs. Gaskell*, ed. J. Chapple and A. Pollard [Manchester, 1966], p. 810). This figure seems greatly exaggerated in view of his modest salary, his respectable but not lavish inheritance from his father, and the following passage from a letter from Maria to Jane Hood in 1838: "You know with our Athenaeum that every farthing that comes in goes out as quickly and would quicker if we had it" (permission to quote granted by Geoffrey Langley, County Reference Librarian at Avon County Library).

17. E. Kintner, ed., *The Letters of Robert Browning and Elizabeth Barrett, 1845–1846* (Cambridge, Mass., 1969), 1:382.

18. For Chorley's account of his introduction to Dilke and the *Athenaeum*, see *Henry Fothergill Chorley: Autobiography, Memoir, and Letters*, comp. Henry G. Hewlett (London, 1873), 1:89–105.

19. Roskill-Dilke Papers; permission to quote granted by Miss Marion Stewart, Archivist, Churchill College, Cambridge. The Keats sonnet was reprinted in *Papers* 1:12. Other "fringe" contributors include (1) Horace Smith, who sent a virtual flood of miscellania between June to December 1830, but whose name does not appear in the Marked File after 1831; and (2) Frank (or William) Fladgate, who reviewed Horace Smith's *Midsummer Medley* (August 14, 1830), contributed some poetry, and acted as drama reviewer for several months in the latter part of 1830. The Fladgates were relatives of Rice and helped draw Reynolds into the "dreary profession." Mentioned several times in Keats's letters, they apparently remained in touch with the Dilkes for many years. Maria wrote to Jane Hood on May 3, 1838, that William and Frank Fladgate and their wives had dined with them on separate occasions during the preceding week (Letter: see Chapter 1, note 87). Also along with Mrs. Chatfield (Wentworth's mother-in-law), W. M. Fladgate was witness to Dilke's will and testament dated December 31, 1863.

20. See Chapter 1.

21. Most contributors in Dilke's reign and after can be identified because beginning June 5, 1830, Dilke wrote the names of contributors (for purposes of payment) at the conclusion of each contribution. This set of volumes is bound in the offices of the *New Statesman* on Great Turnstile Street in London. Volumes for years

1832, 1835, 1836, 1837, 1838, and 1844 are missing, but succeeding editors to the end of the century and after followed his practice. This set is called the Marked File and is usually referred to here as MF. When a contribution is unmarked, it will usually mean that for one of various reasons the contributor will not be reimbursed. In many cases these may be Dilke's, though because other possibilities exist, one cannot assume any given unsigned contributions to be his; such contributions could be offerings from any of the early proprietors who were expected to produce up to a given amount for free. Or after 1833 many unsigned contributions are Chorley's, whose name appears at the bottom of only those contributions over and above that for which he is salaried. Only the Weekly Gossip columns, virtually all unsigned, are the exception; that column is Dilke's own, and his writing style and interests are reflected regularly and consistently in it. It was his gate to the outside world and his medium for changing it, or trying to change it, more to his liking. Virtually any unsigned matter in the Weekly Gossip column between October 1831 and May 1846 can be safely assumed as his.

22. Maria's brother John, who died apparently from too much blood-letting by an apothecary (letter from Maria to Jane Hood, April 21, 1838; permission to quote granted by Geoffrey Langley, County Reference Librarian at Avon County Library).

23. Marianne's husband.

24. Ibid. Permission to quote granted by Geoffrey Langley, Avon County Library. Rowland Hill was a hero to all friends of progress and especially to Dilke and the *Athenaeum*, which praised him for his "penny postage" plan on every possible occasion. Reynolds reported on "Minutes of Evidence Taken before the Select Committee on Postage," printed for House of Commons (*Athenaeum*, April 21, 1838, pp. 281–83.

25. "The Dead Bird," containing overtones of and even a direct quotation from "Ode to a Nightingale" (ibid., January 29, 1848, p. 111). The poem bears explication.

26. In February 1840 when Hood returned to England on pressing business matters with his publisher (see below, this chapter). He stayed with the Dilkes.

27. L. M. Jones, *Letters of J. H. R.*, p. 50. In spite of their "treaty" Reynolds could not forbear to report the following anecdote: something Reynolds had said publicly (undoubtedly in *New Sporting*

Magazine, which he was then editing) was construed by the Dilkes to be against the *Athenaeum*. "I must ... whisper to you a decent reply I could not help making the other day to Eliza [his wife] after she had had an explanatory chat with Mrs. Dilke about my alleged 'speaking against the *Athenaeum*'—the latter had observed that it was like attempting 'to take away their bread'—and Eliza said to me *en passant* 'and why should you attempt to take away their bread.' My answer was 'because it is *so dry*.'" (ibid.). In 1841 Reynolds quarreled, apparently permanently, with Hood.

28. On December 18, 1846, Eliza called on Dilke and went away "quite satisfied and content" to give Milnes "free use of letters & papers" (*KC*, 2:176).

29. Dilke's two notices were first, in the *Athenaeum*, November 27, 1852, p. 1296; and *Notes and Queries* (hereinafter referred to as *NQ*), October 4, 1856, p. 275.

30. The first volume of *Papers* places Dilke's and Hood's first acquaintance in 1816 (p. 54), but *The Memorials of Thomas Hood*, edited by his son, has it in 1821.

31. See Chapter 2.

32. Roskill-Dilke papers; letter from Jane Hood to Maria.

33. Morgan, *Letters of Hood*, p. 244.

34. The Dilkes's first visit to Coblenz was a fiasco, for Hood had to leave almost immediately on their arrival, and Dilke became seriously ill (letter from William Dilke to Maria, Roskill-Dilke papers, December 11, 1836). However, Fanny Lindo apparently came over from nearly Bruges to see them (see Morgan, *Letters of Hood*, p. 282). A second trip, this time to Ostend in 1837 with John and Letitia Snook, was much more pleasurable.

35. Where the Dilkes moved in 1825; Hood visited England in January 1838, January 1839, and January and March 1840; Jane came June 1838 and October 1839.

36. Thereby breaking his own rule that reviewer must be unacquainted with author or publisher; some notices of Hood's works were written by Chorley, who also wrote his obituary.

37. Dilke to Hood, December 27, 1839; permission to quote granted by Geoffrey Langley, County Reference Librarian at Avon County Library.

38. Shortly after he had visited the Dilkes in March (see note 35).

39. Morgan, *Letters of Hood*, p. 663 (dated November 6, 1844).

The *Athenaeum* was published at 14 Wellington Street, Strand, and had sold since 1831 for 4ᵈ; "Heavy Dry" undoubtedly refers to wines.

40. It is certain that the break in friendship was more pronounced with Hood than with Dilke. Indeed, it is possible that Dilke was oblivious to it. After his death the *Athenaeum* continued to champion Hood and his surviving family; Chorley wrote a glowing eulogy; and Dilke in the Weekly Gossip invariably refers to him as "poor Hood." With Dilke this is a sure sign of warm and tender sentiment.

41. Cunningham's first appearance in the Marked File is an "original paper," "The Tam O'Shanter Group" (June 19, 1830, p. 379).

42. Seventeen in all, these papers began appearing in 1831 and continued over the next two years.

43. A monumental series, these papers began October 26, 1833, and continued through December 28, 1833. The list of authors (discussed under the headings of Poetry, Romances, History, Biography, Drama, and Criticism) numbers nearly 150.

44. Marchand suggests, however, that Cunningham's especial favorites, like Sir Walter Scott, received "fervent rather than critical respect" (p. 181). The longest single contribution ever to appear in the *Athenaeum*, occupying an entire issue, was Cunningham's eulogy on Scott occupying some 33 columns (September 29, 1832, pp. 641–53).

45. In 1832 Cunningham introduced Carlyle to Dilke, and in spite of their recognizable differences, they admired each other and quickly became friends. He called Dilke 'an honest kind of creature": exceptional praise from Carlyle. Maria, too, pleased Carlyle with her hospitality (though to his wife Jane he uncharitably called Maria fat). (C. P. Sanders and Kenneth Fielding, eds., *The Collected Letters of Thomas and Jane Welch Carlyle*, [Durham, N.C., 1970–77], 5:386.) Dilke was one of the six people accorded the honor of reading *Sartor Resartus* (then called "Teufelsdreuck") in manuscript, but Carlyle was not pleased with Dilke's less than encouraging response. Having so read the book (in Mss.) written by a friend, Dilke, of course, according to his "religious custom," could not review it in the *Athenaeum*. Like Browning, Carlyle was later criticized for "the manner—not the matter" of his writing.

46. See note 108, Chapter 4.

47. *KC*, 2:7, 8.

48. M. W. Chapman, ed., *Harriet Martineau's Autobiography* (Boston, 1877), 1:317.

49. Hewlett, *Autobiography of H. F. Chorley*, 1:101.

50. Marchand, *Athenaeum*, p. 181.

51. In his *Autobiography* Chorley boasts that his music criticism contributed greatly to the *Athenaeum*'s rank as the largest magazine of its kind in England.

52. *Letters*, p. 52.

53. *Papers*, 1:54.

54. Claude C. Abbott, *The Life and Letters of George Darley, Poet and Critic* (Oxford, 1928, reprinted Oxford, 1967), p. 158.

55. *Athenaeum*, May 28, 1836, p. 371.

56. See, for example, the following reviews: Francis Trollope, *Michael Armstrong, Factory Boy* (ibid, August 10, 1839, pp 587–90); Francis Trollope, *Life and Adventures of Jonathan Jefferson Whittam* (ibid., July 2, 1836, pp. 462–63); Lady Charlotte Bury, *The Divorced* (ibid., February 25, 1837, p. 135); H. B. Stowe, *Uncle Tom's Cabin* (ibid., May 22, 1852, p. 574).

57. Ibid., July 2, 1836, p. 463.

58. Ibid., July 3, 1852, p. 724.

59. Well over 200 contributions are marked "Morgan" in the Marked File. From certain internal evidence concerning stylistic and organizational habits, one can usually separate Lady Morgan's from those of Dr. Charles Morgan's offerings; there is, however, no sure predicting who will write on a given topic.

60. For other notices and comments in reviews condemning puffery see the following: September 4, 1830: "The Literary Gazette" (unsigned); October 23, 1830: "Cabinet Cyclopedia" (unsigned); October 30, 1830: "The Literary Gazette, the Authoress of *Separation* [Lady Charlotte Bury] and Messrs. Colburn and Bentley" (unsigned); December 4, 1830: "The Literary Gazette" (signed Alaric A. Watts); February 5, 1831: "Play-Bill Puffing" (unsigned); January 4, 1834: "Play Bill Puffs" (unsigned); April 9, 1831: "The Englishman's Magazine" (unsigned); April 16, 1831: "The Metropolitan" (unsigned); April 23, 1831: "Play-Bill Puffing" (unsigned); May 24, 1831: "To Correspondents" (unsigned); June 4, 1831: "Address" (unsigned); October 22, 1831: "To Correspondents" (unsigned); April 21, 1831: "Weekly Gossip" (see Chapter 3, note 4); November 10, 1832: "To

Correspondents"; December 1, 1832: "Heath's Book of Beauty"; January 5, 1833: "The Management of Drury Lane Theatre and the *Athenaeum* (unsigned); March 23, 1833: "Drury Lane (unsigned); July 27, 1833: Note to "England and the English" (unsigned); July 15, 1837: "Weekly Gossip" (see Chapter 3, note 4); August 28, 1841: "To Correspondents" (unsigned); June 7, 1845: "Impositions upon Authors . . ." (quoted from *Times*).

61. Taylor's first appearance in *MF* is in the issue of March 12, 1831, p. 167; Hervey's is in that of November 5 of the same year, p. 733; though they appear weekly thereafter, Dilke did not until some years thereafter entrust them with the responsibility of writing *Athenaeum* policy.

62. Sir Charles Morgan's name first appears in the Marked File as author of an "original paper" on criticism, January 29, 1831, pp. 72–73.

63. Sir Charles Morgan eventually would write: "the quantity of sewers is a tolerably accurate index to the degree of civilization and advancement of society" (ibid., August 13, 1842, p. 726).

64. The volume for the year 1836 is unmarked; *Athenaeum*, November 12, 1836, p. 793.

65. Ibid., September 27, 1845, p. 947.

66. See reports on such towns in the July 25, 1846, August 8, 1846, and May 15, 1847, issues.

67. Ibid., December 20, 1845, p. 1222.

68. Ibid., June 27, 1846, p. 655.

69. Ibid., August 13, 1842, p. 725; see also note 63.

70. Minutes of the first meeting were recorded in the *Examiner*, which noted that "Charles W. Dilke was called to the Chair" (*Examiner*, February 5, 1842, p. 90).

71. *Athenaeum*, August 6, 1842, p. 712.

72. Ibid.

73. Ibid.

74. Ibid., pp. 712–13.

75. Usually referring to himself, this is Dilke's term, which he admitted appropriating from the *Times*.

76. Ibid., p. 713.

77. Ibid., September 3, 1842, p. 790.

78. Ibid., November 5, 1842, p. 955.

79. Ibid.

80. Ibid.

81. Ibid., December 3, 1842, p. 1042.

82. See Chapter 2 section on "Views of Public Affairs."

83. Taylor reviewed, for example, *History of Morals* (April 27, 1835), *The Middle and Working Classes* (August 3, 1833), *On Wages* (March 1, 1834), and *On the Education of the Middle Classes* (March 15, 1834).

84. *Athenaeum*, April 23, 1842, p. 359: "Report in Favor of the Abolition of Capital Punishments"; see also note 73, Chapter 2.

85. Ibid.

86. Ibid.

87. Ibid., July 24, 1830, p. 460. In 1830 Dilke had written against art patronage in the *Westminster Review*.

88. Ibid., May 14, 1831, p. 315; for other adverse commentary on art unions, art lotteries, and art patronage, see April 1835: "Weekly Gossip," p. 327 (unsigned); February 15, 1841: "Weekly Gossip," p. 134 (unsigned); April 30, 1842: "Weekly Gossip" p. 383 (unsigned); January 14, 1843: "Weekly Gossip," p. 39 (unsigned); February 4, 1843: "Weekly Gossip," p. 113 (by Hood); February 4, 1843: "Lotteries and Little Goes," p. 117 (quoted from *New Monthly*); March 4, 1843: "Art Unions, Lotteries, and Little Goes...," pp. 218–19 (unsigned); May 6, 1843: "Public Gallery...," p. 440 (unsigned); October 7, 1843: "Progress of Lotteries," p. 909 (unsigned); February 21, 1846: "Fine Arts Gossip," p. 204 (unsigned); April 4, 1846: "Legislation on Art Unions," pp. 353–54 (by Townsend); April 4, 1846: "Fine Arts Gossip," pp. 354–55 (by Hervey); April 4, 1846: "Art Unions," pp. 354–55 (unsigned); June 11, 1846: "Institute of Fine Arts," p. 713 (by Hervey); August 22, 1846: "Weekly Gossip," p. 867 (by Hervey); November 13, 1852: "Gambling Houses," p. 1250 (by Dilke). Those articles marked "unsigned," were possibly by Dilke, and those unmarked in the "Weekly Gossip" column almost certainly were (see note 21, Chapter 3).

89. Dilke regularly attended meetings of the Archeological Association both in London and at the various cities which hosted the annual meetings of the British Association for the Advancement of Science (founded 1830), of which association he was likewise a member. On at least two occasions Dilke exhibited artifacts at the local meetings (objets d'art, ancient portraits, stained glass, etc.: see *Athenaeum*, January 17, 1846, p. 67, and May 9, 1846, p. 478).

90. Pettigrew for some time denied "bolting," claiming that the other side had seceded in that certain members of the organization had departed from the original purposes and ideology and that he was merely leading a movement back to it (see ibid., June 4, 1845, p. 588). Issues dealing with the Pettigrew controversy were April 12, 1845: "Weekly Gossip," p. 314 (Peter Cunningham); May 17, 1845: "The Archeological Association, p. 489 (unsigned); May 24, 1845: "The An-Archaeologists," pp. 16–17 (unsigned); May 31, 1845: "Weekly Gossip," p. 543 (unsigned); June 7, 1845: "Weekly Gossip," p. 548 (Peter Cunningham); June 14, 1845: "The An-Archaeologists," p. 589 (unsigned); June 18, 1845: "Weekly Gossip," p. 618 (unsigned); July 5, 1845: "The An-Archaeologists," p. 669 (unsigned); July 26, 1845: "The An-Archaeologists," p. 745 (unsigned); January 31, 1846: "The Psychological Journal," p. 116 (unsigned); June 13, 1846: "The Archaeological Institute and the Archaeological Association," pp. 604–605 (Peter Cunningham); August 15, 1846: "The Archaeological Institute and the Archaeological Association," pp. 840–41 (Guise and Hervey); August 22, 1846: "The Archaeological Institute and the Archaeological Association," pp. 863–64 (Hervey); September 5, 1846: "The Archaeological Institute and the Archaeological Association," pp. 909–10 (Guise, president of the Gloucester Society). The dispute becomes interesting, if somewhat overplayed, by the fact that the *Athenaeum*'s chief rival, the *Literary Gazette*, took Pettigrew's side.

91. Dilke argued that, line for line, the *Athenaeum* was even cheaper (ibid., February 15, 1834, p. 130).

92. Editor of the rival *Literary Gazette*, which Dilke particularly castigated for its puffing propensities.

93. Ibid., April 28, 1832, p. 274.

94. Ibid., February 23, 1833, p. 121.

95. Ibid., for other references to this subject see April 28, 1832: "The Penny Magazine," p. 274 (unsigned); 1832: "Society for Diffusion of Useful Knowledge," pp. 602–604 (unsigned); February 23, 1833: "The London University and the Society for Diffusing Useful Knowledge," pp. 121–22 (unsigned); February 15, 1834: "Cheap Literature," p. 131 (unsigned); March 8, 1834: "To Correspondents," p. 189 (unsigned); April 5, 1834: "Society for the Diffusion of Knowledge," pp. 260–61 (unsigned).

96. Dilke had previously praised the efforts of Miss Martineau toward liberal reforms, had given favorable reviews to her books, and had even encouraged via the *Athenaeum* a public subscription to alleviate her worsening physical and financial conditions (see *Athenaeum*, October 29, 1842, pp. 930–31 and April 15, 1843, p. 368, and June 17, 1843, p. 569). Later in the 1850s her offerings in the *Daily News* are credited with serving significantly to keep that paper afloat.

97. According to MF, Hervey wrote this column and therefore presumably wrote all the others. Usually Dilke did not mark reviews of second and third notices once the identity of the reviewer had been established in the first notice.

98. Among the letters in the University of Chicago collection of Editors of the *Athenaeum* (1832–1862; Mss. 612) is one in the melancholy scrawl of Hervey to Dilke quoting a correspondent: "I was informed yesterday by a lady who preceded Miss Martineau in her lodgings at Mrs. Holliday's [J's aunt and Miss Martineau's landlady] that she knows the veracious J. to be a thief!!" (quoted by permission of Elizabeth S. Teleky, Mss. Research Specialist of the University of Chicago Library). For other references to this subject, see January 4, 1845, pp. 14–15; March 15, 1845, pp. 268–69; March 22, 1845, pp. 290–91; March 29, 1845, pp. 310–11; April 5, 1845, pp. 333–35; April 12, 1845, pp. 361–63.

99. For Hervey's reports on "The Electric Girl," see issues for February 28, 1846, p. 230; March 7, 1846, pp. 252–53; March 14, 1846, pp. 269–70; April 4, 1846, p. 349.

100. Ibid., October 19, 1850, pp. 1094–95; in the same notice Dilke proceeds to relate how he personally debunked the alleged miraculous "powers" of magnets to discover valuable metals. Dilke caused a square field of 150 yards to be plowed, somewhere within which he buried a "treasure" and then challenged the owners of such magnets to find it. After several failures they acknowledged their bewilderment and error; whereupon Dilke limited their perimeters to a circle with a diameter of 25 yards. But alas, with the same embarrassing results.

101. Ibid., April 7, 1832, p. 226.

102. Ibid., p. 227.

103. Between July 4 and November 7, 1835, Flint contributed eleven original papers on an American authors series.

104. Ibid. April 15, 1837, p. 265; Hood contributed two series of papers headed "Copyright and Copywrong"; the first series was in 1837: April 15 (pp. 263–65), 22 (pp. 285–87), and 29 (pp. 304–6); the second series was in 1842: June 11 (pp. 524–26), and 18 (pp. 544–45).

105. Ibid., April 27, 1837, p. 286; see the same phrase in Dilke's letter to Severn in 1842, condemning Brown's memoir (pp. 49–50). and other such typically Dilkean tones. This suggests that he may have had a hand in Hood's copyright articles.

106. See preceding discussion on art unions.

107. *Athenaeum*, April 29, 1837, p. 305.

108. Ibid., June 18, 1842, p. 544.

109. Ibid.

110. See previous discussion on Hood.

111. Ibid., February 20, 1841, pp. 155–56.

112. Ibid., p. 156; Macauley's argument was that a "long" period of copyright, say sixty years, would deprive the world of some of the works of great artists and authors such as those of Boswell and Richardson, whose descendants would likely choose to suppress their "embarrassing" productions.

113. Ibid., June 11 and 18, 1842 (pp. 524–26 and pp. 544–45).

114. Dilke was reluctant to acknowledge that other journals deserved much mention for their efforts, arguing that "for years and almost single-handed," the *Athenaeum* had been "urging the question on public attention" (July 9, 1842, p. 610).

115. See preceding discussion in Chapter 3.

116. See Chapter 4.

117. *Athenaeum*, July 16, 1842, p. 636.

118. House et al., eds., *Letters of Charles Dickens* (Oxford, 1974), 3:491; the object of this association was to publicize the positive side of bookseller-author relationships and to stress those areas where later their interests were mutually affected.

119. Ibid., p. 492n; see also *Athenaeum*, May 20, 1843, p. 489.

120. All publishers; "and others" at the meeting undoubtedly included Colburn, with whom, according to Hood, Dilke was unaccountably sitting (Morgan, *Letters of Thomas Hood*, p. 546).

121. Which the *Athenaeum* had earlier charged was ineffective.

122. House, *Letters of Charles Dickens*, 3:492n; Hood had indicated to Dickens that he would like to be on the committee but later

confided that "there was a juggle" which succeeded in keeping him off it (Morgan, *Letters of Thomas Hood*, pp. 534–35); Marryat (1792–1848) was a navy captain, novelist, and sometime editor of the *Metropolitan Magazine*.

123. Ibid.

124. *Athenaeum*, February 18, 1843, p. 163.

125. Ibid., April 1, 1843, p. 307; on this date Dilke inserted a squib from Longman, the publisher, who lent his name and prestige to the cause of International Copyright and with whom Dilke and Dickens were on very good terms. Hood, however, did not like him (Morgan, *Letters of Thomas Hood*, p. 537).

126. Ibid.

127. See Chapter 4.

128. See Marchand, *Athenaeum*, p. 70. Other significant contributions concerning copyright were July 21, 1832, p. 178 (unsigned); October 10, 1832, p. 683 (unsigned); August 10, 1833, p. 532 (unsigned); January 28, 1837, p. 65 (unsigned); February 11, 1837, p. 107 (unsigned); June 3, 1837, p. 402 (unsigned); June 29, 1839, pp. 485–86 (by Hood); February 8, 1840, p. 114 (by Hood); November 13, 1841, p. 819 (unsigned); January 8, 1842, pp. 41–42 (unsigned); March 5, 1842, p. 212 (unsigned); May 14, 1842, p. 436 (unsigned); July 9, 1842, p. 610 (unsigned); July 16, 1843, p. 163 (unsigned); February 14, 1843, p. 163 (unsigned); February 25, 1843, pp. 178–79 (Dilke [with Hood's assistance]); April 1, 1843, p. 314 (unsigned); May 27, 1843, p. 508 (unsigned); July 29, 1843, p. 695 (unsigned); October 28, 1843, p. 963 (unsigned). Those unsigned were probably by Dilke.

129. Though the National Education issue continued to receive high priority until the end of the century.

130. Dilke repeatedly stressed that the recognition of the need by Parliament as well as by the public represented half the battle.

131. *Athenaeum*, July 9, 1836, p. 482.

132. Ibid., February 27, 1836, p. 159; italics Dilke's.

133. Ibid., February 18, 1837, p. 113; for other sentiments relative to *need* see ibid., p. 121: "A national system of Education is absolutely required, not only for the moral well-being, but for the prosperity of the country." See also May 27, 1837, p. 384.

134. Ibid., July 9, 1836, p. 482.

135. Ibid., July 18, 1835, p. 542.

136. Dilke assumed that this standard would in the public schools include doctrinal instruction in religion, though he personally disdained such in his education of Wentworth and "Numero Three" (see *Papers* 1:18–23, 72–75). For other statements on moral education, see *Athenaeum*, February 18, 1837, p. 113; March 4, 1837, p. 160; December 16, 1837, p. 905.

137. See the March of Intellect, this chapter.

138. Ibid., February 18, 1837, p. 113.

139. Ibid., August 6, 1836, p. 553.

140. Ibid.

141. Ibid., May 13, 1837, p. 345.

142. Ibid., February 2, 1839, p. 85.

143. Ibid., February 18, 1837, p. 113.

144. Established in 1830 (see note 89, Chapter 3).

145. Ibid., September 10, 1836, p. 658.

146. Ibid., September 17, 1836, p. 676.

147. Ibid., December 17, 1837, pp. 906–907.

148. Ibid., May 27, 1837, p. 383.

149. Ibid., p. 384.

150. Ibid., December 16, 1837, p. 905.

151. Ibid., p. 906.

152. He once told Elizabeth Barrett Browning that she may contribute a series on the Greek Christian poets (which she did), but to avoid opinions on religion. (Frederic Kenyon, *Letters of Elizabeth Barrett Browning* (London, 1897), 2:97, 117).

153. See, for example, *Athenaeum*, December 16, 1837, p. 906; for other references to church authority, see February 13, 1837, pp. 113–14 and May 27, 1837, pp. 383–84.

154. See *Letters*, p. 234, 426.

155. See, for example, *Athenaeum*, December 31, 1831, p. 850; May 24, 1834, p. 397; September 26, 1835, p. 732; May 6, 1840, p. 396; May 21, 1842, p. 458; November 13, 1852, p. 1245; Keats had noted that Dilke expected America to take up the March of Intellect where England left off. Both he and Brown accurately observed that Dilke was not one to relinquish such a prejudice easily.

156. *Athenaeum*, January 5, 1833, p. 1; Dilke's prospectus for the New Year.

157. Sentiments and style are those of Dilke.

158. Ibid., November 28, 1835, p. 886.

159. Ibid., December 26, 1835, p. 968.

160. Ibid., January 2, 1836, p. 15.

161. Ibid., February 20, 1836, p. 145; undoubtedly by Chorley.

162. Ibid., October 15, 1836, p. 739.

163. Ibid., July 2, 1842, p. 583.

164. Ibid.

165. Ibid., June 11, 1836, p. 418; as late as 1852 Dilke was pleased to note that "Institutes and Societies established for the purpose of diffusing knowledge" were "in favor of progress" (November 13, 1852, p. 1245).

Chapter Four

1. *KC*, 2:8.

2. Richard Cobden to Dilke, March 16, 1849; Roskill-Dilke Papers; permission to quote granted by Marion Stewart, Archivist, Churchill College, Cambridge.

3. Baptist W. Noel (1798–1873), a divine who agitated in behalf of the poor in an anticornlaw tract "A Plea for the Poor" (1841); bolted the established church in favor of the Baptists in 1849.

4. Letter, John Bright to Dilke, January 4, 1849. Permission to quote granted by Marion Stewart, Archivist, Churchill College, Cambridge.

5. Ibid.

6. Sometimes Cobden is especially complimentary: "I have completely identified myself with the success of your paper.... You are launching your double sheet with wind and tide in your favor.... The leading matter is now admirably done...." Permission to quote granted by Marion Stewart, Archivist, Churchill College, Cambridge.

7. H. S. Escott, *Masters of English Journalism* (London, 1911), p. 214, credits Dilke with the successful launching of the *Daily News*: "Dilke not only made the *Daily News*; he established for it a tradition of full and early information, unbroken loyalty to which has been the secret of its success. Proprietors, editors, managers changed. The lines laid down by Dilke were never departed from."

8. "The authorship of the Letters...": *Athenaeum*, July 22, 1848, pp. 717–19.

9. Ibid., p. 718.

10. Ibid.

11. Ibid., July 29, 1848, p. 746.

12. General Townshend.

13. *Athenaeum*, July 7, 1849, p. 685.

14. Ibid., p. 686.

15. Ibid.

16. Ibid.

17. Ibid., September 7, 1850, p. 939.

18. Ibid., p. 940; italics Dilke's.

19. Ibid.

20. Ibid.

21. Ibid., September 14, 1850, pp. 969–72.

22. Ibid., p. 969.

23. Ibid., p. 970.

24. Ibid., p. 972.

25. Ibid., September 21, 1850, p. 994.

26. Dilke concluded his attack on the Franciscan theory by saying that he hoped that he would never hear Francis mentioned again until some *"one fact"* had been brought forward "to show a connection between him and Junius." Quoting this statement by Dilke, Mr. C. W. Everett (*The Letters of Junius* [London, 1927], p. 381) concurs: "In the face of so notable a contradiction of the supposed facts, the Franciscan hypothesis must either give way or bring forth its "one fact.""

27. *Athenaeum*, May 17, 1851, p. 520.

28. Ibid., p. 523.

29. Addenda 43,899; permission to quote granted by Dr. M. A. E. Nickson, Department of MSS., British Museum.

30. *Papers*, 1:72; the Dilkes were married in 1806 (see note 15, Chapter 1); her death certificate names "stricture of the ilium" as Maria's cause of death.

31. Ibid.

32. See, however, bibliography under Junius from "Lord Sandwich" (*NQ*, December 1854) to "Political Papers..." (*Athenaeum*, March 1860).

33. January 17, 1852 (Grenville) and January 24, and February 14, 1852 (Rockingham); these are reprinted in *Papers*, where Sir Charles erroneously records the date of the latter of February 4. For

contributions on Walpole see bibliography, "The Correspondence of Horace Walpole...."

34. The Roskill-Dilke Papers contain some forty such letters, some of them lengthy.

35. *Athenaeum*, August 8, 1857, p. 1011.

36. Dilke to Hepworth Dixon, Roskill-Dilke Papers; permission to quote granted by Marion Stewart, Archivist, Churchill College, Cambridge.

37. See note 38 for confirmation of date.

38. William Holman Hunt (1827–1910), Victorian Pre-Raphaelite painter who later wrote on other Pre-Raphaelites. This "anticipatory" notice probably refers to F. G. Stephens's *William Holman Hunt and His Works*... (London: J. Nisbet & Co., 1860), but I do not find that it was reviewed in the *Athenaeum*.

39. Dilke to Dixon, Roskill-Dilke Papers; permission to quote granted by Marion Stewart, Archivist, Churchill College, Cambridge.

40. Ibid.

41. Edward Bean Underhill (1813–1901), *The West Indies: Their Social and Religious Condition* (London: Jackson, Walford & Hodder, 1862); reviewed in the *Athenaeum*, February 15, 1862, pp. 222–24.

42. Dilke to Dixon, Roskill-Dilke Papers; permission to quote granted by Marion Stewart, Archivist, Churchill College, Cambridge.

43. *Athenaeum*, July 8, 1854, pp. 835–39; reprinted in *Papers*, 1:296–312; after this publication a Mr. "Y.Z." (Mr. Kerslake, a Bristol Bookseller) wrote on September 16, to request that "the "writer of the articles in the *Athenaeum*" state his authorities "and when and where the original documents have been found" (p. 219, *NQ*); on September 23, "C" (Peter Cunningham) makes the same request (p. 238); the world still does not know how and where Dilke obtained the Caryll Papers.

44. Ibid., p. 835.

45. Ibid.

46. Ibid., p. 836.

47. Ibid., p. 837.

48. Ibid., September 8, 1860, p. 317.

49. Ibid., p. 316.

50. Ibid., p. 317.

51. Ibid., September 26, 1857, pp. 1206–9; October 3, 1857, pp. 1232–35.

52. Ibid., p. 1234; here Dilke is quoting Walpole's anecdote as reported by Carruthers.

53. "Here is an obtuse rascal by his own confession. Pope, he tells us, 'it is said,' took a thousand pounds to suppress these verses; but since his death, *I* have got hold of a copy, and here they are. *I* publish them, and *my* publication 'is not the first instance where *Mr. Pope*'s practical virtue has fallen very short of his pompous professions'" (ibid.).

54. Ibid.

55. Ibid., August 4, 1860, p. 151.

56. Ibid., p. 153.

57. George Sherburn, *The Early Career of Alexander Pope* (Oxford, 1934), p. 26.

58. Forster was just then collaborating with Dilke, Dickens, and Elwin on the Literary Fund squabble (see below); ironically, on the latter issue, Murray was on the opposite side.

59. The Caryll Papers, which somehow Dilke obtained in 1854; see note 43, Chapter 4.

60. Quoted by permission of Marion Stewart, Archivist, Churchill College, Cambridge; see Chapter 4, note 108.

61. Dilke to Dixon (then the editor): "I grub on while Croker lives," Dilke said of the Tory critic who had (in Dilke's opinion) unfairly castigated his "most affectionate" and "longest" friends: Keats and Lady Morgan. By that he perhaps meant that as long as Croker aspired to a *Life of Pope*, Dilke would continue to produce Pope information important enough to render the value of Croker's *Life* questionable. Permission to quote granted by Marion Stewart, Archivist, Churchill College, Cambridge.

62. Letter, May 21, 1858; permission to quote granted by Marion Stewart, Archivist, Churchill College, Cambridge.

63. Ibid., June 2, 1858; permission to quote granted by Marion Stewart, Archivist, Churchill College, Cambridge.

64. Ibid., June 22, 1858, permission to quote granted by Marion Stewart, Archivist, Churchill College, Cambridge.

65. Ibid., February 14, 1859; permission to quote granted by Marion Stewart, Archivist, Churchill College, Cambridge.

66. Ibid., permission to quote granted by Marion Stewart, Archivist, Churchill College, Cambridge.

67. Crossed through but legible; Dilke was then writing on Swift.

This crossed-out portion is another indication, however, that Dilke had felt that his total immersion in Pope studies had been unhealthy for him.

68. Ibid., Permission to quote granted by Marion Stewart, Archivist, Churchill College, Cambridge.

69. Ibid., October 8, 1862; permission to quote granted by Marion Stewart, Archivist, Churchill College, Cambridge.

70. Ibid., permission to quote granted by Marion Stewart, Archivist, Churchill College, Cambridge.

71. Ibid., permission to quote granted by Marion Stewart, Archivist, Churchill College, Cambridge. The first volume was printed but not released; it would be nearly a decade before a second volume was finished and nearly three decades before the set of ten was completed.

72. According to Warwick Elwin, son of Whitwell, "Dilke was delighted with the Introduction, but doubted whether the public would stand so terrible an exposure of the poet's character" (*Some XVIII Century Men of Letters: Whitwell Elwin*, ed. Warwick Elwin [1902 reissue New York/London: Kennikut Press, 1970], p. 263). Elsewhere Dilke had written to Elwin: "Think of me, devoting these years to Pope—I, who do not admire his poetry, with the exception of the Dunciad!" (ibid., p. 288); see also R. K. Root, "The established edition of Pope's *Works* is still that of Elwin and Courthope in ten volumes ... [1871–1889] [containing] bias curiously hostile to Pope both as a man and as a poet ..." (R. K. Root, *The Political Career of Alexander Pope* [Gloucester, Mass., 1962], p. 227).

73. "Dean Swift and the Scriblerians v. Dr. Wagstaffe" *NQ*, May 17, 1862, pp. 381–84; signed D. S. A.

74. Dilke does not comment on the difference in spelling.

75. Ibid., p. 383.

76. Present editors make no mention of Swift in connection with the *Miscellaneous Works of Dr. William Wagstaffe*.

77. *Athenaeum*, July 8, 1854, p. 835.

78. Though generally ascribed to him, according to the Marked File, Dilke wrote only the final article. Article No. 1 was by Hervey; Nos. 2 and 3 by Peter Cunningham; No. 4 by Lankester (Chapter 4, note 83), the fifth and all subsequent articles herein listed were by Dilke.

79. *Athenaeum*, April 18, 1850, p. 390.

80. For this and other references to Panizzi and the British Museum, I am much indebted to Professor Barbara McCrimmon of Flor-

ida State University for permission to read and to quote certain parts of her dissertation "The Publication of the General Catalogue of Printed Books in the British Museum, 1881–1900." Dr. McCrimmon also loaned me the use of two Dilke letters in her possession. Panizzi's argument for a handwritten catalogue was based on his conviction that a "printed" catalogue must of necessity be rendered obsolete by the addition yearly of vast new holdings, constantly making new printings mandatory and hence too expensive; indeed, the highly respected historian Henry Hallam after much deliberation had concluded that no catalogue could be produced which justified its time and expense.

81. *Athenaeum*, April 25, 1850, pp. 416–17.

82. Ibid., p. 417.

83. Edwin Lankester (1814–1874) physician, professor of natural history at New College, London, friend of Dickens, and writer on diverse topics for the *Athenaeum* after 1840. He was also a regular contributor to the *Daily News,*

84. Ibid., May 11, p. 499.

85. Cooley, William D. (d. 1883), geographer, who specialized on African subjects. It was Cooley who, on the authority of Portuguese explorers, erroneously denied the existence of any snow-capped mountains in Africa, even after Thornton's return from Kilimanjaro in 1863. He was a frequent reviewer in the *Athenaeum*.

86. *Athenaeum*, May 11, 1850, p. 499.

87. Ibid.

88. Keats's sobriquet of Dilke.

89. *Athenaeum*, May 11, 1850, p. 501.

90. Ibid.

91. Ibid., p. 502; the *Athenaeum* often expressed admiration for Mr. Rowland Hill and his "pennypost": "if Mr. Rowland Hill... could have been transferred to the British Museum for three months or less, with all the assistance he might require, we could have a catalogue compiled... and printed within another three months. What ...does Mr. Hill know about Catalogue making? *This* emphatically, that it would be his duty to make a catalogue" (ibid., June 22, 1850, p. 661; see also note 24, Chapter 3). Hill, who lived in Hampstead, was a friend of Dilke.

92. Ibid., June 22, 1850, p. 661.

93. Ibid.

94. See, for example, issues for January 22 and October 29, 1853; see also a three-part notice with the ironic title "Designs on the British Museum," January 14, 21 and 28, 1854.

95. In which his son Wentworth was one of the four commissioners and for which his friend and former associate on the *Daily News*, Joseph Paxton, built the famous Crystal Palace: see issues May 3, pp. 477–79; May 10, pp. 502–3; May 17, pp. 525–26; and May 24, pp. 551–53 for glowing reports on the Exhibition.

96. Ibid., April 20, 1850, pp. 413–15.

97. Ibid., April 12, 1851, p. 403; April 19, 1851, p. 437; December 10, 1859, p. 777.

98. Ibid., February 28, 1852, p. 254; Dilke was not originally in favor of the establishment (in 1826) of the University of London, which was professedly established for the purpose of "extending to those who are not members of the church of England the same privileges and advantages as are enjoyed at Oxford and Cambridge by those who are." He would have preferred instead that the two old universities open their doors to all, "...united...in the ties of brotherhood and affection" (ibid.). But in 1837 he wrote of "one of the principal objects of the founders ⟨was⟩ the creation of an university at which academical degrees could be obtained without reference to religious opinion" (February 25, 1837, p. 142). Dilke's son and grandson were Cambridge men (Trinity Hall College).

99. Ibid., May 15 and June 5, 1852; signed "young morality," Dilke's articles were responses to Jerdan's *Autobiography* (4 vols.) 1852.

100. Ibid., May 22, 1852 (pp. 575–77); November 27, 1852 (pp. 1303–4), December 4, 1852 (pp. 1333–34); to this series may be added a March 26, 1853 "original paper" entitled "The Newspaper and the Literary Paper" (pp. 387–88).

101. This is Dilke's familiar argument that the people of a given age *share*, whether or not they know it, in the aesthetic thrust peculiar to that age. To that extent Dilke shared with Keats and Shelley a belief which perhaps could be called a "platonic aesthetic," but what is herein called an "ethnos of art and literature."

102. Ibid., December 1, 1855, pp. 1406–7.

103. Ibid., p. 1406.

104. Ibid., p. 1407.

105. Ibid.

106. Ibid., signed "No R. A."

107. *Letters of George III to Lord North* (by Lord Brougham), ibid., October 6 (pp. 1143–45); October 13 (pp. 1183–85); October 27, 1855 (pp. 1237–39).

108. Ibid., October 25, 1857, pp. 1299–1301; earlier in the decade J. Payne Collier was charged by P. Cunningham, Dyce, Singer, and others with forgery in the famous mid-century case of the Shakespeare forgeries, which Collier steadfastly denied; Dilke had known Collier as contributor, fellow Shakespearean, and colleague in the Shakespearean society since at least 1840. He supported Collier throughout, although P. Cunningham (son of Allan, d. 1842) did not. While this may have been a "traitorous act" by Cunningham, so far as Dilke was concerned, posterity has apparently proved Cunningham right and Dilke wrong.

109. See Bibliography under heading of "General."

110. See *Athenaeum*, March 11, 1837, p. 175, where Dilke is opposed by Jerdan.

111. Editor of *The Speeches of Charles Dickens* (Oxford, 1960), p. 193.

112. As, for instance, the complaint against the committee's stipulation that any author of "a worthless book" was eligible to receive relief, but that authors of essays or periodical contributions, be they ever so numerous or important, were arbitrarily denied that consideration.

113. *Athenaeum*, March 16, 1850, p. 288.

114. Ibid., June 9, 1855, pp. 675–76. Dickens wrote the Reports of the Special Committee and of the subcommittee, for Dilke was in Paris during the week preceding the general meeting, but he wrote to Hepworth Dixon that though he had not seen Dickens's reports, he "had agreed to the details before he left London." He went on to advise Dixon that "the Charter Committee (i.e., the "Special Committee") appears to be of opinion that it will be best to follow out the original intentions of the founder, and to do something with the existing machinery; but that if what is proposed be not found to be of service to literary men, then there is no alternative but to reduce the cost" (Roskill-Dilke Papers; permission to quote granted by Marion Stewart, Archivist, Churchill College, Cambridge).

115. *Literary Gazette*, March 17, 1855, p. 170.

116. Roskill-Dilke Papers; permission to quote granted by Marion Stewart, Archivist, Churchill College, Cambridge.

117. *The Case of the Reformers of the Literary Fund*, stated by Charles W. Dilke, Charles Dickens, and John Forster (Bradbury and Evans), March 1848, p. 14; in this pamphlet the Reformers are nowhere so specific as they were in the Special Report of 1855.

118. Quoted from Letter of 1 March 1850 in *Speeches of Charles Dickens*, p. 257. The benefactor, as everyone knew, was John Forster.

119. Master at University College School; classical scholar and lexicographer; succeeded Elwin in 1867 as editor of *Quarterly Review*; a "neutral" in the struggle between the Reformers and the Committee.

120. Fielding, *Speeches of Charles Dickens*, p. 258.

121. Dickens in 1862 writes to "Sir" Wentworth (who was almost exactly his contemporary): "Pray let your good Father know that I will not lose the opportunity of discharging an arrow or so at the Literary Fund" (Letter, March 10, 1862, Roskill-Dilke Papers). Earlier in 1857 he had written Dilke "that I have my war paint on—that I have buried the pipe of peace—and I am whooping for committee scalps" (letter March 19, 1857; Roskill-Dilke Papers; also quoted partially in *Papers*, 1:79).

122. Dilke to Dixon, Roskill-Dilke Papers; permission to quote granted by Marion Stewart, Archivist, Churchill College, Cambridge.

123. With W. J. Thoms, who had started a "folklore" column in the *Athenaeum* in 1846, Dilke established *Notes and Queries* in 1849.

124. For a fuller account of this final portion of Dilke's life see Richardson, *The Everlasting Spell*, pp. 135–53, and Stephen Gwynn and Gertrude Tuckwell, *The Life of the Rt. Honorable Sir Charles W. Dilke, bart., M.P.* (New York, 1917), 1:11–48.

125. Ibid., p. 16.

126. Ibid., pp. 12–13.

127. Ibid., p. 13.

128. But see below, pp. 185–86.

129. See especially Keats's "Mansion of Many Chambers" letter to Reynolds, May 1818, Letters, p. 138ff.

130. Gwynn and Tuckwell, *Life of Sir Charles Dilke*, 1:14.

131. Though in 1862 Wentworth had become highly renowned and respected and had been granted a baronetry for his work on the 1851

and 1862 exhibitions, he apparently did not fulfill Dilke's early expectations (Gwynn and Tuckwell, *Life of Sir Charles Dilke*, 1:7) of him.

132. Ibid., p. 40. See also Richardson, *The Everlasting Spell*, p. 143.

133. Ibid., p. 45.

134. Ibid., p. 47.

135. Gwynn and Tuckwell, *Life of Sir Charles Dilke*, 1:47–48; Dilke's death certificate indicates that he died of a granular kidney disease; numerous tributes were written of Dilke by his contemporaries, some of which were reprinted in *Papers* and Gwynn and Tuckwell. But none expressed sentiments more sincere or beautiful than William Dilke's small note of condolences to Wentworth, which concludes with "You have lossed a parent, and I a Brother, and a great mind has passed from amongst us." (Permission to quote granted by Marion Stewart, Archivist, Churchill College, Cambridge.)

136. Ibid., p. 21.

137. See Arnold's *Culture and Anarchy*.

138. Dilke's only known poem was "A Choral Song: After the Manner of the Platonists," *Athenaeum*, July 16, 1831, p. 456.

139. Lady Morgan's term for principal-searching (see Stevenson, *Wild Irish Girl*, p. 161).

140. *Papers*, 1:42–43; Darley harbored identical sentiments.

141. Darley's quip that "When Leviathan is to be fed, we must heave in bushels of garbage, or the bathos of his stomach will never feel itself filled" (Abbott, *Life and Letters of George Darley*, p. 121) is echoed by Dilke's comment on bookseller cupidity, which trade "is chiefly employed in throwing tubs to that great whale the public...."

142. Marchand, *Athenaeum*, p. 52.

143. Roger Wallins, "Victorian Periodicals and the Emerging Social Consciousness," *Victorian Periodicals Newsletter* 8 (June 1975): 47–59.

Selected Bibliography

PRIMARY SOURCES

1. Books and Pamphlets

Dilke, C. W., ed. *Old English Plays, Being a Selection from the Early Dramatic Writers*, 6 vols. London: John Martin, 1814–1815.

Letter to Lord John Russell: The Source and Remedy of the National Difficulties, Deduced from the Principles of Political Economy. London: Rodwell and Martin, 1821.

"The Last Embarkation of the Doge of Venice," in *Gem.* Edited by Thomas Hood (1828), pp. 217–49 (/s/ "Thurma").

Dilke, C. W.; Dickens, Charles; Foster, John. *The Case of the Reformers of The Literary Fund.* London: Bradbury and Evans, March 1858.

Dilke, Sir Charles, ed. *Papers of a Critic.* 2 Vols. London: John Murray, 1875.

2. Articles and Reviews: General

Many of the *Athenaeum* contributions are ostensibly book reviews, which, according to *Athenaeum* practice, usually serve as an excuse to launch into theoretical discussion of the subject matter in general. The authority for assigning the great majority of these contributions to Dilke is (1) the Marked File of the *Athenaeum* (hereinafter referred to as MF) where from June 5, 1830 (the issue wherein Dilke commenced editing) to the end of the century and after, the successive editors marked each contribution for purposes of payment (volumes for years 1832, 1835, 1836, 1837, 1838, and 1844 are missing); (2) Dilke's practice of using the initials of the title and/or the beginning words of the article as his signature; and (3) Sir Charles Dilke's assignments in *Papers*, apparently from Dilke's manuscripts. Contributions assigned as Dilke's for reasons other than these three have been marked and "justified" in parenthesis. This listing of Dilke's contributions is selective; the total number of positive identifications of substantial original papers and reviews amounts to nearly 500 items. A somewhat longer listing is provided in "A Checklist of the

Writings of Charles Wentworth Dilke (1789–1864)," *Victorian Periodicals Review* 14, no. 3 (Fall, 1981):111–18.

Legend: (MF) = assigned to Dilke in the Marked File;
              (AP) = assigned or reprinted in *Papers*;
              (OP) = "Original Paper"
              /s/   = Dilke's signature, usually the initials of the title (see #2 above).

"Artaxerxes." *Champion*, January 11, 1818, p. 27. (Dilke became Drama Reviewer for the *Champion* on January 11 and ceased on February 22, 1818.)

"The Point of Honour. Miss O'Neill." *Champion*, January 11, 1818, pp. 27–28.

"Twelfth Night." *Champion*, January 25, 1818, pp. 57–58.

"Remains of Nithsdale and Galloway Song, &c. Cadell and Davies, 1810." *Champion*, January 25, 1818, pp. 58–59 (assigned on evidence from *Athenaeum*, April 1832, p. 265). (Second Notice). February 1, 1818, pp. 74–75.

"Guy Mannering. Mrs. Garrick." *Champion*, February 1, 1818, pp. 73–74.

"The Belle's Stratagem." *Champion*, February 1, 1818, p. 74.

"Point of Honor." *Champion*, February 8, 1818, p. 90.

"The Illustrious Traveller; Or, The Forges of Kanzel." *Champion*, February 8, 1818, p. 90.

"Bride of Abydos." *Champion*, February 8, 1818, pp. 90–91.

"Farzio." *Champion*, February 15, 1818, pp. 106–7.

"Bride of Abydos." *Champion*, February 22, 1818, p. 122.

"Falstaff's Death Scene." *Champion*, February 22, 1818, p. 122.

"A Discourse Inscribed To the Memory of The Princess Charlotte Augusta. By An Under-Graduate Of the University of Oxford. Taylor and Hessey 1817." *Champion*, March 22, 1818, pp. 186–87 (assigned on Bailey's authority).

"The Antiquary." *London Magazine*. September 1821, pp. 253–56. (This and the next two articles are signed "Thurma," known to be one of Dilke's signatures).

"Westminster Abbey." *London Magazine*, December 1821, pp. 651–54.

"Pleasant And Unpleasant People." *London Magazine*, February 1822, pp. 125–28.

Numerous contributions to "View of Public Affairs" Columns, *London Magazine*, May 1823–March 1825.

"Thomas Heywood's Plays." *Retrospective Review* 11; Part 1 (1825), pp. 127–55 (assigned in *Papers*: hereinafter referred to as AP).

"Imperial Fate." In *The Table Book*. Edited by William Hone, Vol. 2. London: Hurd and Clark, 1828, column 395–97 (see note 99, Chapter 2).

"The Will of John Keats, The Poet." In *The Table Book*. Edited by William Hone, Vol. 2. London: Hurd and Clark, 1828, column 430 (see preceding entry).

"Patronage of Art." *Westminster Review*, July 1830, 197–217 (on authority of *Liverpool Journal*, Sept. 7, 1833, p. 286).

"Illustrations of Popular Works," by George Cruikshank. Part 1, Royal 5 Vo. London: Longman & Co., 1830 (Review). *Athenaeum*, June 5, 1830, p. 348 (Marked File: [assigned to Dilke in Marked File: hereinafter referred to as MF]).

"A Visit to Arqua" (O.P. [Original Paper]). *Athenaeum*, June 12, 1830, p. 361 (MF).

"Character of the Belgians" (O.P. Foreign Correspondent). *Athenaeum*, August 21, 1830, pp. 524–25 (MF).

"Royal Academy" (O.P.). *Athenaeum*, May 14, 1831, pp. 315–16 (MF).

"A Choral Song by Beatified Spirits to Welcome a Returning Spirit. Somewhat after the Opinions of the Platonists" (poem). *Athenaeum*, July 16, 1831, p. 465 (MF).

Numerous contributions to "Weekly Gossip" column, October 15, 1831–May 1846.

"The Maid of Elvar; a Poem, in twelve parts," by Allan Cunningham. London: Moxon, 1832 (Review). *Athenaeum*, April 28, 1832, p. 265 (see note 27, Chapter 2).

"The Dutch Athenaeum." "Our Weekly Gossip," *Athenaeum*, May 13, 1837, p. 345.

"Up the Rhine," 2nd notice, December 21, 1839, pp. 960–63.

"Thomas a Becket: A Dramatic Chronicle, in Five Acts..." by George Darley. London: Mason (Review). *Athenaeum*, March 14, 1840, p. 204. (Darley's authority; see Abbot entry).

"The Comic Annual for 1842," by T. Hood (Review). *Athenaeum*, November 20, 1841, pp. 890–92.

"Stained Glass" (O.P.). *Athenaeum*, October 24, 1846, p. 1098 (MF).

"Life, Letters and Literary Remains of John Keats," by Richard M.
   Milnes. London: Murray (2nd notice. Review). *Athenaeum*,
   August 19, 1848, pp. 824–27 (MF).
"The British Museum." *Athenaeum*, January 26, 1850, p. 101 (MF).
"The History of England," by John Lingard, D.D., 5th Edition, 10
   Vols. Dolman (Review). *Athenaeum*, April 13, 1850, pp. 394–
   95 (MF).
"The Fourth Estate: Contributions towards a History of Newspapers,
   and of the Liberty of the Press," by F. Knight Hunt, 2 Vols.
   Bogue (Review). *Athenaeum*, April 20, 1850, pp. 413–15
   (MF).
"A Classed Catalog." *Athenaeum*, May 11, 1850, pp. 499–502 (MF).
"The Universal Catalogue." *Athenaeum*, June 22, 1850, pp. 660–61
   (MF).
"Our Weekly Gossip" (Dilke's experiment with Magnets). *Athe-
   naeum*, October 19, 1850, pp. 1094–95 (MF).
"Personal History of King Charles the Second, from his Landing in
   Scotland on June 23, 1650, till his Escape out of England, Oc-
   tober 15, 1651, &c.," by Rev. C. J. Lyon. Edinburgh: Stevenson
   (Review). *Athenaeum*, March 29, 1851, pp. 348–49 (MF).
"The Grenville Papers: being the correspondence of Richard Gren-
   ville, Earle Temple, K. G., and the Right Hon. George Gren-
   ville, their friends and Contemporaries," with notes by W. J.
   Smith, esq. 2 Vols. Murray (Rev.) *Athenaeum*, January 17, 1852,
   pp. 71–73 (MF); [second notice], January 24, 1852, pp. 110–12.
"Memoirs of the Marquis of Rockingham and his contemporaries,
   with Original Letters and Documents now first published," by
   George Thomas, Earl Albemark. 2 Vols., Bentley (Rev.) *Athe-
   naeum*, January 24, 1852, pp. 103–4 (MF); [second notice]
   February 14, 1852, pp. 195–97; (MF); [concluding notice]
   February 21, 1852, pp. 218–19.
"The Invasions and the Projected Invasions of England, from the
   Saxon Times: with Remarks on the Present Emergencies," by
   E. S. Creasy, M. A. Bentley, and "The French in England; or,
   Both Sides of the Channel," by Bradbury & Evans. *Athenaeum*,
   February 28, 1852, pp. 252–53 (MF).
"Peter Pindar" (defense of charges in Jerdan's autobiography). *Athe-
   naeum*, May 15, 1852, p. 555 (MF).
"The Book Trades." *Athenaeum*, May 22, 1852, pp. 575–77 (MF).

"Peter Pindar" (answer to Jerdan's letter). *Athenaeum*, June 5, 1852, p. 637 (MF).

"Robert Heron." *Notes and Queries*, October 23, 1852, pp. 389–90 (RH).

Obituary of John Hamilton Reynolds. *Athenaeum*, November 27, 1852, p. 1296 (MF).

"Practical Art." *Athenaeum*, November 27, 1852, pp. 1303–4 (MF).

"Second Report of the Commissioners for the Exhibition of 1851, to the Right Hon. Spencer Horatio Walpole, &c., &c., one of Her Majesty's Principal Secretaries of State." *Athenaeum*, December 4, 1852, pp. 1319–22 (MF).

"The Post Office in 1763" (O.P.). *Athenaeum*, December 4, 1852, p. 1329 (MF).

"Letter to David Garrick." *Notes and Queries*, December 18, 1852, pp. 531–32 (L.D.G.)

"Churchill's Death." *Notes and Queries*, December 18, 1852, pp. 591–92 (C.D.)

"The Scientific Societies" (a letter from G. B. Airy with an answer by Dilke concerning his support of Her Majesty's Commissioners for the 1851 G. E.). *Athenaeum*, December 25, 1852, p. 426 (MF).

"Talpa; or, the Chronicles of a Clay Farm. An Agricultural Fragment," by C. W. H. Reeve & Co. (Review). *Athenaeum*, January 1, 1853, pp. 10–11 (MF).

"The British Museum." *Athenaeum*, January 22, 1853, pp. 109–10 (with Hervey: MF).

"Art Education at Home and Abroad," by G. W. Yapp (Review). *Athenaeum*, January 29, 1853, p. 134 (MF).

"Uncle Tom's Cabin, Bleak House, Slavery and the Slave Trade" (Review of 6 books: 5 by Lord Denman and 1 by Sir George Stephen). Longman & Co. *Athenaeum*, February 12, 1853, p. 188 (MF).

"Historic Society of Lancashire and Cheshire" (O.P.). *Athenaeum*, February 12, 1853, p. 191 (MF).

"The Newspaper and the Literary Paper" (O.P.). *Athenaeum*, March 26, 1853, pp. 387–88 (MF).

"The Literary Fund and Its Reporter" (O.P.). *Athenaeum*, April 2, 1853, pp. 416–17 (MF).

"The Royal Literary Fund. Report of the Anniversary, corrected to

October 1, 1852. With the Auditor's Report for 1851" (O.P.).
Athenaeum, April 9, 1853, pp. 439–42 (MF). Also April 16,
1853, p. 484 (MF).

"The Archaeological Institute" (O.P.). *Athenaeum*, July 23, 1853,
pp. 889–90 (with Hervey: MF).

"Life of William Lord Russell," by Lord John Russell, 4th Edition,
(Review). *Athenaeum*, August 6, 1853, p. 943 (MF).

"The British Catalogue of Books published from October 1837 to
December 1852," compiled by Sampson Low. Vol. 1. General
Alphabet (Review). *Athenaeum*, October 29, 1853, p. 1290
(MF).

"The Letters of Rachel Lady Russell," London: Longman & Co.
(Review). *Athenaeum*, December 24, 1853, p. 1549 (MF).

"Autobiography of William Jerdan," Vol. 4 (Review). *Athenaeum*,
December 31, 1853, p. 1592 (MF).

"Designs on the British Museum" (O.P.). *Athenaeum*, January 14,
1854, pp. 53–54 (with Dixon: MF); also January 21, 1854,
p. 87 (with Dixon: MF); also January 28, 1854, pp. 118–19
(with Dixon: MF).

"Cawley the Regicide." *Notes and Queries*, March 18, 1854, p. 247
(C.T.R.).

"Edward Gibbon, Father & Son." *Notes and Queries*, June 3, 1854,
pp. 511–12: /s/ (E.G.F.S.).

"Biographies of Living Authors." *Notes and Queries*, October 14,
1854, pp. 313–14 (B.L.A.).

"Campian's Decem Rationes." *Notes and Queries*, March 3, 1855.
(C.D.R.).

"The Literary Fund." *Athenaeum*, June 23, 1855, pp. 732–34 (MF).

"The Louvre; or, Biography of a Museum," with Two Plans by Bayle
St. John. Chapman and Hall (Review). *Athenaeum*, July 7,
1855, pp. 787–88 (MF).

"The Archaeological Epistle." *Notes and Queries*, July 14, 1855, p. 35
(T.A.E.).

"The Whig Examiner." *Notes and Queries*, July 21, 1855, p. 47
(T.W.E.).

"Cathedral Registers." *Notes and Queries*, September 1, 1855, p. 173
(C.R.).

"Letters of George the Third to Lord North. Appendix to 'Historical
Sketches'" by Henry Lord Brougham; Griffin & Co. (Review).

Athenaeum, October 6, 1855, pp. 1143–45 (MF); [second notice], October 11, 1855, pp. 1183–85 (MF).

"Fine Art Gossip" (State and Condition of Art in this Country!!). *Athenaeum,* December 1, 1855, pp. 1406–7. No RA (MF).

"Hugh Speke and the Forged Declaration of the Prince of Orange" *Notes and Queries,* January 12, 1856, pp. 28–29 (H.S.F.D.P.); [second notice] January 19, 1856, pp. 46–48 (H.S.F.D.P.).

"Papers in Relation to the Case of Silas Deane," Philadelphia (1st work issued by a Society: "The Seventy-Six Society"). (Review). *Athenaeum,* February 16, 1856, pp. 195–97 (MF).

"Shakespeare and 'The Passionate Pilgrim.'" Letter by J. Payne Collier, *Athenaeum,* May 17, 1856, pp. 616–17 (AP).

"Think of Me" & "The Garden of Florence" and "J.H.R." *Notes and Queries,* October 4, 1856, pp. 271–72 (T.M.T.).

"Seven Lectures on Shakespeare and Milton," by S. T. Coleridge, "A List of all the MS. Emendations in Mr. Collier's Folio, 1632: and an Introductory Preface," by J. Payne Collier, Esq. Chapman & Hall (Review). *Athenaeum,* October 25, 1856, pp. 1299–1301 (MF).

"Shakespeare's Portrait," *Notes and Queries,* January 24, 1857, pp. 61–62 (S.P.).

The Literary Fund. *Athenaeum,* March 7, 1857, pp. 309–10 (MF).

The Literary Fund. *Athenaeum,* March 6, 1858, pp. 304–6 (AP); also March 20, 1858, pp. 370–71 (MF); May 1, 1858, pp. 559–63 (AP).

"On Treasure Trove," by G. V. Irving (Review of a paper read at a meeting of the British Archaeological Association). *Athenaeum,* February 26, 1859, p. 285 (MF).

"The Physiology of Shakespeare," by J. C. Bucknill, M.D., Longman & Co., and "Strictures on Mr. Collier's New Edition of Shakespeare," by Rev. A. Dyce. Smith. *Athenaeum,* September 24, 1859, p. 397 (MF).

"Our Weekly Gossip" (Archaeology of Hampshire). *Athenaeum,* December 10, 1859, p. 777 (A Hampshire Man: MF).

"Memoirs of the Insurrection in Scotland in 1715," by John, Master of Sinclair. With notes, by Sir Walter Scott. (Printed for the Abbotsford Club.) (Review.) *Athenaeum,* December 31, 1859, pp. 879–81 (MF).

"Some Account of the Family of Smollett of Bonhill. Some Account of the Family of Dennistun of Colgrain. History of Dumbartonshire," by Joseph Irving, 2nd edition, Dumbarton (Review). *Athenaeum*, January 21, 1860, pp. 92–93 (MF).

"The Origin of Species," a report by Prof. Asa Gray, botanist (Review). *Athenaeum*, August 4, 1860, p. 161 (MF).

"The Beggar's Petition." *Notes and Queries*, November 24, 1860, pp. 401–2. (T.B.P.).

"Admiral Sir Thomas Dilkes." *Notes and Queries*, January 19, 1861, p. 52 (A.S.T.).)

"The Letters and Works of Lady Mary Wortley Montagu." Edited by Lord Wharncliffe, 3rd edition with Illustrated Notes and a New Memoir, Bohn (Review), *Athenaeum*, April 6, 1861, pp. 460–63 (AP) W. Moy Thomas, (Dilke's secretary); [second notice] April 13, 1861, pp. 492–94, (AP); [concluding notice] October 5, 1861, pp. 437–39 (AP).

"Satirical Print Against Lord Bolingbroke." *Notes and Queries*, November 22, 1862, pp. 401–3 (S.P.B.: AP).

"Sussex Archaeological Collections, relating to the History and Antiquities of the Country," published by the Sussex Archaeological Society, Vol. 15. Lewes (Review). *Athenaeum*, December 12, 1863, pp. 764–65 (MF).

3. Junius

"The Authorship of the Letters of Junius Elucidated," by John Britton. J. R. Smith (Review). *Athenaeum*, July 22, 1848, pp. 717–19; [second notice] *Athenaeum*, July 29, 1848, pp. 745–47 (MF).

"The History of Junius and his Works—Identity of Junius with a distinguished living Character—A Critical Enquiry regarding the Real Author of the Letters of Junius, &c., &c., &c.," by Sir David Brewster, North British Review (Review). *Athenaeum*, July 7, 1849, pp. 685–88 (MF).

"Junius; with New Evidence as to the Authorship, and an Analysis by the late Sir Harris Nicolas," by John Wade, Vol. 1, Bohn (Review). *Athenaeum*, February 2, 1850, pp. 125–26 (MF); [second notice] February 9, 1850, pp. 154–57 (MF).

"Junius Identified." *Notes and Queries*, July 13, 1850, p. 103 (R.J.: AP).

"Junius," by John Wade, Vol. 2, "Containing the Private and Miscellaneous Letters and a New Essay on the Authorship," Bohn (Review). *Athenaeum*, August 17, 1850, pp. 863–64 (MP).

"Sir Philip Francis, And His Claims To Be Considered The Writer Of The Letters of Junius": "Some New Facts and a Suggested New Theory as to the Authorship of the Letters of Junius," by Sir Fortunatus Dwarris, Knt. (Privately Printed) "The History and Discovery of Junius," by John Wade———Junius. 2 Vols. Bohn (Review). *Athenaeum*, September 7, 1850, pp. 939–41 (AP); [second notice] September 14, 1850, pp. 969–72 (AP); [concluding notice] September 21, 1850, pp. 993–96 (AP).

"Mr. Taylor And The Authorship of Junius," *Athenaeum*, September 28, 1850, pp. 1021–22 (AP).

"Junius And 'Junius Identified'" (O.P.) *Athenaeum*, October 12, 1850, p. 1071 (in answer to a lettter from Mr. John Taylor on case of friendship with Mr. Dubois) (MF).

"Junius and his Works compared with the Character and Writings of Philip Dormer Stanhope, Earl of Chesterfield," by William Cramp. Lewes, Baxter & Son. "Fac-simile Autograph Letters of Junius, Lord Chesterfield, and Mrs. C. Dayrolles," by W. Cramp. Hope & Co. (Review). *Athenaeum*, March 22, 1851, pp. 323–24 (MF).

"The Vellum Bound Junius." *Notes and Queries*, April 5, 1851, p. 262. V.B.

"The Junius Autograph." *Athenaeum*, April 5, 1851, p. 388 (a letter from Mr. Netherclift) (MF).

"The Correspondence of Horace Walpole, Earl of Oxford, and Rev. William Mason," ed. by the Rev. J. Mitford (Review). *Athenaeum*, May 10, 1851, pp. 493–95 (MF); [second notice] May 17, 1851, pp. 520–23; [third notice] May 24, 1851, pp. 548-50.

"MacLean Not Junius." *Notes and Queries*, May 24, 1851, pp. 411–12 (M.J.).

"Walpole and Junius." *Notes and Queries*, November 15, 1851, p. 395 (W.J.).

"The Quarterly Review," #179. Murray. *Athenaeum*, January 17, 1852, pp. 78–81 (note: in this article Thomas, Lord Lyttelton is announced as "The Junius of our contemporary...") (MF).

"Junius Rumors." *Notes and Queries*, February 14, 1852, p. 159 (J.R.).

"Junius and the Quarterly Reviews." *Notes and Queries,* February 28, 1852, p. 194 (J.Q.R.).

"The Vellum Bound Junius." *Notes and Queries,* March 27, 1852, pp. 303–4 (V.B.J.); also April 3, 1852, p. 332 (V.B.J.).

"Colonel or Major-General Lee." *Notes and Queries,* June 26, 1852, p. 611 (C.M.L.).

"Letters of Junius." *Notes and Queries,* September 4, 1852, p. 224 (L.J.).

"The Early Piratical Editions of Junius." *Notes and Queries,* September 11, 1852, pp. 239–41 (L.J.); also, September 18, 1852, pp. 261–63 (L.J.); also September 25, 1852, pp. 285–86 (L.J.).

"The First Genuine Edition of Junius's Letters." *Notes and Queries,* October 23, 1852, pp. 383–85 (L.J.).

"Collins." *Notes and Queries,* October 30, 1852, pp. 412–13 (C.S. AP).

"David Garrick." *Notes and Queries,* January 8, 1853, p. 40 (G.D.: AP).

"Touching the Identity of Junius." *Dublin University Magazine.* "The Ghost of Junius," by Francis Ayerst. Bosworth (Review) *Athenaeum,* February 19, 1853, pp. 219–20 (AP); concluding notice June 18, 1853, pp. 733–35 (AP).

"Junius, Lord Temple. The Stowe Letters.—The Grenville Papers," edited, with notes by W. J. Smith, Esq. Vols. 2 & 4 (Review). *Athenaeum,* June 11, 1853, pp. 698–700 (AP); [concluding notice] June 18, 1853, pp. 733–35 (AP).

"Park the Antiquary." *Notes and Queries,* July 2, 1853, p. 8 (P.T.A.).

"Carefully Examined and Well-Authenticated." *Notes and Queries,* July 2, 1853, pp. 8–9 (V.B.) (see "The Vellum Bound Junius" above).

"That Swinney (Junius)." *Notes and Queries,* September 3, 1853, pp. 213–15 (T.S.J.); also, September 10, 1853, pp. 238–39 (T.S.J.).

"Lord Sandwich." *Notes and Queries,* December 9, 1854, p. 465 (S.L.: AP).

"Penny Post." *Notes and Queries,* December 30, 1854, p. 523 (N.E.P.: AP).

"Junius, Mr. George Woodfall, etc." *Notes and Queries,* July 14, 1855, pp. 22–24 (L.J.) (AP: see "Letters of Junius" and "The Early Piratical Editions of Junius" above).

"The Pertinent Anecdote." *Notes and Queries*, September 8, 1855, p. 193 (T.P.A.).

"The Vellum-Bound Junius." *Notes and Queries*, October 20, 1855, p. 299 (T.V.B.).

"Bohn's Junius." *Notes and Queries*, October 20, 1855, pp. 299–300 (B.J.).

"The Vellum-Bound Junius." *Notes and Queries*, January 12, 1856, pp. 36–37 (V.B.).

"Mr. Macauley and Sir Philip Francis" (O.P.). *Athenaeum*, March 8, 1856, pp. 305–6 (AP).

"Who Was Junius." *Notes and Queries*, March 8, 1856, pp. 185–87 (W.W.J.).

"Was Daniel Wray Junius." *Notes and Queries*, September 13, 1856, p. 212 (W.D.W.).

"Philip Francis and Pope Ganganelli in 1772." *Athenaeum*, January 9, 1858, pp. 50–52 (AP).

"Junius Discovered" by Frederick Griffin. Boston: Little & Co., and "Junius, Lord Chatham: a Biography," by William Dowe. New York: Miller & Co. (Review). *Athenaeum*, July 17, 1858, pp. 78–79 (AP).

"William Burke the Author of Junius," by Jelinger Cookson Symons. Smith, Elder & Co. (Review). *Athenaeum*, July 2, 1859, pp. 13–14 (MF).

"The Bibliographer's Manual of English Literature," by William Thomas Lowndes. Bohn (Review) *Athenaeum*, February 25, 1860, pp. 265–66 (MF).

"Political Papers from St. James' Square." *Athenaeum*, March 10, 1860, pp. 341–42 (AP); also, March 17, 1860, p. 375 (AP).

"A Few Words on Junius and Macaulay." *Cornhill Magazine*, Smith, Elder & Co., (Review) *Athenaeum*, March 17, 1860, pp. 366–69 (with Dixon: MF).

"Political Papers From St. James' Square." *Athenaeum*, March 24, 1860, pp. 409–10 (AP).

"Papers of John Wilkes." *Notes and Queries*, December 22, 1849, p. 125 (W.)

"The Wilkes MSS. and 'North Briton.'" *Notes and Queries*, March 29, 1851, p. 241 (W.M.S.). Apparently the first instance of of Dilke's "personal signature"; the initials of the beginning of the title or the first words of the article.

"John Wilkes. History of England," by Lord Mahon, Vols. 5 & 6 (Review). *Athenaeum*, January 3, 1852, pp. 7–10 (MF); [concluding notice] January 10, 1852, pp. 46–49 (MF).

"History of England, from the Peace of Utrecht to the Peace of Versailles," by Lord Mahon, Vol. 5, 1763–1774, 3rd edition, revised. Murray (Review). *Athenaeum*, September 17, 1853, pp. 1090–92 (AP).

"Wilkes' Copy of Junius' Letters." *Notes and Queries*, February 13, 1855, p. 84 (W.C.J.).

"Wilkes and the 'Essay on Women,'" *Notes and Queries*, July 4, 1857, pp. 1–2 (D: AP); also, July 11, 1857, pp. 21–22 (D: AP); also July 18, 1857, pp. 41–42 (D: AP).

"Essay on Women." *Notes and Queries*, January 23, 1858, p. 77 (D: AP).

"Wilkes' Last Speech In Parliament." *Notes and Queries*, April 26, 1862, p. 339 (W.L.S.).

"Arms of Wilkes." *Notes and Queries*, May 24, 1862, p. 415 (W: AP).

4. Burke

"Foreign Reminiscences," by Henry Richard Lord Holland, ed. by his Son Henry Edward Lord Holland. Longman & Co. (Review). January 11, 1851, pp. 44–45 (MF); [second notice] January 18, 1851, pp. 77–78 (MF).

"The Public and Domestic Life of Edmund Burke," by Rev. Peter Burke, Esq. Ingram, Cooke & Co. (Review). *Athenaeum*, December 3, 1853, pp. 1147–49 (AP).

"The 'Domestic Life' of Edmund Burke" (O.P.). *Athenaeum*, December 10, 1853, pp. 1476–69 (AP); [second notice] December 17, 1853, pp. 1512–15 (AP).

"The Life of the Right Honourable Edmund Burke," by James Prior. Bohn (Review). *Athenaeum*, February 17, 1855, pp. 195-97 (AP).

"Spence's Anecdotes." *Notes and Queries*, January 2, 1858, p. 17 (S.A.).

"Dunning's Eloquence." *Notes and Queries*, February 13, 1858, pp. 121–23 (D.E.).

"The Candor Pamphlets." *Notes and Queries*, February 20, 1858, p. 141 (D.E.). (See preceding entry; also February 27, 1858, p. 161–63 [D.E.]).

"The Life and Times of Edmund Burke," by Thomas MacKnight. Vols. 1 & 2. Chapman & Hall (Review). *Athenaeum*, February 20, 1858, pp. 236–38 (AP); also, July 3, 1858, pp. 16–17 (D.E). (see "Dunning's Eloquence," above); [concluding notice] Vol. 3. Chapman and Hall. *Athenaeum*, December 22, 1860, pp. 866–67 (AP).

"Authorship of the Candor Pamphlets." *Notes and Queries*, July 17, 1858, p. 54 (A.C.P.).

"Chatterton's Papers." *Notes and Queries*, June 8, 1861, p. 457. W. Moy Thomas (Dilke's secretary, who sometimes signed for him).

"Edmund Burke." *Notes and Queries*, March 1, 1862, pp. 161–62 (E.B.S.). The article begins "Some years since...." (Dilke often enhanced the initials of the title with those of the first word or words in the text.) Also, March 15, 1862, p. 212 (T.C.B.). The article begins "There can be no doubt..."; also March 15, 1862, pp. 212–13. (I.A.W.: AP); the article begins, "I agree with your correspondent..."; also, March 22, 1862, pp. 221–22 (I.R.T.: AP). The article begins "I rejoice that a spirit..."; also, April 26, 1862, p. 326 (T.S.F.). The article begins, "The smallest facts..."; May 31, 1862, pp. 429–31. (I.R.T.).

"More Mysteries About Burke." *Notes and Queries*, April 5, 1862, p. 269 (M.M.A.).

"Burke and Beaconsfield." *Notes and Queries*, August 2, 1862, pp. 81–82 (J.R.T.). (Signature used by Dilke in earlier notes in March 22, and May 31 issues.)

"Our Library Table," Column: "Edmund Burke: a Lecture," by the Right Hon. Joseph Napier, L.L.D. Dublin: Hodges & Smith (Review). *Athenaeum*, August 2, 1862, p. 144 (MF).

5. Pope

"Pope and John Dennis." *Notes and Queries*, June 3, 1854, pp. 516–17 (P.J.D.).

"The Life of Alexander Pope" (O.P.). *Athenaeum*, July 8, 1854, pp. 835–39 (AP); second notice, July 15, 1854, pp. 875–79 (AP); third notice, July 22, 1854, pp. 907–10 (AP).

"Pope's Epitaph on Mrs. Corbet." *Athenaeum*, July 29, 1854, p. 942. (AP).

"Leonard Welstid." *Notes and Queries*, August 5, 1854, p. 104 (W.L.). In his signature Dilke often reversed the initials of persons.

"Old Lady Blount of Twickenham." *Notes and Queries*, September 2, 1854, p. 184 (O.L.B.).

"Pope and the Pirates." *Notes and Queries*, September 9, 1854, pp. 197–200: /s/ by the Writer of the Articles in the *Atheneum*.

"The Poetical Works of Alexander Pope," by the Rev. G. Croly, London: Scott (Review). *Athenaeum*, September 9, 1854, p. 1089 (AP).

"Lewis Theobald." *Notes and Queries*, September 16, 1854, p. 219 (T.L.).

"The Dublin Reprint of 'The Dunciad.'" *Notes and Queries*, September 23, 1854, p. 239: /s/ by The Writer of the Articles... etc.

"Mr. Murray's Edition of Pope." *Notes and Queries*, September 30, 1854, p. 258 (M.E.P.).

"Pope's Skull." *Notes and Queries*, November 25, 1854, p. 418 (P.S.).

"James Moore Smyth." *Notes and Queries*, December 9, 1854, p. 459 (J.M.S.).

"Satirical Print of Pope." *Notes and Queries*, January 6, 1855, p. 7 (S.P.P.).

"The Dunciad." (O.P.). *Athenaeum*, January 13, 1855, p. 50 (MF).

"Arthur Moore and the Moores." *Notes and Queries*, March 3, 1855, pp. 157–59: /s/ by the Writer of the Articles... etc.; also, March 3, 1855, pp. 177–78: /s/ by the Writer of the Articles... etc.; also, March 17, 1855, pp. 197–98: /s/ by the Writer of the Articles... etc.

"Signor Carolini, Dr. Barnveldt, and the author of 'Key to the Dunciad.'" *Notes and Queries*, March 3, 1855, p. 175 (S.C.B.).

"Pope and Donne's Satires." *Notes and Queries*, April 7, 1855, p. 261 (P.D.S.).

"Lives of the Most Eminent British Poets," by Samuel Johnson, with Notes by Peter Cunningham, F.S.A., Vol. 3. London: John Murray (Review). *Athenaeum*, April 4, 1855, pp. 424–25 (MF).

"Alexander Pope." *Notes and Queries*, July 21, 1855, p. 46 (A.P.I.). (The article begins, "Inquiries are just now....")

"The Jersey Muse." *Notes and Queries*, July 21, 1855, p. 52 (T.J.M.).

"Pope and Bathurst, the Bookseller." *Notes and Queries*, July 28, 1855, p. 60 (P.A.B.); also November 17, 1855, p. 379 (P.A.B.).

"Dryden, Pope, and Curll's 'Corrina.'" *Notes and Queries*, October 13, 1855, pp. 277–79 (W.M.T.: William Moy Thomas, Dilke's secretary, who signed for him occasionally).
  p. 325 (W.M.T.).
"Carruther's Life of Pope." *Notes and Queries*, October 27, 1855,
"Curll's 'Corinna.'" *Notes and Queries*, December 1, 1855, pp. 431–32 (W.M.T.).
"Pope's Letters." *Notes and Queries*, December 15, 1855, pp. 463–64 (W.M.T.).
"Caryll of the 'Rape of the Lock.'" *Notes and Queries*, November 24, 1855, p. 415 (C.R.).
"Roscoe's Edition of Pope." *Notes and Queries*, February 7, 1856, p. 135 (W.M.T.).
"Pope's Ode for Music." *Notes and Queries*, June 7, 1856, p. 449 (P.O.).
"Mr. Carruthers And The Pope Manuscripts At Maple-Durham—a Review of New Editions to be coming out of Mr. Carruther's 'Life and Poems of Pope.'" *Athenaeum*, June 28, 1856, pp. 810–11 (MF).
"Pope and Warburton." *Notes and Queries*, September 6, 1856, p. 182 (P.A.W.).
"Rape of the Lock." *Notes and Queries*, September 6, 1856, pp 181–82 (R.O.L.).
"Pope's 'Letters to Cromwell.'" *Notes and Queries,* September 27, 1856, p. 242 (P.L.C.).
"Stray Notes on Edmund Curll, His Life, and Publications." *Notes and Queries* (#1), October 18, 1856, pp. 301–303 (AP: S.N.M.). The article begins with a quotation from "Man of Taste"; also (#2), October 25, 1856, pp. 321–24 (S.N.M.; also (#3), November 1, 1856, pp. 341–44 (S.N.M.); also (#4), November 8, 1856, pp. 361–64 (S.N.M.); also (#5), November 22, 1856, pp. 401–4 (S.N.M.); also (#6), November 29, 1856, pp. 421–24 (S.N.M.); also (#7), December 6, 1856, p. 441 (S.N.M.); also (#8), February 21, 1857, pp. 141–44 (S.N.M.); also (#9) June 27, 1857, pp. 501–3 (S.N.M.); also (#10), June 19, 1858, pp. 489–92 (S.N.M.), June 26, 1858 (S.N.M.); also (#11), September 15, 1860, pp. 201–4 (M.N.S.): perhaps because his last, Dilke inverted the order of initials).

"The Pope and Blount Letters." *Notes and Queries*, November 1, 1856 pp. 344–45 (T.P.B.).

"Additions to Pope." *Notes and Queries*, November 1, 1856, p. 345 (A.T.P.)

"The Poetical Works of Alexander Pope. With Memoir, Critical Dissertation, and Explanatory Notes," by Rev. George Gilfillan, 2 Vols. Edinburgh: James Nichol (Review). *Athenaeum*, November 15, 1856, pp. 1397–99 (AP).

"Pope's Letters." *Notes and Queries*, January 24, 1857, p. 70 (W.M.T., Dilke's secretary).

"Pope's 'Ode on St. Cecilia's Day.' " *Notes and Queries*, February 7, 1857, p. 110 (P.O.S.).

"The Dying Christian." *Notes and Queries*, February 7, 1857, p. 110 (P.O.S.: see preceding entry).

"Pope, Belinda, and 'The Man of Merit.' " *Notes and Queries*, February 28, 1857, p. 161 (P.B.A.).

"Pope and Theobald." *Notes and Queries*, April 25, 1857, pp. 324–25 (P.T.).

"Essay on Man." *Notes and Queries*, April 25, 1857, p. 325 (E.O.M.).

"The MSS at Mapledurham." *Notes and Queries*, May 23, 1857, p. 403 (T.M.S.).

"Pope's Father—His First Wife—And Pope's Half-Sister, Mrs. Rackett." (O.P.). *Athenaeum*, May 30, 1857, pp. 693–95 (AP); also, June 13, 1857, pp. 461–62 (P.F.).

"Alexander Pope, Broad Street." *Notes and Queries*, June 13, 1857, p. 462 (D: AP).

"Pope and his Aunt-Godmother, Christina Cooper." (O.P.). *Athenaeum*, July 18, 1857, pp. 911–12 (AP).

"The Life of Alexander Pope. Including Extracts from his Correspondence," by Robert Carruthers. 2d edition. Bohn (Review). *Athenaeum*, September 26, 1857, pp. 1206–9 (AP).

"Pope: His Descent and Family Connections. Facts and Conjectures," by Joseph Hunter. J. R. Smith (Review). *Athenaeum*, November 21, 1857, pp. 1451–52 (AP); also, December 5, 1857, p. 445 (P.H.D.).

"A Patent Fact." *Notes and Queries*, November 21, 1857, pp. 405–6 (D:AP).

"Bolingbroke's Letter to Pope." *Notes and Queries*, December 5, 1857, pp. 445–46. /s/ W. Moy Thomas (Dilke's secretary).

"Odell and Pope." *Notes and Queries*, December 5, 1857, p. 447 (O.A.P.).

"Pope's Aunt." *Notes and Queries*, December 26, 1857, p. 507 (P.A.).

"Lines on the Dunciad." *Notes and Queries,* December 26, 1857, p. 508 (L.D.).

"Additions to the Works of A. Pope." *Notes and Queries*, December 26, 1857, pp. 508–509 (A.T.T.).

"Mrs. Corbet." *Notes and Queries*, December 26, 1857, p. 509 (M.C.A.). (The article begins, "According to...")

"Mannick." *Notes and Queries*, January 2, 1858, p. 506 (M.A.C.). (The article begins, "A correspondent asks...")

"Pope's Father." *Notes and Queries*, February 6, 1858, pp. 103–4 (P.F.).

"Pope's Father Residing at Kensington." *Notes and Queries*, February 6, 1858, p. 104 (P.F.R.).

"Baptism of Catholics." *Notes and Queries*, February 6, 1858, p. 104 (B.O.C.).

"Mr. Pottinger, Pope's Cousin." *Notes and Queries*, February 6, 1858, p. 105 (M.P.P.).

"Pope, Editions of 1735 and 1736." *Notes and Queries*, March 6, 1858, pp. 183–84 (P.E.).

"The Poetical Works of Alexander Pope.: ed. by Robert Carruthers, 2 Vols. Bohn. (Review). *Athenaeum*, May 8, 1858, pp. 585–87 (AP); [second notice] May 15, 1858, pp. 622–25 (AP).

"Pope: additionel Facts concerning his Maternal Ancestry," by Robert Davies. J. R. Smith (Review). *Athenaeum*, May 22, 1858, pp. 654–55 (AP).

"Arthur Moore And The Moores." *Notes and Queries*, July 3, 1858, pp. 13–14 (A.M.T.).

"Pope and Dennis." *Notes and Queries*, November 20, 1858, p. 412 (P.D.).

"James Moore." *Notes and Queries*, September 3, 1859, p. 195 (J.M.); also, September 17, 1859, p. 235 (J.M.).

"Unpublished Letter." *Notes and Queries*, December 10, 1859, pp. 466–67 (U.L.).

"On the Relations of Alexander Pope with the Duchess of Marlborough and the Duchess of Buckinghamshire; and on the Character and Characteristics of Atossa." (O.P.). *Athenaeum*, August 4, 1860, pp. 151–54 (AP).

"A Search into the History of the Publication of Pope's Letters" (O.P.). *Athenaeum*, September 1, 1860, pp. 279–80 (AP); also September 8, 1860, pp. 316–19 (AP); also, September 15, 1860, pp. 348–50 (AP).

"Bowes vs. Roscoe." *Notes and Queries*, November 17, 1860, pp. 318–82 (B.V.R.).

"Pope's Letters." *Notes and Queries*, December 22, 1860, pp. 485–87 (D: AP); also December 29, 1860, pp. 505–507 (D: AP); also January 26, 1861, pp. 61–62. (Unsigned.)

"The Impertinent." *Notes and Queries*, August 9, 1862, pp. 111–12 (D: see preceding entry).

"Swift or Pope." *Notes and Queries*, May 2, 1863, pp. 350–51 (S.O.P.).

6. Swift

"Swift's Letters." *Notes and Queries*, September 16, 1854, p. 219 (S.L.).

"Letters of Swift and his Contemporaries." *Notes and Queries*, December 9, 1854, p. 459 (L.S.C.).

"Jonathan Swift." *Notes and Queries*, July 21, 1855, p. 45 (J.S.A.) (The article begins, "A new edition...")

"Swift or Bolingbroke: Which or Neither?" *Notes and Queries*, September 8, 1855, p. 177 (S.B.W.).

"Sir Richard Steele's Daughter Elizabeth," ed. by Mr. Nichols (Review). *Athenaeum*, January 5, 1856, p. 19 (S.R.).

"Portrait of Swift." *Notes and Queries*, September 6, 1856, p. 199 (P.O.S.).

Reply to "Swift, Portrait of, and Edit. of 1734." *Notes and Queries*, December 27, 1856, p. 150 (P.O.S.).

"Jonathan Swift, Dean of St. Patrick's." *Notes and Queries*, August 15, 1857, pp. 124–25 (J.S.D.).

"The Vonhomrigs." *Notes and Queries*, January 9, 1858, p. 27 (T.V.).

"Faulkner's Edition of 'Swift's Works.'" *Notes and Queries*, January 9, 1858, pp. 27–28, (F.E.S.).

"Dean Swift and Life of Bonnell." *Notes and Queries*, March 13, 1858, p. 207 (D.S.).

"Sir Richard Steele and Dean Swift." *Notes and Queries*, March 13, 1858, pp. 206–7 (E.B.T.: AP). In reply to query as to authorship of the surreptitious "Essays By The Author of 'Tale of a Tub.'"

"Molly Mog." *Notes and Queries*, July 30, 1859, pp. 84–85 (M.M.).

"The Tale of a Tub." *Notes and Queries*, October 1, 1859 (T.T.T.); also, October 8, 1859, p. 290 (T.T.T.).

"Poetry, A Rhapsodey." *Notes and Queries*, January 12, 1861, p. 27 (P.A.R.).

"Dean Swift and the Scriberlerians v. Dr. Wagstaffe." *Notes and Queries*, May 17, 1862, pp. 381–84 (D.S.A.); also, September 27, 1862, pp. 253–54 (D.S.A.).

"The Letter from Dr. Andrew Tripe." *Notes and Queries*, November 15, 1862, p. 396 (T.L.F.).

SECONDARY SOURCES

1. Books and Articles

Abbot, Claude C. *The Life and Letters of George Darley, Poet and Critic*. Oxford: Clarendon Press, 1928. Darley was one of Dilke's four "art-group" spokesmen and was nearest him in terms of ideas and writing style.

Adami, Marie. *Fanny Keats*. London: John Murray, 1937. Includes several details of Dilke's trusteeship of Fanny's fortunes between 1824 to 1848.

Bauer, Josephine. *London Magazine*. Copenhagen: Roskenkilde and Baggers, 1953. Best biography of this famous magazine to which Dilke and friends contributed and for which he served as editor from 1824 to 1825.

Brown, Charles. *Walter Hazlebourn*, c. 1838. Brown's unpublished "full length caricature of Dilke."

Chapman, N. W. *Harriet Martineau's Autobiography*. Boston: James R. Osgood, 1877.

Chapple, J., and Pollard, A., eds. *The Letters of Mrs. Gaskell*. Manchester: University Press, 1966.

Edgcombe, Fred. *Letters from Fanny Brawne to Fanny Keats*. New York: Oxford University Press, 1937. Several letters detail the moral and psychological support given both Fannys.

Elwin, Warwick, ed. *Some XVIII Century Men of Letters: Whitwell*

Elwin. New York/London: Kennikut Press, 1970. Elwin tells the history of how his father, Whitwell Elwin, persuaded Dilke to assist in Elwin's edition of Pope.

Escott, T. H. S. *Masters of English Journalism.* London: Adelphi Ter race Press, 1911. Contains a good account of Dilke and the *Athenaeum* and especially of his role in salvaging the *Daily News.*

Everett, C. W. *The Letters of Junius.* London: Faber and Gwyer, 1927.

Fielding, K. J., ed. *The Speeches of Charles Dickens.* Oxford: Clarendon Press, 1960. Contains much information about Dilke-Dickens crusades between 1840 and 1860: copyright, Artist Benevolent Fund, Metropolitan Improvement Society (pollution nuisances), and Literary Fund Reform.

Forman, M. B., ed. *Letters of John Keats.* London, New York, Toronto: Oxford University Press, 1952. Several letters and numerous references to Dilke show most facets of the Keats-Dilke relationship from 1817 to 1820.

Francis, John C. *A Literary Chronicle of Half a Century.* London: Richard Bentley & Son, 1888. Son of the printer Francis who was part owner of the *Athenaeum* and friend of Dilke. John C. Francis includes a chapter on Dilke and the *Athenaeum.*

Garrett, William. "The Glaucus Episode: An Interpretation of Book III of *Endymion*." *Keats-Shelley Journal* 27 (1978):23–24. Shows Keats's consciousness of "Cultural Continuity," which he shared with Dilke.

———. "Hazlitt's Debt to C. W. Dilke." *Keats-Shelley Memorial Bulletin* 15 (1964):37–42. In his 1821 *Lectures on the Elizabethan Age,* Hazlitt cribbed ideas and phrases from Dilke's 1815 Introduction to *Old English Plays.*

———. "A Checklist of the Writings of Charles Wentworth Dilke (1789–1864)," *Victorian Periodicals Review,* 14:3 (Fall, 1981), 111–18.

———. "Two Dilke Letters," *Keats-Shelley Memorial Bulletin,* 27 (1976), 1–9.

Gittings, Robert. *The Keats Inheritance.* New York: Barnes and Noble, 1965. A defense of George Keats in the Keats-Dilke-Brown controversy with the Keats Brothers finances.

Hewlett, Henry G. *Henry Fothergill Chorley: Autobiography Memoir & Letters.* London: Richard Bentley & Son, 1873. Chorley was Dilke's only full-time staff member and came to be a distinguished music critic; virtually his entire career was spent in connection with the *Athenaeum*.

Hone, William. *The Everyday Book and Table Book III*. Part 2, 1828.

House et al., eds. *Letters of Charles Dickens*. 3 Vols. Oxford: Clarendon Press, 1974. Several references to Dilke and their crusades with Hood in the early 1840s.

Jones, Leonidas G., ed. *The Letters of John Hamilton Reynolds*. Lincoln: University of Nebraska Press, 1973. From the years 1816 to 1838 Reynolds's career is often intertwined with Dilke's. They remained fast friends.

Kinter, E., ed. *The Letters of Robert Browning and Elizabeth Barrett, 1845–1846*. Cambridge, Mass.: Harvard University Press, 1969.

Marchand, Leslie. *Athenaeum: A Mirror of Victorian Culture*. Durham: University of North Carolina Press, 1941. Contains the best biography of the *Athenaeum*, and still probably the fullest account of Dilke.

Milnes, Richard H. *Life, Letters and Literary Remains of John Keats*. London: John Murray, 1848. Keats's first biographer, detailing Dilke's and others' relationships with Keats.

Morgan, Peter F. *The Letters of Thomas Hood*. Toronto: University of Toronto Press, 1973. Hood's long, lonesome, entertaining and often painful letters between 1835 and 1840 show his deep friendship with Dilke.

Muir, Kenneth, ed. *John Keats: A Reassessment*. Liverpool: Liverpool University Press, 1958.

Richardson, Joanna. *The Everlasting Spell*. London: Jonathan Cape, 1963. A sensitive feeling biography of Dilke and Brown, their quarrel and of Sir Charles's devastating fire which destroyed Dilke and perhaps Keats memorabilia.

———. *Fanny Brawne: A Biography*. New York: Vanguard Press, 1952. Defends Fanny against detractors (such as Sir Charles Dilke, Dilke's grandson).

———. "Some Dilke Papers." *Times Literary Supplement*, August 29, 1952.

Rollins, H. E., ed. *The Keats Circle*, 2 Vols. Cambridge: Harvard University Press, 1965. The collection of letters indispensable to all students of Keats or of any member of his circle.

"More Letters and Poems of the Keats Circle." Reprinted in *KC*, 2, 1965.

Root, R. K. *The Political Career of Alexander Pope.* Gloucester, Mass.: Peter Smith, 1962.

Sanders, C. P., and Fielding, Kenneth, eds. *The Collected Letters of Thomas and Jane Welch Carlyle.* Duke of Edinburgh Edition, 1970–1977. Brief references to the "kindness" and "honesty" of Dilke.

Sharp, William. *Life and Letters of Joseph Severn.* New York: C. Scribner's Sons, 1892. Generally pro-Brown and anti-Dilke.

Sherburn, George. *The Early Career of Alexander Pope.* Oxford: Clarendon Press, 1934. Contains high praise of Dilke's scholarship on Pope.

Stevenson, Lionel. *The Wild Irish Girl.* New York: Russell and Russell, 1969. Lady Morgan and her husband were among the two or three of Dilke's most prolific, valued and capable writers.

Stillinger, Jack, ed. *The Letters of Charles Armitage Brown.* Cambridge: Harvard University Press, 1966. An excellent edition of one of Dilke's closest friends in the early and middle parts of his life.

Wallins, Roger. "Victorian Periodicals and the Emerging Social Consciousness." *Victorian Periodicals Newsletter VIII*, June 1975. An excellent article highlighting a facet of early Victorian social consciousness; acknowledges that subject admits of greater detail and length.

Index